D0216589

Privatisation and Supply Chain Management

Privatisation and Supply Chain Management brings together two of the most important issues in current management thinking: the impact of privatisation on the performance and behaviour of the companies involved, and the increasingly important role of purchasing and supplier relationships. The notion that efficiency is improved with privatisation is critically examined, as is the idea that privatised organisations have recognised the importance of the procurement role and developed both their procurement functions and supplier relationships so as to enhance competitiveness.

Grounded in economic theory, and providing rich case study material, this volume makes a major contribution to an increasingly important area. It will be of interest to students and researchers in economics, business and management studies and specialist courses in procurement management.

Andrew Cox is Professor of Strategic Procurement Management and Director of the Centre for Strategic Procurement Management at Birmingham Business School, University of Birmingham, UK.

Lisa Harris works in supply management for the BMW/Rover Group.

David Parker is Professor of Business Economics and Strategy and Head of the Strategic Management Group at the Aston Business School, Aston University, Birmingham, UK.

Routledge studies in business organizations and networks

1 **Democracy and Efficiency in the Economic Enterprise**
Edited by Ugo Pagano and Robert Rowthorn

2 **Towards a Competence Theory of the Firm**
Edited by Nicolai J. Foss and Christian Knudsen

3 **Uncertainty and Economic Evolution**
Essays in honour of Armen A. Alchian
Edited by John R. Lott Jr.

4 **The End of the Professions?**
The restructuring of professional work
Edited by Jane Broadbent, Michael Dietrich and Jennifer Roberts

5 **Shopfloor Matters**
Labor–management relations in twentieth-century American manufacturing
David Fairris

6 **The Organisation of the Firm**
International business perspectives
Edited by Ram Mudambi and Martin Ricketts

7 **Organising Industrial Activities Across Firm Boundaries**
Anna Dubois

8 **Economic Organisation, Capabilities and Coordination**
Edited by Nicolai Foss and Brian J. Loasby

9 **The Changing Boundaries of the Firm**
Explaining evolving inter-firm relations
Edited by Massimo G. Colombo

10 **Authority and Control in Modern Industry**
Theoretical and empirical perspectives
Edited by Paul L. Robertson

11 **Interfirm Networks**
Organization and industrial competitiveness
Edited by Anna Grandori

12 **Privatisation and Supply Chain Management**
On the effective alignment of purchasing and supply after privatisation
Andrew Cox, Lisa Harris and David Parker

13 **The Governance of Large Technical Systems**
Edited by Olivier Coutard

14 **Managing the New Product Supply Chain**
An industrial organisation perspective
Michael Schwartz

Privatisation and Supply Chain Management

On the effective alignment of purchasing and supply after privatisation

Andrew Cox, Lisa Harris and David Parker

London and New York

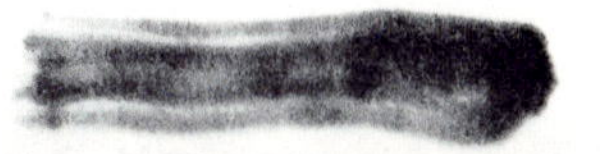

London and New York
First published 1999
by Routledge
11 New Fetter Lane, London EC4P 4EE

Simultaneously published in the USA and Canada
by Routledge
29 West 35th Street, New York, NY 10001

Typeset in Times by Pure Tech India Ltd, Pondicherry
http://www.puretech.com
Printed and bound in Great Britain by Biddles Ltd, Guildford and King's Lynn

British Library Cataloguing in Publication Data
A catalogue record for this book is available from the British Library

Library of Congress Cataloging in Publication Data
Cox, Andrew W.
Privatisation and supply chain management: on the effective
alignment of purchasing and supply after privatisation/Andrew Cox,
Lisa Harris, and David Parker.
p. cm. — (Routledge studies in business organizations and
networks ; 12)
Includes bibliographical references and index.
1. Industrial procurement—Great Britain. 2. Privatization—
Great Britain. I. Harris, Lisa. II. Parker, David, 1949 Sept. 28–
III. Title. IV. Series.
HD39.5.C69 1999 98–38317
658.7′2–dc21 CIP
ISBN 0–415–17300–0 (hbk)

Contents

Figures

Tables

Acknowledgements

This study of the purchasing and supply activities of recently privatised companies in the UK would not have been possible without the support of the Leverhulme Trust, who provided the finance to enable the empirical research to be undertaken. We are indebted to the Trust for its financial support and encouragement of this research into what is a relatively new area of academic enquiry.

The research could not have been undertaken without the willing co-operation of all of the privatised companies and public organisations that are discussed in this volume. We are also particularly indebted to all of the hard-pressed practitioners who gave up a substantial amount of their valuable time to complete the survey questionnaire and participate in the interviews, without which this study could not have been completed. The conclusions that have been drawn as a result of their participation are, however, those of the authors, who alone are responsible for all of the sins of omission and commission which appear here.

We would like to thank Jackie Potter and Michele Donovan at the University of Birmingham and Vicky Bond at Aston University for their support and assistance in preparing the manuscript for publication.

If the ideas contained in this work assist practitioners and academics to understand how privatised companies might better utilise their resources in the future then it will have served its purpose.

Andrew Cox, Lisa Harris and David Parker
Birmingham and Aston, June 1998

1 Privatisation, corporate supply management and procurement competence

This book is about the extent to which privatised companies have, or have not, achieved an operational increase in the professionalisation of their purchasing and supply function, or have developed a more strategic approach to procurement competence through an understanding of supply chain alignment. The differences between these two approaches to the effective management of external resources have been described in detail elsewhere (Cox, 1997a, 1997b and 1998), but these are summarised under the following headings.

Purchasing and supply functional professionalism

By purchasing and supply functional professionalism is meant that process by which corporate decision-makers recognise the need to improve their existing structures and processes, as well as practitioner skills and capabilities, within the purchasing and supply function in their company. This recognition normally involves, first, a focus on immediate cost reduction, through a reduction in headcount internally, or through the immediate aggressive renegotiation of external supply contracts. Only after this search for (what economists refer to as) static efficiency gains may come a second stage. In this stage, a reappraisal of the purchasing function in relation to existing in-house functions (in particular the existing manufacturing and production function) may occur. This may involve a reappraisal and a repositioning of the purchasing and supply function within the corporate hierarchy, with an increasing focus on ways to improve the internal and external cost structure behind the delivery of the function.

Relatedly, this reappraisal can lead to a new commercial role and responsibility for purchasing and supply management. Instead of its historic role as a reactive administrative function, purchasing can become more actively involved in internal and external supply chain management. This process normally involves the function developing a more active approach to supplier appraisal, development and performance. This new approach normally involves a rejection of price offerings from suppliers in favour of a focus on the total costs of ownership, and the development of a more sophisticated understanding of the range of supply relationships that are available to achieve long-term value for money. This may also involve an emphasis on the total integration and management of the existing logistics and supply chain, as the basis for waste reduction and operational efficiency throughout the corporate supply chain for current products and services. It may also involve a significant reappraisal of the insourcing and outsourcing of historic support service to the company. This focus on new processes and ways of doing things is normally referred to (by economists) as the search for dynamic efficiency.

Procurement competence and supply alignment

The professional approach to purchasing and supply functionalism described above can still be seen, however, as primarily reactive in conception. While there is little doubt that a reappraisal of the purchasing and supply function, and the interventions that are necessary to achieve this, require a more proactive and innovative approach by purchasing professionals, this approach is still primarily located within an operational effectiveness way of thinking about competitive advantage. The reason for this is because the modus operandi of this approach is based on two distinct, but linked views of how to achieve operational effectiveness for existing products and services. The first goal is the desire to improve the internal alignment of the current purchasing function with other operational silos within the company by redefining roles and responsibilities. The second aspect is a linked attempt to deliver current products and services in a more operationally efficient way through a more professional approach to existing logistics and supply chain processes and relationships.

As effective as this may be in improving the current operational effectiveness of the way in which products and services are delivered, it can be argued that this innovation is still within the existing product and service delivery paradigm. The company is still trying to find a more effective way of delivering existing products and services. This is a relatively reactive way of thinking about corporate success when it is compared with a truly proactive approach that focuses on how a company can realign the structure of power within current supply chains in order to create competitive advantage. Such an approach might focus on the wholesale outsourcing of existing primary production (rather than support) processes, in order to deliver supply chain functionality to customers in a superior way, which competitors would find difficult to imitate (Lonsdale and Cox, 1998; Cox and Lonsdale, 1998). It might also lead to the search for ways in which completely new products and services can be created to transform the current focus of the company entrepreneurially.

Sustained competitive advantage in the long term requires that companies must do more than simply innovate with the internal and external delivery of existing products and services. Clearly, sustained competitive advantage requires that companies *also* focus on how to create new products and services in the primary supply chains within which they are involved.

This proactive and innovative way of thinking about supply chain power and functionality requires more than just a focus on purchasing and supply professionalism, it requires an understanding of effective resource leverage and procurement competence throughout a company. The reason for this resides in the fact that product and service innovation is almost always a supply chain phenomenon. This means that an understanding of the importance of supply innovation and control is an essential requirement for the effective management of corporate strategy and operational practice in well-run businesses, whether they have been recently privatised or not. This way of thinking about corporate strategy and operational practice is referred to here as procurement competence and supply alignment.

This study assesses the degree to which the newly privatised companies in the UK have been able to come to terms with the need to focus simultaneously on static and dynamic efficiency through cost reduction and purchasing and supply functional professionalism, and transformational efficiency through supply alignment and procurement competence. Overall, the research findings demonstrate that, while a majority of the privatised companies analysed (and even some of the public sector organisations studied as a control group) have made tremendous improvements in the professionalism of their internal and external purchasing and supply functions, *very few have demonstrated any real understanding of* supply alignment and procurement competence. This finding can mean only one of two things. Either corporate decision-makers do not understand what procurement competence and supply alignment is, or, they can only arrive at this after a learning process.

The research in this study suggests – as outlined in Figure 1.1 – that this learning process is a three-stage phenomenon. The first stage involves an immediate cost reduction phase with a focus on internal and external process restructuring. This may be equated with improvements in static efficiency. Most of the privatised companies studied in this work have clearly developed this approach, although at different times and in a variety of ways. The second stage involves a professional development phase in which the company improves the competence of its existing purchasing and supply function, and seeks to find ways to improve operational effectiveness for the existing logistical supply chains, delivering current products and services. This second phase may be equated with improvements in dynamic efficiency through changes to create new processes and ways to deliver existing products and services more effectively and efficiently. Only some of the privatised companies in our survey had developed this approach, although a majority of those studied were clearly focused on moving in this direction. The third stages involves the procurement competence and supply alignment phase.

In this final phase, corporate decision-makers begin to understand that effective resource leverage through the development of procurement

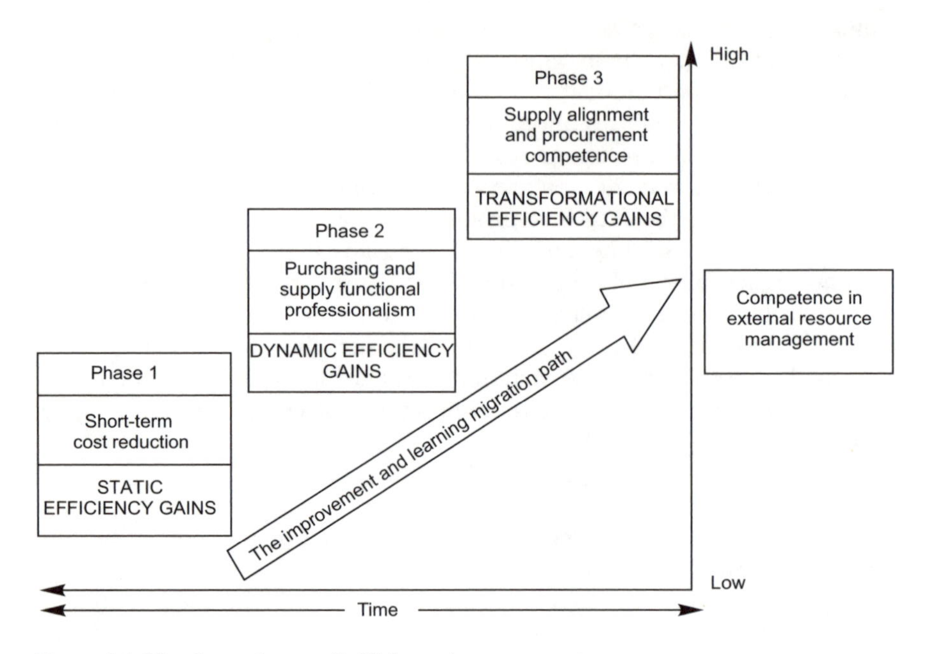

Figure 1.1 The three phases of efficiency improvement.

competence and supply alignment is a strategic, as well as an operational competence (Cox, 1997a). Once this is understood, the new competence begins to drive the strategic goals of the company. This third phase appears to indicate a new form of efficiency and effectiveness, which is referred to here as transformational efficiency. In this phase the company seeks to achieve improvements in its ability to make profits (or deliver exceptional public service) by shifting the boundary of the firm in line with the structure of the supply chains within which it operates. It also demonstrates an ability to manage existing or new products and services with a more flexible approach to make–buy decision making in the organisation's primary, as well as support, supply chains (Lonsdale and Cox, 1998; Cox and Lonsdale, 1999).

Only one or two of the companies involved in this study appear to have begun to recognise the importance of this way of thinking and, even in these cases, only halting steps have been made in this direction. This leads one to conclude that far from this learning process being inevitable, it may only be developed by extremely competent individual decision-makers within particular companies. This finding confirms the argument, developed theoretically elsewhere by one of the current authors, that the development of procurement competence and supply alignment is not inevitable, but requires a high degree of intellectual sophistication by corporate decision-makers (Cox, 1997a, 1997b and 1998).

THE STRUCTURE OF THE BOOK

If the summary above provides an insight into the basic findings of this study of privatisation, purchasing and supply management and procurement competence, it is important to understand how these conclusions have been arrived at. This is assisted by a description of the structure of this book.

In Part I, the context within which privatisation occurred in the UK is described and a basic summary of the research methodology is provided. Chapter 2 outlines the reasons why nationalisation was used in the UK and why it was replaced by privatisation and with what expectations by the Conservative governments of the 1980s and 1990s. The chapter shows that, while the policy was opportunistically conceived and demonstrated little concern for improving purchasing and supply management as such, in theory and practice it was inevitable that once privatisation had occurred there would be an inevitable pressure to increase the professionalism of the purchasing and supply function. The primary reason for this was the need to find immediate cost improvements in existing operational structures and processes, as shareholders replaced the government as owners.

It is further argued in this chapter that, whether or not this immediate pressure for cost improvement in existing functional processes and competencies (gains in static and dynamic efficiency) will give way to continuous corporate improvement and innovation (gains in transformational efficiency) is an open question. There is no inevitability about privatised companies moving beyond the search for immediate short-term cost reductions and becoming supply chain aligned and competent in procurement. This is the major theme that underpins everything in this book. It equates to the earlier distinction made between the three phases of cost reduction, developing professionalism and supply alignment. Overall, the research in this study demonstrates, in terms of Figure 1.1 (see page 4), that privatised companies have achieved considerable improvements in static efficiency (phase 1) and in dynamic efficiency (phase 2), but have a considerable way to go in achieving transformational efficiency (phase 3).

Chapter 3 provides an overview of the way in which these research findings were arrived at. The basic methodology in the study is explained and the rationale for the choice of the twenty-eight privatised companies and four public sector control organisations in the survey established. The basic structure of the study was built around a survey questionnaire of these participating companies. The key questions asked focused on four operational hypotheses about expected changes in purchasing and supply behaviour in public bodies after they had experienced privatisation. These hypotheses tested primarily for static and dynamic efficiency gains, and were structured around cost reduction and purchasing and supply functional professionalism.

In order to understand in more detail the reasons for these changes, and to understand the operational difficulties which privatised companies experience in achieving these static and dynamic efficiency gains, ten interviews were conducted with a sample of the participating companies. Since these interviews did not provide complete answers regarding the difficulties experienced in achieving transformational efficiency gains, in-depth case studies were undertaken of five of the participating companies. These were undertaken in order to see to what extent they had moved beyond cost reduction and functional professionalism in the direction of supply alignment and procurement competence. The aim was also to understand, if they had made only halting progress in this direction, what were the major reasons for this relative failure.

The basic empirical research findings of the study are presented in Parts II and III. In Part II there are four chapters concerned primarily with evidence about the degree to which both privatised companies and public bodies have been able to achieve static and dynamic efficiency gains through cost reduction and purchasing functional professionalism. Chapter 4 summarises the key findings from the questionnaire survey of twenty-eight privatised companies in the UK. It shows that virtually all of the companies are pursuing static and dynamic efficiency gains, but not necessarily in the same ways or with the same degree of success. While almost all of the respondent companies have introduced immediate cost reduction programmes after privatisation, fewer have developed a fully professional approach to the management of the purchasing and supply function. Despite this, it is clear that well over 50 per cent of respondents are pursuing the developmental phase outlined earlier. There is little evidence, however, that many of the companies are in fact even beginning to think about the transformational efficiency gains available through the third, supply aligned, phase.

In order to understand the reasons for these trends, as well as to understand the causes of differential performance within and between different types of privatised companies, three additional chapters are provided in Part II. These chapters give more detailed evidence of the history and development of the purchasing and supply function and the specific reasons why particular processes, structures and competencies have been developed since privatisation. Chapter 5 provides an insight into the recent developments in UK utilities companies since privatisation. The particular case studies are British Gas, Welsh Water, South West Water, PowerGen, Scottish Hydro-Electric and NORWEB. Chapter 6 provides a similar service but for privatised, non-utilities companies. The case studies here are the Rover Group and Rolls Royce. By way of a control, to test whether any of the static and dynamic efficiency gains were being developed independently of privatisation, two case studies drawn from existing public agencies are provided in Chapter 7. The case studies provided here are of London Underground and the Civil Aviation Authority.

The case studies presented in Part II provide detailed evidence about the difficulties experienced by a range of private and public bodies in achieving static and dynamic efficiency gains, when moving from an immediate cost reduction focus (phase 1) to a more developmental, functionally professional approach (phase 2). As one might expect, this reappraisal of the purchasing and supply role is, other things being equal, relatively easier in the private than in the public sector. The case studies show, however, that, when the public sector has intelligent people in place in purchasing and supply, and a conducive senior management and government environment to work within, the developmental phase can also be achieved. Relatedly, even though a company has been privatised, the case material reveals that there may still be serious obstacles to functional professionalism within some companies. Privatisation is, therefore, not an automatic guarantee of the speedy achievement of dynamic efficiency gains, even if it reduces the range of constraints on static efficiency normally experienced by those operating within the public sector.

This conclusion is interesting because, irrespective of the relative degree of success that privatised and public bodies appear to have experienced in achieving static and dynamic efficiency gains, it is clear that the majority of public and private practitioners analysed do not appear to aspire to anything more than a relatively more professional, reactive role. By this, one means a desire to provide current products and services within *existing* supply chains as efficiently as possible. This being the case, and because there was so little evidence of the search for transformational efficiency gains in our initial research findings, it was decided to undertake a further five in-depth case studies. These case studies, which are presented in Chapters 8 to 12, include the utilities companies, Severn Trent and South West Electricity, the non-utility companies British Airways and British Steel, and the publicly owned Post Office. These case studies were undertaken in order to ascertain to what extent the four privatised and one public enterprise have begun to address the issue of transformational efficiency gains. It was also important to understand, if they had not begun to move towards supply alignment and procurement competence, what were the most important obstacles to the achievement of a simultaneous focus on static, dynamic and transformational efficiency.

Part IV provides the final conclusions to the study. In Chapter 13, a summary of the findings within the study is provided, and some ideas as to why many of the privatised companies have failed to move beyond the static and dynamic efficiency approach are presented. The major finding here is that the relative slowness in the development of functional professionalism in some privatised companies is clearly a result of the relative lack of procurement competence, both of the existing senior management and of the purchasing staff left when privatisation occurred. When privatisation also resulted in a major change in the personnel within senior management and purchasing there is clear evidence that the development of a more professional dynamic efficiency approach was made much easier. On the other hand, there is evidence that even when this occurred this has not always led to a parallel understanding of the need for transformational efficiency, predicated on supply alignment and procurement competence.

There would appear to be two primary reasons for this. The first is that many of the newly privatised companies were transferred from the public sector, but with their relative monopoly or oligopoly position in the supply chain still intact. Given this, it is hardly surprising that neither the senior management nor the purchasing staff in these companies should recognise the need for anything more than improvements in static or dynamic efficiency. The second reason is perhaps more worrying, and this is the fact that very few management practitioners in the private sector as a whole appear to understand the different approaches and ways of thinking that are required to achieve a simultaneous focus on static, dynamic and transformational efficiency. Given this malaise, which is not confined exclusively to the managers of the newly privatised companies, some clues as to how practitioners might begin to think appropriately about supply alignment and procurement competence are provided in the final chapter.

Part I

Privatisation and the management of purchasing and supply

2 Privatisation, business restructuring and purchasing and supply management

Introduction

In 1979 a new Conservative government was elected in Britain with a mission to reduce the role of the state in the economy. After 1979 the Conservatives gradually implemented a large-scale reform of the public sector with a view to improving the country's economic performance (Martin and Parker, 1997). By 1997, when the Conservatives lost office, the programme had involved:

- lower income and corporation taxes and public spending controls;
- competitive tendering for the provision of state services in place of monopoly government provision (such as in refuse collection, cleansing services, the cleaning of government buildings and later the provision of certain white-collar local government services);
- the devolution of powers and establishment of agencies to run certain functions previously operated by central and local government departments, e.g. the so-called 'Next Steps' initiative for central government departments, local management of schools and National Health Service trusts;
- the introduction of more competition in public procurement, including but extending well beyond, Ministry of Defence supplies;
- the disposal of the state's housing stock through a series of 'right to buy' initiatives aimed at existing tenants; and
- the sale of state industries.

This book is concerned with the latter policy, the sale of state industries – the policy usually referred to as 'privatisation' – although all of the above policy initiatives should be seen as complementary. All are concerned with reducing the role of the state in the economy.

This book discusses specifically the impact of privatisation on the purchasing and supply management strategies of British privatised companies. The content is based upon a major research programme that looked at the management of purchasing and supply in a total of twenty-eight companies privatised after 1979, mainly through flotation on the stock market. The research was conducted by the authors between 1995 and 1997. In principle, buyer–supplier relationships have important implications for the management and operation of firms. It can be argued that they offer, during and following privatisation, a means of reducing costs and improving the quality and reliability of outputs so as to achieve sustainable competitive advantage. Also, the changes in privatised companies took place at a time of considerable interest in industry in more effective mechanisms for the management of external resources. The aim of these new initiatives in industry was to raise competitiveness through the use of tools and techniques such as lean supply, partnership and network sourcing and outsourcing methods (Lamming and Cox, 1995; Cox, 1996a; Owen and Parker, 1997; Lonsdale and Cox, 1999). The advocacy of an almost universal application of such methods has been criticised for being an unthinking application of 'fads', rather than the adoption of appropriate methods given the nature and environment in which the particular firm operates (Cox, 1996a, 1996b, 1997; Parker and Hartley, 1997; Cox and Thomson, 1999). This book asks whether or not the privatised industries have adopted these fashionable approaches to external resource management and with what effect? More generally, the book also seeks to address the general question of whether or not the privatised companies have adopted an appropriate methodology to understand where the effective boundary of the firm should be, and how each particular company should manage its sourcing and external resources strategy.

This chapter sets the scene for later chapters, which focus specifically on purchasing and supply management strategies, by considering the nature of both nationalisation and privatisation in Britain. Only by understanding the process of privatisation, and of the nature of the nationalisation that preceded it, can we obtain a complete understanding of the changes in purchasing and supply practices that go on within privatised companies, both at the time of privatisation and afterwards, and the appropriateness of any new methods adopted subsequently.

The rise and fall of nationalisation

In the nineteenth century, during the country's industrialisation, a number of activities came under the control and direction of municipal authorities. In spite of an essentially *laissez-faire* economic policy, public provision of water and sewerage, gas and later electricity supplies, was found to be more satisfactory than private provision. By the 1930s most local tram and bus services were also operated by the municipalities.

In the UK, central government departments had managed a few facilities and services for long periods, such as the Royal dockyards and The Post Office. The Post Office traces its origins back to at least the sixteenth century and in 1912 it was granted an entire monopoly of telecommunications facilities (except in the City of Kingston-upon-Hull which retained a municipal telecommunications operation) to add to its postal monopoly. In the 1920s and

1930s a number of other activities came under central state control; notable additions were the BBC (radio and later television broadcasting), the Central Electricity Board (electricity transmission) and London Transport. But the main period of nationalisation came between 1945 and 1951, when the first majority Labour government, and with a socialist mandate, nationalised the railways, coal mining, electricity, gas and steel industries and road haulage. Nationalisation of the latter two activities had not been completed when Labour lost office in 1951 and what had been brought under state control was largely denationalised in the early 1950s. Steel was renationalised in 1967 and the remaining state road transport activities were brought together as the National Freight Corporation in 1969.

Broadly speaking, from the 1950s to 1979 successive governments, both Labour and Conservative, accepted the existence of state-owned industries and with the exception of steel and road transport, there were no major denationalisations. Between 1970 and 1974 a Conservative administration sold certain state-owned public houses in the Carlisle area and the travel agents, Thomas Cook, but these were of little economic significance. Indeed, in the 1970s the state sector expanded. The Labour government between 1974 and 1979 established a state oil company, the British National Oil Corporation in 1976, to ensure a public stake in the burgeoning North Sea Oil sector. The government already owned a majority stake in the integrated oil company, BP, through a shareholding dating back to the outbreak of the First World War. Also, two large industries were saved from economic failure by government takeover, namely shipbuilding and British Leyland (later the Rover Group) and the country's three main aircraft manufacturers were merged to form a new public corporation, British Aerospace, in 1977.[1] Therefore by 1979, when the Conservatives took office again, the state, in the form of nationalised industries and municipal services, dominated large parts of the UK economy, including energy supplies (gas, thermal and nuclear electricity and oil), transport (bus, coach, rail, ferry services, London Underground and air travel but to a lesser degree road haulage), steel, telecommunications, posts, aerospace, shipbuilding, motor vehicle manufacture and water and sewerage services (municipal water and sewerage services had been merged into ten regional water authorities, each a public corporation, in 1973). To place the scale of the subsequent privatisation programme in context, by 1997 the only sizeable state-owned enterprises remaining in public ownership were The Post Office and the London Underground rail system. By 1997 all of the other state enterprises of any real economic significance had been sold. Moreover, the Conservatives had slated both The Post Office and the London Underground for possible privatisation and had already attempted to privatise The Post Office. The attempt had been defeated in 1994 by backbench Members of Parliament, fearful of the effect of private ownership on rural postal services. In total, between 1979 and 1997 Conservative governments were responsible for privatising over £60bn. of industrial assets. In the same period, the share of employment in Britain accounted for by state industries fell from 7.2 per cent to under 2 per cent and the state industries' share of GDP to less than 2 per cent from 10.5 per cent (Parker, 1998).

In the 1920s and 1930s the Labour Party had deliberated over the type of socialist industry that should be created by a future Labour government (Barry, 1965). Some members advocated a form of workers' control, including syndicalism. Others preferred control by government departments. In the end neither of these options was chosen. On the one hand, workers' control seemed too risky because consumers' interests might be neglected and economic power would be transferred to local officials. Workers' control also seemed incompatible with the central economic planning at the time favoured by Labour. On the other hand, departmental control of state industries would mean that civil servants were responsible for running large parts of the economy. There was recognition that civil servants were ill-suited in terms of experience and training to run commercial concerns efficiently.

By 1945 the leadership of the Labour Party had decided upon a third option for state ownership – the public corporation. The public corporation was essentially the form of organisation adopted for the BBC from 1927 and by Herbert Morrison for London Transport in 1933 (Morrison, 1933). Herbert Morrison was a leading figure in the post-1945 Labour government. Hence, the public corporation form is still sometimes referred to in Britain as 'the Morrisonian corporation'.

The public corporation is intentionally similar to the joint-stock company in the private sector. A joint-stock company involves a separation of ownership and control between shareholders (owners) and board directors (control). In principle, it is a primary duty of the directors to manage the company in the interests of the shareholders. Generally, this means ensuring that the company maximises profitability over time or, more technically, the net present value of the future profit stream. In this form of ownership there is a clear *agent–principal* relationship with shareholders as the principals and the board of directors as the agents. Effective corporate governance requires that the agents operate the company in the interests of the principals and not in their own interests – something discussed further below.

The public corporation after 1945 was structured similarly to the joint-stock company, but it did have a number of important differences that were to prove important in explaining the performance of the nationalised industries in the postwar period. Each industry had a board with a chairman appointed by the secretary of state (government minister of the sponsoring department). When appointing other members of the board the secretary of state would consult with the chairman. These boards included executive and non-executive members and commonly numbered between eight and fifteen. Non-executive appointees were typically from political, academic and business circles and sometimes from trade unions. The chairman and non-executive members were part-time appointments, salaried and appointed for fixed periods (they could be reappointed). While the appointments were ostensibly non-political, it was not unknown for a new incoming government to fail to renew a chairmanship and instead to appoint its own nominee.

The boards, through their chairmen, were accountable to the secretary of state and through him/her to a government department ('the sponsoring department') and onwards to the cabinet and parliament. Each year the board was required to present a corporate plan to the secretary of state setting out its future business plans and financing needs. This corporate plan was intended to guide the strategic management of the corporation. In practice, changes in the external environment (e.g. demand changes, changes in input prices) and political intervention frequently negated the plan.

The Morrisonian corporation is often referred to as an 'arm's length' form of ownership, mirroring the relationship between shareholders and directors in the private sector. The government agreed the corporate plan with the board and could issue directives of a general nature on the running of the industry, but was otherwise not supposed to intervene in the industries and especially in their day-to-day management. The board was accountable for the management of the industry and this would be inconsistent with interference by government. Political interference would undermine the accountability of the board for the success of the enterprise.

The boards were directed under the nationalisation acts to manage the industries in pursuit of a number of goals, typically relating to economic development, employment, union recognition, exports, innovation, etc. In other words, there were a number of goals not all of which were necessarily consistent. Overall, the industries were to be operated in 'the public interest', although this was not well defined in the nationalisation acts. This left the industries open to political intervention, including the overruling of corporation boards by ministers, 'on public interest grounds'. Unclear and inconsistent objectives could leave management uncertain as to the direction to take in managing the businesses and this problem was compounded by frequent political intervention, especially in those enterprises which were loss making or needed to finance large investments, where the Treasury could be expected to take a view. Opaque objectives and political intervention were a lethal combination, one that was almost certain to lead to inefficiencies. In practice, the day-to-day contacts between the industries and their sponsoring departments encouraged political influence in corporate strategy, including matters such as pricing, investment, plant closures and redundancies.

Like joint-stock companies on which they were modelled, the nationalised industries were given independent finances with their own accounts and published annual reports. However, there was no equity capital (shares) as such and the industries' capital derived from government loans, internally generated funds and occasional government subsidies. Each industry was given powers to borrow but only with government agreement. The Treasury argued that, as the state industries' loans were effectively guaranteed by the government, the government must have a veto over loan issues.[2] From time to time loss-making enterprises, notably coal mining and the railways, benefited from capital restructuring, including the writing-off of debts. The burden fell on the taxpayer.

In the 1970s a growing interest in monetarism – the notion that the growth in the quantity of money in circulation is a primary cause of inflation – led to stricter controls on the level of government borrowing. Government borrowing, especially through the financial markets, is recognised to be a potential source of monetary growth. In the UK one important measure of government borrowing has been the public sector borrowing requirement (PSBR), which is the sum of the borrowings of central government, local governments and state-owned industries. To hold down inflation, successive governments set targets for the PSBR. For the nationalised industries, external financing limits (EFLs) were imposed from 1976. These capped the amount of borrowing by each enterprise and in a number of cases profitable industries (in recent years notably The Post Office) were set negative EFLs. Negative EFLs meant that the enterprise could not borrow net amounts and instead was required to pay sums to the Treasury. These payments contributed to holding down the total PSBR.

As early as the mid-1950s it was evident that there were serious weaknesses in the management of the state industries in the UK (HMSO, 1956). Some industries were perennial loss makers (coal mining and the railways), whose performance could be blamed only partially on unfavourable market conditions. Increasingly, it became difficult to recruit and retain good-quality management because of the frustrations caused by political interference and because of uncompetitive salaries. Senior management pay in the nationalised industries was depressed by successive prices and incomes policies, which in practice fell most heavily on the public sector.

In 1961 a government White Paper suggested that state industry should face stricter financial objectives with a view to raising performance.[3] In the 1940s nationalisation legislation, the principal financial target imposed was one requiring that the industries should break even 'taking one year with another'. This meant that losses could be excused for long periods. The break even period was now defined as five years and, in addition, each industry was given a profit or other financial target. Usually the profit target took the form of a rate of return on net assets.

In 1967 a further White Paper advocated the use in the nationalised industries of marginal cost pricing and the discounted cash flow method for investment appraisal. The objective was to raise allocative efficiency by bringing prices for extra supplies into line with the costs of producing them and by improving capital investment. The test discount rate to be used in investment appraisal was based on an estimate of the social opportunity cost of capital. It was expected to reflect the rate used in comparable private enterprises, thereby ensuring that capital was not used to expand investment in nationalised industries by reducing more economically beneficial investments in the private sector.[4] The target rates of return remained, although this meant that there could be inconsistency between the pricing rules under marginal cost pricing and the prices needed to achieve the profitability target. In practice, management in state industries paid more attention to achieving the target rate of return. It was easier to operate and the Treasury proved more interested in the accountants' profit than the economists' allocative efficiency.

In the 1970s the finances of the state-owned firms declined sharply in the face of high inflation, especially of fuel costs following the OPEC (Organisation of Petroleum Exporting Countries) price rises between 1972 and 1974. Successive prices and incomes policies held down or froze prices in the state sector. By 1975 many of the major state industries were making losses squeezed by higher costs and static revenues. Unsurprisingly, there was evidence of a serious decline in morale among state industry employees and management. The nationalised industries were affected by waves of strikes. Pay restraint imposed by the government at a time of high inflation led to serious industrial unrest, the most important dispute being in coal mining in 1973–74. This led to a general election in February 1974 and the fall of the then Conservative government.

It was quite clear by the mid-1970s that the high expectations for state ownership in the Labour movement in the 1940s had proved optimistic, perhaps naïve. They had foundered on the practicalities of managing giant enterprises efficiently and effectively in the public sector, an environment which is essentially political and not commercial. In 1976 the National Economic Development Office (NEDO) issued a major report on the nationalised industries identifying considerable weaknesses in their management, control and financing.[5] In response, in 1978 a Labour government White Paper introduced new financial goals involving a 5 per cent (raised to 8 per cent in 1981) 'required rate of return' on investment (in real terms before tax), while still retaining profit targets. The required rate of return differed from the earlier test discount rate by applying to the overall investment programme rather than individual investments.[6] The NEDO report concluded that the 1967 instructions on marginal cost pricing had proved troublesome to operate. Hence, the 1978 White Paper suggested that marginal cost pricing should be adopted where feasible, but more generally it downgraded the importance of this economic objective. The paper also permitted the issuing of specific directives to the industries by the secretary of state, where it was felt that certain management action should be taken in the public interest. These directives would be published and open to parliamentary scrutiny. Finally, the White Paper recommended that state industries should publish performance targets, including service targets, as a spur to good management.

The 1978 White Paper recommended a number of important changes aimed at raising performance. However, it was quickly overtaken by the election of a new Conservative government in 1979. The Conservatives offered a more radical vision for the public sector. In political opposition, between 1974 and 1979, the party under a new leader, Margaret Thatcher, formulated a free-market economic strategy for Britain based on encouraging private enterprise, the profit motive and individual initiative (Parker, 1987). This vision implied a significant break with the postwar political consensus based on the acceptance of a 'mixed economy', though the future privatisation programme was as yet neither planned nor agreed in government.

The rise and rise of privatisation

In spite of the clear failings of nationalisation, especially in the 1970s (Pryke, 1981) and the Conservative Party's new vision for Britain, plans for large-scale privatisation did not form part of the new government's election manifesto in 1979. The manifesto flagged the 'denationalisation'[7] of British Shipbuilding and British Aerospace (only recently nationalised) and the possible introduction of some private capital in other areas, but no other important changes in ownership were signalled. Instead, privatisation emerged gradually in the 1980s as a consequence of the need to fund government expenditure without raising the public sector borrowing requirement (PSBR), and as a logical development of the government's programme of cutting the public sector, reducing trade union power and introducing more competition. The first sales of state assets occurred on a small scale and were relatively uncontentious since what were considered to be 'core' state enterprises – telecommunications, gas, electricity, water and sewerage, the railways (the public utilities or network industries) and coal mining – were unaffected. Only from 1982 did the government begin to plan the privatisation of these industries.

There were broadly two reasons for the expansion of the privatisation programme in the early 1980s. First, the sale of state assets produced a flow of funding to the Exchequer at a time when the government was keen to cut taxes and public sector borrowing. Second, privatisation proved popular with the management of the state industries and there was little opposition from the public. Senior management of state industries welcomed privatisation because it freed them from political interference in their decision making. Also, movement to the private sector meant that management salaries could rise to free-market levels. Management salaries remained depressed in the public sector. Senior managers gained. The public who bought shares in the state enterprises benefited because usually the share price rose dramatically following privatisation (Parker, 1998). This occurred because the shares were generously priced to ensure the success of the sales and because these industries had large capitalisations. This meant that their shares were sought after by institutional investors in the first days of stock market trading. Institutional investors aim to hold a cross-section of leading company shares.

Table 2.1 provides a list of the major enterprises sold by the government and in each case the date of the first sale of shares (in some cases the shares were sold in tranches). The acceleration of the privatisation programme after 1983 is evident, as is the extension of the programme to the network industries starting with British Telecom (1984) and moving on to British Gas (1986), the water and sewerage companies (1989), the electricity industry (1990–91) and finally the railways (1995–97).

Table 2.1 Privatisations in the UK (major sales)

Corporation/sector	*Date of sale*[a]
British Petroleum (BP)	1979
National Enterprise Board investments	1980
British Aerospace	1981
Cable & Wireless	1981
Amersham International	1982
National Freight Corporation	1982
Britoil	1982
British Rail Hotels	1983
Associated British Ports	1983
British Leyland (Rover)	1984
British Telecom (BT)	1984
Enterprise Oil	1984
Sealink	1984
British Shipbuilders & naval dockyards	1985
National Bus Company	1986
British Gas	1986
Rolls Royce	1987
British Airports Authority (BAA)	1987
British Airways (BA)	1987
Royal Ordnance Factories	1987
British Steel	1988
Rover Group	1988
Regional Water and Sewerage Companies	1989
Regional Electricity Companies (RECs)	1990
Electricity generation (National Power and PowerGen)	1991
Electricity Generation (Scottish Power and Scottish Hydro-Electric)	1991
Trust Ports	1992
British Coal	1995
British Rail (BR)	1995/97
British Energy (nuclear power)	1996

Note

a Date refers to first sale of shares when shares were sold in tranches.

From time to time government ministers articulated the case for privatisation. The rationale can be summarised in the following terms:

1 increasing consumer choice;
2 raising revenue for the Exchequer;
3 extending share ownership;
4 reducing trade union power; and
5 raising economic efficiency.

Economists tend to concentrate upon the final argument, raising economic efficiency. This is because more consumer choice is dependent upon increasing competition in the market place rather than ownership *per se* (Vickers and

Yarrow, 1988). In principle, consumer choice could be achieved by having a number of competing state firms or by allowing private sector firms to compete with an existing nationalised enterprise.[8] It is certainly not achieved by privatising monopolies as monopolies. With regard to the raising of state revenue, privatisation is only an efficient means of financing public spending if it is cheaper than other forms of revenue raising, namely taxation and state borrowing. It is not self-evident that this will be the case, especially if to attract investors state assets are sold at a sharp discount to their true market value. In terms of extending share ownership and creating a large number of small shareholders, the economic rationale for this remains unclear (although there were potential political gains to a Conservative government from expanding the numbers of people with a stake in a 'property-owning democracy'). It is not at all self-evident that having a large number of small shareholders in a privatised enterprise is advantageous. This is discussed further below.[9] Turning to reducing trade union power, Conservative ministers were mindful of the coal miners' dispute of 1973–74, which led to the collapse of the previous Conservative government, and were keen to limit union strength to avoid a repetition. The nationalised industries were highly unionised and collective bargaining was universal. Privatisation offered a way of reducing the role of the unions. It is also possible that some Conservatives wanted revenge against the miners' union – something achieved during the lengthy miners' dispute of 1983–84. Nevertheless, from an economic perspective, reducing union power is best treated as a component contributing to the raising of economic efficiency in (former) state industries.

Although nationalised industries were usually giants in their industrial sector, most privatisations in the 1980s involved the sale of the state firm as a single entity. The firm was not broken up into competing parts. This meant that the sale price was high; for example, the first tranche of British Telecom shares sold in November 1984, amounting to 50.2 per cent of the issued share capital, had a total market valuation of £3.9bn.; the later sale of British Gas, in late 1986, was valued at over £5bn. Such large valuations seemed to rule out a direct sale to an existing business or a management buy-out or buy-in. Moreover, there were fears that such large sales might be beyond the scope of the domestic institutional investors to finance with ease. One solution was to attract the interest of small investors in the privatisation stock. Arguably however, effective corporate governance is better achieved by having a small number of large shareholders. Unlike small shareholders, larger investors have more motivation to monitor and change the behaviour of management to ensure the efficient use of the enterprise's resources. They have more to lose from the failure of the enterprise and more to gain from its economic success. Generally, economists equate effective corporate governance with a smaller number of larger investors rather than large numbers of small owners. A number of researchers (e.g. Walking and Long, 1984; Argawal and Mandelker, 1987; Baker and Weiner, 1992) have suggested that firm performance improves when ownership interests and managerial interests correspond through concentration of ownership or some kind of equity participation by management, such as stock options.

In the economics literature on privatisation, agency theory provides a theoretical grounding (see, for example, Bos, 1991). The central premise of agency theory is that goal conflict exists when parties with different goals engage in cooperative behaviour (Ross, 1973; Jensen and Meckling, 1976; Eisenhardt, 1989). An agent is a person contracted to perform some activity on behalf of a principal and receives some remuneration or benefit for services performed. The principal will benefit provided that the agent works efficiently and effectively to meet the principal's goals. This will occur when the agent's and the principal's utility functions are identical. This can be expected to occur very rarely, if at all, in the absence of appropriate constraints and incentives. For this reason, the potential for goal conflict exists. Without adequate constraints or incentive mechanisms, agents can be expected to pursue their own goals (utility) leading to a welfare loss to the principals. Hence, the principal will design and implement constraints and incentive mechanisms (e.g. performance-related pay for agents) to minimise the agent's deviation from pursuit of the principal's goals.

For joint-stock companies in the private sector, the directors are the agents and the shareholders the principals. The higher welfare of shareholders occurs when the present value of the future profit stream is maximised since this is associated with high dividends and share price appreciation (capital gains). The constraints and incentives on directors' behaviour include performance-related pay, stock options, other equity interests, bonuses, etc. as 'carrots' and censure and dismissal as the main 'sticks'. Directors can be censured at companies' annual general meetings (AGMs) and at other times when shareholders, especially major shareholders, and directors meet. They can also be voted off the board at AGMs and can expect to lose their positions whenever hostile takeover bids occur. Where shareholders lose confidence in the company's directors, they can be expected to sell their shares, leading to a fall in the share price, perhaps triggering a takeover bid by new management. A company with capital that is not producing a competitive return (equal to the return that could be earned elsewhere on an investment with the same risk) is unlikely to remain attractive to existing investors but is likely to be attractive to potential predators.[10]

In a number of economic writings the private capital market and especially the takeover threat is seen as a major constraint on managerial behaviour. This is so despite the fact that studies of actual takeovers have suggested that it is not necessarily poorly performing managements that are affected by bids (Mayer, 1997) and that takeovers do not necessarily raise performance. It seems that, on average, mergers produce either small or negative benefits to shareholders of the predator company (Singh, 1975; Meeks, 1977; Franks and Harris, 1989). Also, some research has questioned the extent to which dissatisfied shareholders can be expected to sell their shares (Grossman and Hart, 1980). It could pay an investor to 'free ride' waiting for other shareholders to sell. They thereby reap the benefits of a subsequent rise in the share price at the time of a bid or higher returns if the existing management respond by improving the firm's performance (however, this argument sits uneasily alongside the existence of high takeover activity in the UK; see Hughes, 1993: 15).[11]

What is clear is the much rarer incidence of hostile takeovers in many other economies, including the economies of Germany and Japan. Over the last half century these countries (and others) have had an economic performance far superior to that of the UK. This suggests, at the very least, that effective corporate governance does not *necessarily* require the takeover threat. Indeed, the threat may promote 'short-termism' in management decision making, damaging firms' long-term economic performance; while fighting takeovers may divert management effort from running their businesses. As Bishop and Kay (1993: 8) conclude: '...expansion by merger and takeover have been British and American preoccupations and have not been a primary concern of our more successful competitors'. Some form of long-term 'relationship investing', as found in Germany and Japan, may be superior and this may be promoted by having fewer, large investors and low levels of share trading.

Whatever the nature of an effective capital market in producing high economic performance and the merits of the British capital market in this respect, it is the case that on the face of it the agent–principal relationship is more complex and potentially less effective in the state sector. In the state sector, the ultimate principals, the public, have no shares in state enterprises to trade. There cannot be a hostile takeover bid, certainly without government sanction, and there are no AGMs to which the public are invited. At the same time, management tend to be paid fixed salaries and tend to lack incentives such as stock options and performance bonuses. Finally, politicians, civil servants and public sector board directors, as agents of the public, may pursue their own goals (at least from time to time). Their utility may depend upon such considerations as maximising votes, maximising budgets and pursuit of a comfortable or easy lifestyle. Information asymmetries in monopoly bureaucracies may favour bureaucrats leading to an overexpansion of departmental budgets.

Ayub and Hegsted (1986) comment in a study of public sector performance in thirteen countries:

> One of the major causes of financial...problems that most large public enterprise sectors...face is the lack of a clear separation between the management...of enterprises on the one hand and political considerations and processes on the other. In many cases this results in diffuse and conflicting objectives, limitations on managerial autonomy,...and a civil service culture where CEOs are more administrators than entrepreneurial businessmen.

The so-called public choice or economics of politics literature has blossomed since the 1960s as a critique of state provision (Downs, 1957;

Buchanan, 1968; Tullock, 1976). In the words of James Buchanan (1978: 17), a leading proponent of public choice theory:

> In one sense, all of the public choice or the economic theory of politics may be summarised as the 'discovery' or 're-discovery' that people should be treated as rational utility-maximisers in all of their behavioural capacities . . .

William C. Mitchell, reviewing the literature, remarks:

> Traditional treatments by political science of government failure proceeds [sic.] in both an *ad hoc* and moralistic manner complaining about this or that blemish on perfect democracy. The major assumption has always been that politics – the very process of electing representatives – poses no problem. Accordingly, institutional tinkering and the discovery of new leaders will, it is thought or implied, bring about the desired effects.
>
> Public choice, however, questions the fundamental nature of politics: it probes the very representative processes by which representatives *choose with other representatives for people they are intended to represent.* And it does so by applying the most rigorous and relevant standard of all: comparable efficiency of institutions, economic and political.
>
> (Mitchell, 1988, pp. 45–6)

Some theoretical and empirical studies have suggested that public choice theory exaggerates the extent to which homo economicus applies to state employees. State employees may be dedicated to their task; while McMaster and Sawkins (1996) contend that the predictions of public choice theory are based on the restrictive assumption that trust is absent in state provision. It is also the case that public sector managers may be motivated and obtain job satisfaction from doing a job well, like their counterparts in the private sector (Parker, 1985). Nevertheless, it is not necessary to accept public choice theory at face value to appreciate its powerful warning against complacency about the motives of politicians and state officials.

Clearly the fundamental question is, how 'comparatively' efficient is the political allocation of resources compared with the obvious alternative of the market? The public choice literature, through a mixture of deduction and empirical study, concludes decisively in favour of the market. In essence, politicians and state management are considered:

1 not to know the public's utility and therefore be incapable of maximising it (the *information* problem); and
2 to lack the desire to maximise the public's utility even if they knew it (the *incentive* problem).[12]

In politics the ballot box is the ultimate means by which the public articulates its demands. But the ballot box is a poor vehicle for members of the public to indicate their views on individual items of public spending and state provision. The economist Kenneth Arrow has demonstrated that: 'If we exclude the possibility of interpersonal comparisons of utility, then the only methods of passing from individual tastes to social preferences which will be defined for a wide range of sets of individual orderings are either imposed or dictatorial' (Arrow, 1963, p. 59). Overall, developments in economic theory in the postwar period have provided a more thorough intellectual argument against state ownership and political resource allocation than existed previously. More specifically, agent–principal theory and public choice theory provided intellectual foundations for the Conservative government's policies from 1979 – policies that were aimed at reducing the role of the state and transferring production from the state to private sector firms.[13]

Privatisation and corporate restructuring

The economics literature on privatisation tends to emphasise improvements in the use of labour and capital inputs following privatisation rather than attention to other possible cost savings (e.g. Vickers and Yarrow, 1988; Ott and Hartley, 1991). State-owned firms have been associated with overmanning, capital rationing and the use of too low a discount rate when appraising capital projects. The result, in terms of economic welfare, is a non-optimal employment of labour and capital inputs under state ownership. Following privatisation, the expectation is that labour productivity will rise and the capital/output ratio will fall.

Possible post-privatisation efficiency improvements can be separated into static and dynamic gains: 'static efficiency . . . involves a continuous search for improvements within a fixed set of initial conditions and dynamic efficiency . . . involves continuous reconsideration of initial conditions' (Ghemawat and Costa, 1993). More specifically, static gains relate to constraints imposed by a fixed production function, waste and other inefficiencies in the use of inputs are removed and the output is produced at lower cost. *Dynamic efficiency* is concerned with changing the parameters of the production function and hence gains will normally materialise over a longer period of time. The result is ongoing improvements in production processes and outputs.

In consequence, immediately before and following privatisation we might expect to see a spurt in efficiency as waste is removed, and generally this is borne out by statistical analysis of the impact of privatisation on performance (see e.g. Martin and Parker, 1997). More difficult will be sustaining such efficiency gains. Static efficiency emphasises attention to existing functional capabilities, but dynamic efficiency requires a fundamental reassessment of the organisation to create an environment conducive to continuous improvement in production processes and outputs. This may require the introduction of a new 'culture' or fundamental changes in the ways of doing things within the organisation (Johnson and Scholes, 1997, pp. 213–23). This in turn may require new management (perhaps from outside the business), a new people-focused orientation (to facilitate the creation of a change mentality) and considerable organisational restructuring (to improve products and processes) (Parker, 1995a). A change in buyer–supplier relationships could occur as part of the search for static efficiency gains – reducing waste in existing purchasing, but would need to be ongoing and more strategic if purchasing is to contribute to dynamic efficiency.

It follows, therefore, that changes in purchasing and supply practices could occur around the time of privatisation and perhaps continue or that they could be delayed until the need to pursue dynamic gains becomes more pressing. What is clear is that some form of organisational response to the new challenges of private sector operation is implied. This might eventually lead to a complete rethinking of the position of the firm in its current supply chains, and/or the development of completely new products and services. If this occurs it may be possible to point to transformational efficiency gains, as defined in the introduction to this book (see page 3).

The process of privatisation involves the conversion of the public corporations into joint-stock companies financed by shares as well as loan capital (a process in some countries called 'corporatisation'; however, the term can be confusing in the UK context where public corporations already existed and were converted into joint-stock companies). At a later stage, these shares are sold to the private sector usually through share flotations but sometimes through direct sales (for example, Rover Group to British Aerospace in 1988) and management and worker buy-outs (e.g. the National Freight Corporation in 1982 and some bus operators from 1986).

Study of the impact of privatisation on companies suggests that cultural change is central to successful privatisation. In a survey of managers in privatised companies and companies undergoing privatisation in Europe, by Gemini Consulting, 78 per cent of respondents expressed a belief that cultural change was essential. A movement away from public sector ways of doing things to private sector modes of thinking and operation was considered essential. This involved a 'customer focus' at all levels in the organisation and a start to making 'people . . . believe that the customer is their employer' (Garret, 1997). This is also associated with organisational restructuring.

The concept and role of culture in organisations is controversial. It is easy to use the term as a meaningless catch-all. Nevertheless, organisations, due to their history and circumstances and the personalities that have shaped them, do take on peculiar ways of doing things. Their routines, structures and strategies reflect past learning that becomes deeply institutionalised. The degree of 'cultural change' and refocusing that takes place with privatisation can be expected to vary depending upon the extent to which the organisation previously adopted commercial goals. Another possible consideration is the financial health of the business. Unsurprisingly, in the UK the largest reorganisations seem to have occurred where the businesses were making large losses, e.g. British Steel, British Airways, coal mining and the railways, or where new competition threatened losses, e.g. BT and British Gas. It is also important to note that some enterprises that did not restructure appreciably before privatisation have done so some time afterwards, in response to the changed external environment including shareholder pressures and new competition. This was certainly the case at BT and British Gas (Parker, 1994; Harper, 1997).

Looking specifically at employment, it is evident that some enterprises delayed sharp job cuts to some time after privatisation (e.g. British Gas and the electricity companies), while others (e.g. British Steel) demanned well ahead of privatisation. Employment at British Steel fell from 191,500 in 1979 to 55,200 in 1988, the year of sale. Where extensive job losses occurred ahead of sale, this reflected the managements' attempts to restructure the business and improve the finances to ensure a successful sale. In passing, it is also worth noting that government reconstructed balance sheets ahead of privatisation. This not only enabled larger profits to be made afterwards, it also left enterprises lowly geared in financial terms (i.e. there was little debt in the balance sheet). This enabled the management post-privatisation to embark on ambitious diversification and takeover policies financed by debt. For example, this has occurred in the case of some of the privatised water and sewerage companies of England and Wales, which hurried into investments outside the water industry that subsequently proved unprofitable. Arguably, the government should not have left the companies with such low gearing at privatisation. Little debt in the balance sheet may have encouraged excessive risk taking with investors' funds. At the same time, of course, low gearing made the enterprises attractive to buyers.

A number of studies have now been undertaken into the performance of firms after privatisation. These studies suggest that privatisation can lead to efficiency gains but that gains do not always materialise. Not all privatised firms show obvious improvements in economic efficiency, whether measured by profitability or productivity (for a full review, see Martin and Parker, 1997). Competition appears to be a consideration alongside ownership: where firms are privatised with their monopoly position more or less intact, efficiency gains may depend upon the effectiveness of the continuing state regulation. In the UK, a number of regulatory offices have been established, namely the Office of Telecommunications (Oftel), the Office of Gas Supply (Ofgas), the Office of Water Services (Ofwat), the Office of Electricity Regulation (Offer) and the Office of the Rail Regulator (ORR). A main piece of the regulatory armoury is the RPI-X price cap. This links permitted price rises to inflation (as measured by the RPI) less an efficiency factor, X. The efficiency factor represents expected efficiency gains over the price cap period, usually five years, after which it is then revised. If management achieve greater efficiency gains (termed 'outperformance') then higher profits can be earned for shareholders (for critical reviews of the regulation of privatised utilities in the UK, see, for instance, Parker, 1997; Waterson, 1997).

Competition, state regulation and the type of ownership can, therefore, be considered together to impact on incentives for management to manage their firm efficiently, thus reducing unit costs and introducing new products and production processes. Figure 2.1 illustrates how economists typically perceive the impact of ownership, regulation and competition on production efficiency. Incentives for management to manage their businesses efficiently are maximised only where there is extensive competition or the threat of competition in product markets,[14] low, non-distortionary state regulation or no regulation, and private property rights.

This combination is shown as point B in Figure 2.1. Performance is likely to be least satisfactory where there is monopoly supply protected by barriers to market entry, high state regulation which reduces incentives to produce efficiently, and state ownership. In this case there are neither product market (competition) nor capital market (shareholder) incentives to be efficient and management decision making is further damaged by burdensome regulation (regulatory distortions). This is shown as point A in Figure 2.1. Other positions, such as point C with private ownership, monopoly supply and high state regulation, can be viewed as intermediary outcomes giving only partial management efficiency incentives. Privatised, regulated utilities will be at or close to point C. The actual position depending upon the degree and form of state regulation and the sustainability of their monopoly rights. A point such as D is

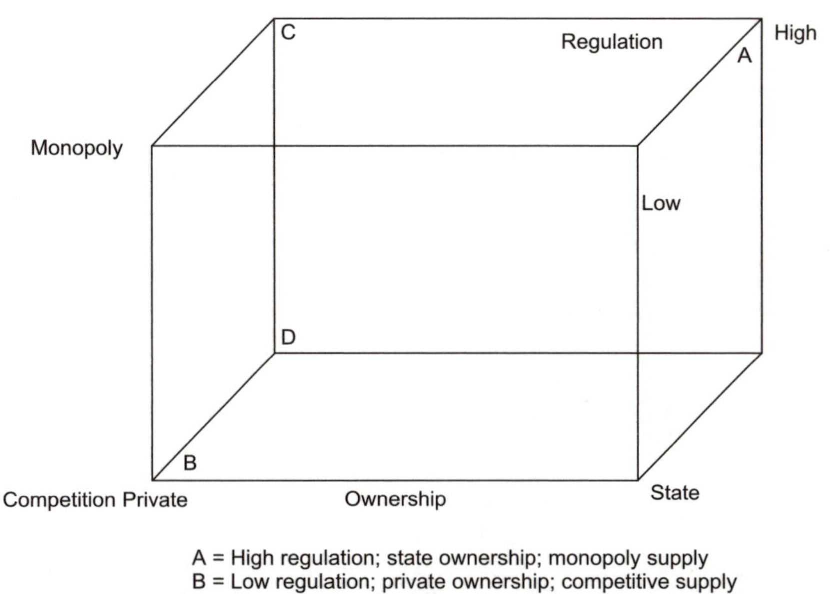

A = High regulation; state ownership; monopoly supply
B = Low regulation; private ownership; competitive supply
C = High regulation; private ownership; monopoly supply
D = High regulation; private ownership; competitive supply

Figure 2.1 Ownership, competition and efficiency.

most likely to be found where the state considers that private sector competition should be regulated, for example on health and safety grounds.

This kind of approach to the study of production efficiency by economists is useful in clarifying possible outcomes. However, arguably, it has distinct limitations for it assumes a common behavioural response; in this case, of management to the same environmental factors (competition, regulation and ownership). In fact, this may be a gross oversimplification of actual behaviour. A study undertaken into ten organisations that changed their status within the public sector (e.g. government department to public corporation) or which crossed the ownership line from private to public or vice versa (nationalisation and privatisation) suggested that the effects on operating efficiency depended upon the degree of internal organisational change, which equated with the specific managerial responses (Dunsire *et al.*, 1991; Parker, 1995a). The explanation for efficiency changes when ownership changed seemed to lie in the extent to which the enterprises shook off their public sector ways of working and internally reorganised. In other words, changes in the internal environment of the firm proved critical in determining the firm's ability to 'fit' to the new external environment (changes in competition, regulation and ownership). Changes in the internal environment came down to particular organisational/management responses.

In general terms, internal changes in response to privatisation may involve:

1 management – in terms of personnel (e.g. new management), competence and training;
2 employment – in terms of numbers employed, forms of collective bargaining (including the role of trade unions) and training of staff;
3 internal architecture – involving the structure and organisation of the business. Since public sector activities tend to be highly centralised, this could involve decentralisation into profit centres, adopting a holding company structure and outsourcing;[15]
4 the nature and location of the business – including investments and divestments;
5 the mission and goals of the organisation – involving a new focus on commercial goals including profit making and a new consumer orientation. This in turn may be associated with changes in vocabulary used in the organisation, for example use of the term 'customer' rather than 'passenger' or 'subscriber'; and
6 internal communications – public sector activities tend to be rules and procedure oriented, involving a keen interest in 'doing it right' according to the rule book. A failure of procedure in arriving at a decision may cause more political embarrassment than the decision itself. This rule-bound management culture in turn leads to a frequent referring up of decisions to appropriate ranking officers. Individual discretion is not encouraged. This environment can be expected to be reflected in the kind of information collated within the organisation and reported to senior management.

Since commercial, non-bureaucratic organisations tend to be more interested in outcomes rather than procedures, *per se*, privatisation is likely to be associated with changes in internal communications and reporting systems. This may involve the introduction of new management accounting and IT systems, to obtain accurate and speedy results-oriented information and a change in the kind of information circulated within the organisation. There may be less referring up and more horizontal information flows.

Table 2.2 summarises that type of differences that tends to exist between public sector and private sector organisations. The emphasis is on *tend* since the list is something of a caricature. Not all private sector organisations are entrepreneurial and non-bureaucratic, by any means. Private sector banks and insurance companies, for instance, are renowned for their rule books and procedures. Equally, some public sector organisations have demonstrated a high degree of commercialism, such as The Post Office in recent years. Nevertheless, privatisation can be expected to lead to changes under at least some of the six headings above. Alternatively, if internal changes do not occur before, at or following privatisation then improved economic performance is unlikely. Merely transferring an organisation from the state to the private sector changes nothing – a name change is merely a name change. Privatisation should be viewed as a means to an end not as an end in itself.

In general terms, the expectation of the proponents of privatisation is that before, during or after privatisation an inward-looking, hierarchical, production-oriented organisation will metamorphose into an outward-looking, profit-centred, customer-focused operation. Organisational structures and behaviour perpetuate ideas, norms and ways of working, and indeed distributions of power or authority in organisations, that over time are accepted as normal and inevitable. Successful transition to a privatised environment requires a fundamental reassessment of this status quo. Privatisation implies considerable restructuring at various levels. *What all of this amounts to is the effectiveness with which management manages strategic change.*

Johnson and Scholes (1997, p. 10) define the characteristics of strategy as 'the *direction* and *scope* of an organisation over the *long term*: which achieves *advantage* for the organisation through its configuration of *resources* within a changing *environment* to meet the needs of *markets* and to fulfil *stakeholder* expectations.'[16] In this sense privatisation is a strategic opportunity (though some, such as the workforce and middle-management grades, may see it as a threat). The approach adopted to strategy formulation and implementation in this book, and more specifically the approach adopted to purchasing and supply strategy, is akin to that of Mintzberg (1987) and others (e.g. Hamel, 1991). They argue that decision-makers are not detached from their environment but deeply embedded in it. Strategy emerges from pragmatic learning and compromise rather than simply from grand masterplans and major leaps forward (Kochan *et al.*, 1984). The approach adopted is complementary to an

Table 2.2 Differences between public and private organisations

Public sector	*Private sector*
Management	
Orientation: inward/production/ professional interests	Consumer/marketing focus
Style: reactive	Proactive
Politically constrained	Stakeholder interests but less constrained
Employment	
High unionisation/centralised bargaining	Lower unionisation/decentralised bargaining
Salary gradings	Employment based on performance
High security of employment	Less security of employment
Internal architecture	
Hierarchical pyramid/centralised	Decentralised/diversified
Functional	Business based/profit centres
	Outsourcing
Nature and location of the business	
Politically and geographically constrained	Commercially determined
Business development politically constrained	Diversification, investment and divestment/mergers/overseas ventures
Limited overseas investment and sourcing	International/global
Mission and goals	
Multiple and sometimes vague and conflicting (public interest)	Commercial
Equity and probity	Consumer orientation
Closed system leading to continuity/ consistency	Open/adaptable
Focus on inputs	Focus on outputs/outcomes
Non-market prices/state subsidies	Market prices/subsidy free
Internal communications	
Bureaucratic and formal	Less bureaucratic/informal
Input oriented	Output oriented
Internal communication via written memoranda	More face to face
Formal committee structures	Ad hoc team working
Rule book procedures	Financial targets
Accounting and management information systems underdeveloped	Strong accounting and MISs[a]

Source: based on Martin and Parker (1997), table 9.1, p. 178.

Note
a MIS: Management information system.

'evolutionary' approach to strategy, in that strategy is seen to evolve over time in response to environmental changes, but, critically, the approach is not deterministic. Different behavioural responses add unpredictability to the precise evolutionary change. In other words, and among other things, *the quality of management decision making matters.* The approach adopted sees the organisation as a normative system and thereby provides a role for effective management. The approach is anchored in a resource-based view of the firm. The resources of the organisation are critical determinants of strategy outcomes, including procurement strategy.

Certainly, the approach adopted stands in stark contrast to the classical view of strategy, now widely criticised, which sees strategy formulation and implementation as involving a rational process of deliberate management calculation and analysis. Instead, strategy in privatised companies is viewed as organic and in terms not of management (and workers) passively reacting to changes in their external environment, brought on by privatisation, but as active shapers of both the challenges and solutions. In other words, like all organisations, privatised firms will have developed a distinctive culture with attitudes, behaviour and expectations that are supportive. This internal environment determines a set of policy options which may no longer be appropriate following transfer to the private sector. Former, conditioned behaviour may now have to be redirected and changed.

Argyris and Schon (1978) have pointed out that organisations tackle day-to-day management issues with what they call 'single-loop' learning. That is to say, management obtain information about their operating environment, make decisions based on that information and act in a fairly consistent and predictable manner. This leads to an incremental form of management, akin to the notion of continuous improvement. At the same time, it leads to a form of *lock-in* or *path dependency*, where the organisation continually refines the way it has done things in the past but essentially continues to do the same things in the same way (Arthur, 1988; Parker, 1995b). There is, in terms of Johnson and Scholes's 'paradigm' (1997, pp. 54–7), no paradigm change. Nelson and Winter (1982, p. 111) refer to the possibility that routines in organisations foster 'the dikes of vested interests'. This is very much in the same spirit.

Single-loop learning, lock-in, path dependency, dominant paradigms and routines are all the products of past success. They work well in supporting consistent and successful production, but ultimately, over time, threaten to undermine the organisation by reducing its flexibility and responsiveness to non-incremental changes in the external environment. Occasionally there are changes in the business environment, for example a new competitor or technological change, which require much more root and branch rethinking. This rethinking Argyris and Schon have labelled 'double-loop' learning and Johnson and Scholes a 'paradigm shift'. Figure 2.2 illustrates the differences between learning with a 'single loop' and 'double loop'. Double-loop learning necessitates a more fundamental change in thinking and a new mental map of the organisation and its place in the world.

Public sector organisations may survive for long periods on single-loop learning since often their environment is highly stable, especially where changes in government do not involve major shifts in policy. For example,

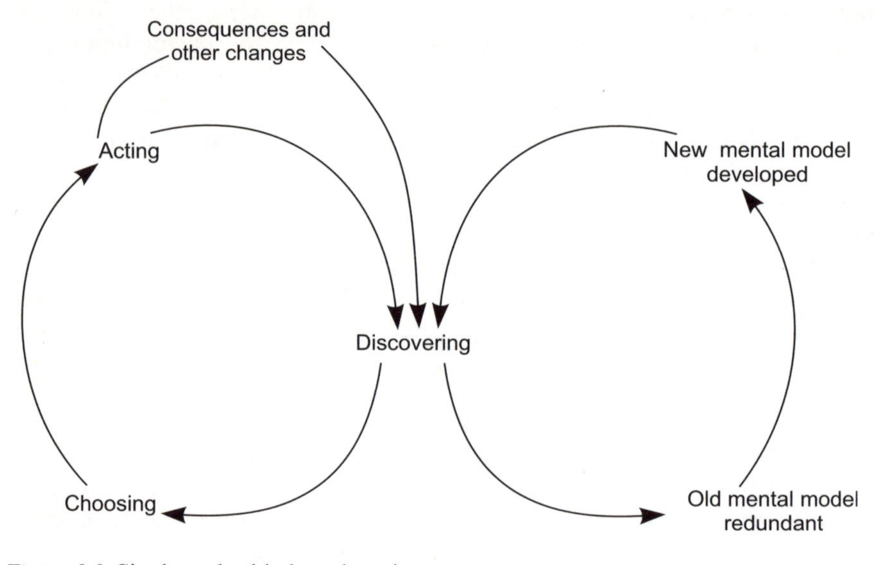

Figure 2.2 Single to double-loop learning.
Source: based on Argyris and Schon (1978).

from the 1940s to the 1980s the NHS (National Health Service) underwent only limited structural reorganisation and changes in funding. From 1950 to 1979 successive governments in the UK managed the nationalised industries in very similar ways. There was a high degree of political consensus in Britain regarding the management of the nationalised industries, as mentioned earlier. Also, a number of the major nationalised firms were protected from competition by statute and were not subject to rapid technological advances, for instance the National Coal Board and the water and sewerage companies. There was, therefore, a high degree of stability in their business environment – a stability conducive to reliance on single-loop learning within management.

The evolving policy of privatisation after 1979 marked a major shift in attitude at the government level. For the first time, the postwar political and economic consensus in Britain based around the mixed economy and with it the efficacy of single-loop thinking within public sector organisations was threatened. The management of the nationalised industries faced the prospect of both being financed by a competitive capital market rather than the state (taxpayers) and enhanced-product market competition. Some were also faced by new forms of state regulation through the new regulatory offices mentioned earlier.

British Gas is a case in point. The company had more or less a complete monopoly over gas supply in the UK prior to privatisation in December 1986. Starting with gas supplies to large users and from 1995 for domestic consumers, British Gas has faced growing competition from new gas suppliers. In consequence, the company has seen its market share dip, dramatically, provoking various bouts of restructuring and senior management changes. Today, British Gas has only around 30 per cent of the large-user market for gas and the domestic gas consumer market was fully liberalised in April 1998. In trial areas from 1996 the company lost around 20 per cent of its domestic customers to competitors, in spite of cutting its charges. At the same time, the company has fought frequent battles with its regulator, Ofgas, over performance targets and new competition. It has also suffered periodic monitoring of its activities by the competition watchdog, the Office of Fair Trading, and three enquiries by the Monopolies and Mergers Commission (MMC, 1988, 1993, 1997). In the face of growing competition and a tough regulatory environment, profits have declined and along with them returns to investors (Parker, 1998). In response, the company divided into two in February 1997 – Centrica, principally responsible for gas trading and servicing, and BG plc, responsible mainly for gas storage and transportation.

Privatisation has necessitated double-loop learning or a paradigm shift at British Gas. As competition has increased and regulation has proved harsher than expected at privatisation, the management have had to rethink their whole way of doing business, in terms of products, processes and structures. At first this involved reorganising functions and duties and limited management and workforce changes. Eventually it led to the abolition of the existing company structure by division into two parts with separate share listings. Figure 2.3 illustrates the shift in British Gas from single-loop learning to double-loop learning. From privatisation in 1986 to the arrival of effective competition in 1992, single-loop learning continued to dominate with relatively little in the way of dramatic change within the company. Since 1992 the

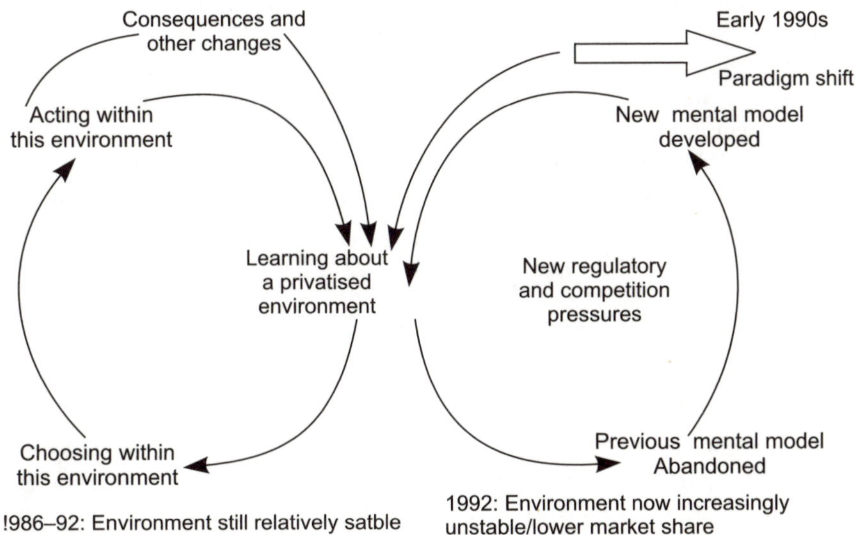

Figure 2.3 Learning at British Gas.

effect of competition has driven management to adopt more radical surgery involving something more akin to the double loop.

More generally, privatisation can be expected to lead to internal changes on the lines outlined earlier where it is associated with real and substantial changes in the business environment. It is to be expected that as part of this reconsideration, the purchasing and supply (or external resource) management activity will come under scrutiny. The privatised companies buy in large amounts of components, materials and fuel supplies. Economies in this area can help to drive down costs and satisfy the profit expectations of the new investors in the City, but, *as importantly*, effective purchasing and supply strategies can be central to determining the overall competitive advantage of firms, especially when this leads to a fundamental rethink about the effective boundary of the firm, and the way in which a growing external spend can be managed appropriately.

Privatisation and purchasing and supply management: some initial comments

Although the impact of privatisation on the boundary of the firm and buyer–supplier relationships has been neglected, one can anticipate that, as part of the reorientation of the business to meet the opportunities and challenges of private sector operation, there will be a new interest in the make–buy issue and appropriate purchasing and supply methods. Following privatisation, there should be more incentive to manage the supply and value chains effectively to maximise profit. In particular, as transactions change so would one expect the contracts that govern them to alter (Spicer and Ballew, 1983). Hence, transactions and contracts will be affected by new environmental forces or 'drivers' impacting on the firm.

Certain hypotheses can be derived regarding the nature and scope of the *efficiency*-related changes in purchasing and supply management that one might expect immediately prior to, during and following privatisation.

First, commensurate with the desire to obtain cost efficiencies, it is to be expected that purchasing and supply will come under pressure to obtain cost savings, including a reduced headcount.

Second, this cost pressure is likely to involve a change in the role and profile of purchasing and supply within the organisation and an increased professionalism among procurement staff.

Third, supplier relationships and performance assessment are likely to change to reflect the new, more professional role of procurement.

Finally, a more strategically aligned approach to make–buy and external resource management may develop as attention centres on developing procurement as part of a wider organisational strategy to achieve dynamic efficiency and competitive advantage through supply alignment.

Privatisation, especially when coupled either with an increase in competition or a hostile regulator, provides 'shock therapy' to the organisation. This necessitates a sharp organisational response if the firm is to survive. More specifically, the firm can be expected to review its core competencies, reposition itself in the market, revisit its products and processes to ensure that they are still 'fit for purpose' and attempt to reduce transaction costs. Transaction costs are the costs of negotiating, monitoring and enforcing contracts with suppliers. To economise on transaction costs the firm will need to align its internal processes to the new external drivers. It will need to reconsider what are its distinctive capabilities to ensure sustainable competitive advantage. An adjustment to the boundary of the firm, including the externalisation or internalisation of activities, may be an important component of this change, as purchasing strategy aligns with the new corporate strategy (Caddick and Dale, 1987). This process requires answers to the following questions:

1 What is the effective boundary of the firm in the new environment brought about by privatisation? This will necessitate a strategic view of outsourcing.
2 What type of relationships externally are now needed? Need they be more co-operative or more arm's length? What is the scope for joint ventures, use of collaborative sourcing, preferred suppliers and so on? The aim should be to achieve a best-practice relationship.
3 Where and how should we source? This may involve a review of vendor accreditation, domestic as against international sourcing (state enterprises have tended to favour domestic suppliers, notwithstanding recent EU procurement directives), and supplier performance measurement.

In practice, the reaction of management and the extent of the resulting changes within the organisation may be expected to vary depending upon the new strategic drivers of the business. The key drivers of change following privatisation can be postulated as a change in demand and cost conditions arising from the new legal status, stock market pressures, competition and regulation, and perhaps the need for faster technological change so as to survive in the private market place. Managers can be expected to alter their behaviour according to the new external environment they face (e.g. tranquil or turbulent; simple or complex) (Burns and Stalker, 1961; Dunsire *et al.*, 1988).

Following privatisation, the environment may seem less complex because the threat of unpredictable political intervention is removed. Also, for example, capital programmes no longer have to be agreed with a government department and are no longer constrained by public sector borrowing limits or EFLs. Alternatively, the environment can seem more turbulent, uncertain and threatening because of the removal of taxpayer funding, the introduction of more competition and uncertainties about the behaviour and demands of the new regulatory offices and of investors.

The nature of the organisational change may be expected to vary from one privatised industry to another and perhaps within the same industry over time, depending upon the particular circumstances. In particular, one might expect a quicker reaction in terms of internal reorientation, including changes in purchasing and supply practices, from management in privatised–competitive industries than from management in privatised firms that retain considerable monopoly power, especially where they are lightly regulated. The impact of regulation on economic performance has been pursued in the literature mainly in terms of capital and labour usage and service levels (e.g. Bailey, 1973; Swann, 1988). However, regulation may have implications for the restructuring of supply chains. In so far as efficiency incentives are reduced by continued state regulation, the expectation would be that there would be fewer innovations in purchasing and supply practices.

Conclusions

If privatisation is to operate as intended and improve organisational performance, then changes must occur in the way that the business is managed and organised so as to achieve coherence or a 'fit' between the new external environment and the internal organisation. Earlier studies have looked at the impact on labour relations, wages and employment (Pendleton and Winterton, 1993; O'Connell Davidson, 1994; Parker and Martin, 1996). There has also been exploratory work on the effects on management and organisational structures (Parker, 1994). Surprisingly, perhaps, there seems to have been no systematic study of the results for purchasing and supply management, even though the importance of good procurement in achieving competitive advantage is now widely recognised (Pearson and Gritzmacher, 1990; Lamming, 1993; Lamming and Cox, 1995; Cox, 1996b, 1997a; Cox and Hines, 1997). This present book fills this gap.[17] The following chapters are concerned with advancing knowledge by reporting the results of a questionnaire survey of purchasing, supply and procurement managers in a cross-section of UK privatised companies and follow-up interviews. The objective is to assess to what extent and in what ways purchasing and supply practices have changed, and are changing, as a consequence of privatisation and how these might be impacting on performance.

Privatisation is an important part of industrial policy in a large number of countries worldwide. The policy has been promoted because of expected efficiency gains when enterprises are transferred from the public to the private sector. At the same time, however, research has suggested that organisational restructuring within the privatised firms may be critical in determining the outcome, although the precise nature of the restructuring still requires investigation. In particular, there has been no systematic study of privatisation and purchasing and supply practices.

Corporate strategy is contingent upon the external environment faced by the firm after privatisation, changes in that environment and the precise management response. Privatisation in the UK has led to a considerable shrinking of the state sector, but some enterprises seem to have taken more advantage than others of the opportunities created. These enterprises seem to be, not surprisingly, the ones that have improved their performance most noticeably. The research which forms the basis of the content of this book sets out to address a number of related issues concerned with purchasing and supply strategies in privatised companies. The main issues are:

1. Has there been a reorganisation of the purchasing and supply function within the organisation as a whole?
2. Has there been a change in the scope, role and responsibility of the purchasing personnel? For example, does purchasing now control a higher proportion of company spend; has the scope of responsibility of the head of purchasing changed?
3. Has purchasing become more strategic as opposed to tactical and reactive?
4. Has the internal profile of purchasing improved? Was it seen as a 'Cinderella activity' in the past and is the purchasing function now gaining more respect in the rest of the company?
5. Has purchasing increased its involvement in non-traditional spend, e.g. consultancy or financial services?
6. Has the level of outsourcing increased or decreased?
7. Has purchasing been involved proactively, reactively, or not at all in the decisions on whether to outsource? This should give an indication of whether purchasing is becoming more involved in strategic issues, or whether it is still seen merely as a 'service' function to the rest of the organisation.
8. Has the use of professional purchasing tools increased? Examples could include the use of benchmarking, strategic source planning, and purchase price cost analysis.
9. Has there been a change in the qualification levels of purchasing staff?
10. Has there been an improvement in supply base management?
11. Has there been a rationalisation of suppliers?
12. Is the organisation becoming more competitive or collaborative in its supplier relationships? Are the private sector trends towards partnerships and increased collaboration with suppliers being followed?
13. Has a new head of purchasing and supply been appointed, either from within the company or from outside?
14. Is make–buy and supply alignment a fundamentally understood methodology in the company?

The results of the research into these broad questions are provided in the following chapters. The next chapter provides a summary of the empirical methodology used in the research. This forms the basis for the empirical work reported later.

3 The research project and methodology

Development of hypotheses and proxy indicators on the functional professionalisation of purchasing and supply management

Although no previous detailed investigation has been carried out into the links between privatisation and changes in purchasing and supply management, there is a growing body of literature in the two separate disciplines: the general effects of privatisation on organisational behaviour (for example, Garrett 1997; Harper 1997); Parker 1994, 1995a; and the development of supply chain management as a functional and strategic competence (Lamming and Cox 1995; Cox 1997a). A review of this work enabled the development of some general expectations or hypotheses relating to changes in purchasing and supply in a privatised company. Following this, the next stage was to develop proxy indicators for these hypotheses so that they could be tested in the field. The four central themes and related indicators are summarised in Table 3.1 and explained below. The indicators are important to note at this stage as they effectively shape the rest of the book: both the questionnaire and follow-up interview results are structured around these themes.

Hypothesis 1 The purchasing and supply function will come under pressure to reduce internal operating costs

Privatised companies are likely to focus much more heavily on achieving cost efficiencies than when they were in the public sector. This is due to the change in ownership and, in some cases, to either increased competition in product markets or regulatory pressures. The ownership change creates shareholders who expect competitive dividend payouts every six months, as well as the threat of takeover, resulting in a focus on profitability and hence cost efficiency. The introduction of product market competition will redouble the focus on costs, for the obvious reason that a competitor producing the same good at a cheaper price will gain market share, everything being equal. Although this second factor of product market competition has not affected all privatised companies (British Gas has retained a monopoly in some

Table 3.1 The four key hypotheses and a summary of the proxy indicators tested in the research

	Expectation		*Proxy indicator*
1	The purchasing and supply function will come under pressure to *reduce internal operating costs.*	⟶	**Structure of purchasing and supply** – employment in purchasing.
2	A more *professional approach* to purchasing and supply will develop at the functional level.	⟶	**Professional purchasing Functionalism** – formal strategy, mission statements, use of new 'tools & techniques', performance measurement of purchasing.
3	There will be a change in the *role and profile* of purchasing and supply management.	⟶	**Role & profile** – involvement in company spend, position of most senior purchasing and supply manager, qualifications of personnel.
4	There will be pressure to reduce the costs of internal operations and external spend.	⟶	**Outsourcing & supplier relationships** – changes in make–buy, supplier relationships, types of supplier performance measurement & actual supplier performance.

markets until very recently and the water companies remain monopolistic in their regions), the industry regulator offers a surrogate for competition by, for example, setting price caps on the companies concerned through the RPI-X formula explained in Chapter 2.

It follows that the purchasing and supply function, along with the rest of the organisation, will come under pressure to reduce internal operating costs. It is difficult to pinpoint any single area within purchasing and supply where cost pressure will show because a consideration for costs is involved in almost every decision that an organisation takes. However, for the sake of presentation, the structure of purchasing and supply is assessed – how this has changed since privatisation, and whether the numbers employed in procurement have changed over the same period. *Has the function been centralised as part of a rationalisation/cost reduction process? Has the number of purchasing personnel been reduced as part of a headcount freeze, or increased as the importance of effective purchasing and supply has been recognised?*

Hypothesis 2 A more professional approach to purchasing and supply will develop at the functional level

In a newly competitive market, privatised companies should begin to develop strategies to achieve competitive advantage and to gain ground on their rivals. As part of this effort, it is expected that a more strategic approach to purchasing and supply management will develop. In most public sector organisations purchasing was often little more than an administrative, order–placer role (as we discovered in our research). This would not suffice in a company aiming to develop sustainable competitive advantage, where the importance of procuring bought-in goods effectively is recognised. Thus, the need for a more strategic approach will arise, and the task of the staff should change accordingly.

Indicators used to test how 'professional' the function has become are: the existence of a formal purchasing and supply strategy, the use of mission statements, and the use of various purchasing tools and techniques ranging from highly reactive practices such as organising bids to more sophisticated techniques such as purchase price cost analysis and strategic source planning. How the performance of the purchasing department was measured and how this had changed since privatisation were also investigated. The result could also indicate increased cost pressure, if performance measurement had been introduced as part of an efficiency drive.

Hypothesis 3 There will be a change in the role and profile of purchasing and supply management

Following on from the second hypothesis, the development of a more strategic approach to purchasing and supply is likely to be reflected in a change in the role and internal profile of the function. This results from senior management increasingly realising the importance of effective supply management, through its effect on the cost and quality of bought-in goods and services. This might result in the function becoming more involved in strategic organisational decisions as opposed to mere order-placing, gaining ground in terms of its position in the organisational hierarchy and, possibly, more respect from elsewhere in the organisation.

The indicators tested here are the position of the most senior purchasing manager/director, and the involvement of the function in company spend – testing how both of these had changed since privatisation. An open question was asked about how the role had changed generally. This change in role and profile may also be reflected in the calibre of procurement staff – as the company realises that higher-calibre individuals are required to carry out the more demanding role. Average levels of qualification are a key indicator here too, and changes in the qualifications of purchasing staff were investigated during the interviews.

Hypothesis 4 There will be pressure to reduce the cost of internal operations and external spend

As companies are released from public sector constraints, where they were often mandated to provide a given service, and as they face increasing competitive and cost pressures, they are likely to re-evaluate their make–buy strategy in an attempt to reduce transaction costs (Parker and Hartley, 1997). Given that the majority of public sector organisations were vertically integrated and performed most activities in-house, it is expected that an increase in outsourcing of support services will result.

Given the increased cost pressures, it can also be expected that privatised companies will begin to monitor supplier performance more carefully, and that this increased pressure will be felt by suppliers, pushing them to improve their performance. It is also likely that the nature of relationships with suppliers will change. While traditional public sector relationships with suppliers have tended to be arm's length and sometimes adversarial, the tendency in the private sector in recent years has been to build more collaborative, partnership-type relationships with suppliers, believing (rightly or wrongly) that this is best practice. Our hypothesis is that privatised companies will follow this trend, in their attempts to gain competitive advantage through adopting so-called 'best practices' from the private sector.

All of these indicators – outsourcing of support services, supplier performance measurement, actual supplier performance, and forms of supplier relationship, are analysed in the research.

The research approach

As explained above, the research project focused on changes in purchasing and supply since privatisation and revolved around four key hypotheses. Based upon this structure, the key objectives were first to unearth general trends in purchasing and supplier relationships in the privatised sector, and second to delve more deeply into any developments that were discovered. This enabled the research team to 'get behind' the trends, and to discover the reasons for any changes in the companies concerned. These objectives necessitated a two-tiered approach, the first stage being a questionnaire survey of all organisations concerned, the second a series of follow-up interviews of a representative selection of companies. These two stages are now explained in more detail.

Stage 1 Questionnaire survey

A standard questionnaire was designed and sent to companies identified as undergoing privatisation since 1979. Before the questionnaires were sent, the companies involved were telephoned in order to make direct contact with a purchasing manager or director to explain the project to them and, it was hoped, to increase the response rate. A copy of the questionnaire can be found in the Appendix on page 235.

Questionnaires were sent to the senior purchasing management of 48 privatised companies in total and completed returns were received from 28 companies, giving a respectable response rate of 58 per cent. The companies that participated in this initial stage are listed in Table 3.2 on page 42. The next stage involved a full analysis of the returns, and the results form the subject of Chapter 4.

Table 3.2 Privatised companies involved in the survey

Organisation	*Year of privatisation*
British Aerospace	1981
Cable & Wireless	1981
Associated British Ports	1983
British Gas	1986
British Airways	1987
British Airports Authority	1987
Rolls Royce	1987
British Steel	1988
The Rover Group	1988
RJB Mining	1995
Railtrack	1996
Water companies	
Northumbrian Water	1989
Severn Trent Water	1989
Southern Water	1989
South West Water	1989
Thames Water	1989
Welsh Water (later, Hyder)	1989
Yorkshire Water	1989
Electricity companies	
Eastern Electricity	1990
Midlands Electricity	1990
Northern Electricity	1990
Norweb	1990
SWEB	1990
Yorkshire Electricity	1990
National Grid	1990
Nuclear Electric[a]	1996
PowerGen	1991
Scottish Hydro-Electric	1991

Note

a Most of Nuclear Electric was merged with the nuclear electric industry in Scotland to form British Energy, which was privatised shortly afterwards, in July 1996. The questionnaire was completed at Nuclear Electric just prior to the merger and privatisation.

Stage 2 Follow-up interviews

While this first stage answered the project's initial questions as to the general static efficiency and dynamic efficiency trends in privatised purchasing and supply management, the research would have been of limited value if it had not looked further into the reasons behind the changes witnessed. Hence a series of follow-up interviews was conducted with senior managers in purchasing departments. Twelve companies were chosen from the list above to participate in this second stage of the research. Privatisation has affected many different industries, and it is known that industry structure can affect company behaviour and performance (see for example Bain, 1959; Scherer, 1970; Porter, 1985) and vice versa. It seems reasonable to assume that industrial structure would also influence purchasing and supply strategy, and so, by studying a selection of industries, it was felt that it would be possible to go some way in testing this hypothesis.

In order to introduce some form of counterfactual,[1] a limited study of organisations remaining in the public sector was carried out. Three public sector organisations: The Post Office, the Civil Aviation Authority and London Underground Limited were interviewed, after a questionnaire had been completed. A fourth public sector organisation also completed a questionnaire but cannot be named for reasons of confidentiality. Questionnaire results for these four public sector organisations appear at the end of Chapter 4, page 63.

The fifteen organisations that took part in the interview stage, together with any relevant aspects of their industrial environment or status, are listed in Table 3.3. In all cases at least one senior manager involved in purchasing was interviewed. The interviews were structured and generally based around issues raised by the questionnaire return. The idea was to gain a deeper understanding of the changes noted in the questionnaire, explore further the reasons for any developments mentioned in the questionnaire returned, and invite the interviewee to note any additional information that was felt to be relevant in the case of their company.

Table 3.3 The fifteen organisations involved in the detailed interviews

Organisation	*Year of privatisation*	*Industrial environment/status*
British Gas	1986	Utility; privatised as a monopoly but competition now introduced; regulated by Ofgas.
Welsh Water South West Water *Severn Trent*	1989	Utility; privatised with monopoly intact; yardstick comparisons between water companies available; regulated by Ofwat.
PowerGen	1991	Power generator privatised as part of a duopoly with National Power; competition increasing; regulated by Offer.
Scottish Hydro-Electric	1991	Power generator, distributor & supplier; competition in generation and supply increasing; regulated by Offer.
NORWEB *SWEB*	1990	Regional Electricity Companies (recs); competition in large-user supply from privatisation; full competition in supply by the spring of 1999; regulated by Offer.
Rolls Royce	1987	Aerospace and marine engines; operates in a globally competitive market.
Rover Group	1988	Motor vehicles manufacturer; operates in a globally competitive market.

Table 3.3 (Contd.)

Organisation	*Year of privatisation*	*Industrial environment/status*
British Airways	1987	Airline; operates in a competitive but regulated market facing continuing liberalisation worldwide.
British Steel	1988	Steel producer; operates in a globally competitive market.
The Post Office	–	Monopoly in < £1 postal market; privatisation considered & rejected in 1994.
Civil Aviation Authority	–	Monopoly; privatisation considered & rejected. June 1998 government announces future sale of the National Air Traffic System (NATS).
London Underground	–	Monopoly; some privatisation or private capital injection considered and now planned.

The interview results appear in Chapters 5, 6 and 7. They have been organised by company into separate case studies, and each one follows the same structure as the questionnaire results, i.e. based on changes since privatisation[2] in the four key hypothesised areas. The five organisations in italics in Table 3.3 formed the subject of a more detailed study and are reported in Part III of the book.

Stage 3 In-depth case studies

The results at this stage of the research were very interesting because, while the questionnaire results had revealed very strong trends in the development of purchasing and supply management, such as significant changes in structure, the interviews suggested wide-ranging differences in the actual, detailed structures and strategies adopted by the different organisations. For example, while over 80 per cent of the companies noted a change in structure, half of them centralised and the other half decentralised. In order to investigate the reasons for this disparity, five more in-depth case studies were organised to look at a number of issues in more detail: was it their differing industrial structures and/or regulatory environments that caused differences, or were there other, more important factors involved in determining the structure and strategy of purchasing and supply? Had the company organised purchasing and supply in such a way that best suited its particular industrial environment, or had it just developed in an ad hoc way throughout the history of the organisation? In effect, this section of the research sought to assess whether the participating companies had shifted from a search for static and dynamic effects to one based on transformational efficiency linked to a supply alignment and procurement competence way of thinking.

In order to answer this question, the structure and strategy, as well as other internal and external factors which might be influential in shifting the strategic focus, were analysed. These included competitive rivalry and supplier markets. The first tier of interviewing had suggested that the industry which a company was in did influence the organisation of purchasing and supply, and this led to a deliberate decision to select organisations from five different industrial environments for this more detailed part of the study. The selection was made from the original group of fifteen and included:

1 Severn Trent
2 South West Electricity (SWEB)
3 British Airways
4 British Steel
5 The Post Office

The research methodology involved further structured interviews with each of the organisations (each was interviewed twice for this part of the research), combined with an analysis of relevant internal and public documentation. In each case, senior procurement executives in the organisations concerned were interviewed. The results are given in Part III in the form of detailed case studies. It follows that these five companies do not appear in Part II. The aim of this work was to place each company in its unique industrial context, map out its primary supply chain position, and assess its procurement competence in relation to this. In Part III, the research moved beyond testing the static and dynamic effects of privatisation, because the aim was to discover whether (or how) procurement aligned with the company's position in its primary supply chain(s). In this sense we were concerned to understand whether the company had accepted the need to develop an approach that would allow for transformational efficiency effects, based on continuous improvement, through developing supply alignment and procurement competence. The research shows that a transformational, as opposed to a static and dynamic efficiency perspective, is underdeveloped, at least in the companies studied.

The study involved a questionnaire and follow-up interviews with senior personnel involved in the purchasing function. Time, resources and obtaining co-operation from the companies and public sector organisations that feature in the book ruled out extending the fieldwork to consider the views of procurement and procurement's contribution to organisational strategy held by other sections of senior management, for example in marketing, finance or operational areas. This is a recognised weakness of the study. Or putting this differently, future research needs to address the coherence of attitudes to purchasing across *all* levels of senior management in organisations. Notwithstanding this need for a fuller study of procurement in privatised companies and the public sector, the book contains research results which go a long way to removing ignorance about purchasing's role in organisational change, most specifically when businesses are privatised. This was the purpose of the study.

Part II

Empirical findings: the survey results and case material

4 The impact of privatisation on the purchasing and supply function

Introduction

This chapter reports the results of the questionnaire survey into twenty-eight privatised companies introduced in the previous chapter, and we also discuss results for the four public sector organisations that were surveyed as part of the major research programme into procurement which is the focus of this book. The chapter is structured around the four hypotheses posited in Chapter 3. These relate to: internal cost reduction; professional purchasing functionalism; changes in the role and profile of purchasing and supply; and external cost reduction and make–buy pressures. In some cases, results from the follow-up interviews are given to illustrate further the points raised by the questionnaire responses. Section 1 presents the results from the privatised sector, and section 2 for the public sector. Both are structured in the same way to allow comparability of results.

In all cases, the questionnaire respondents were purchasing staff in the organisations concerned. These were mainly purchasing managers or directors, or a variant on this title such as supply chain manager or procurement manager/director. It is possible that this might cause some personal bias in the information provided since the interviewees will give a purchasing perspective, and the reader should bear this in mind when considering the results.

Section 1 Questionnaire results: twenty-eight privatised companies

Regarding the twenty-eight privatised companies, the main findings of the questionnaire survey can be summarised as follows. First, there was evidence of considerable internal cost pressures with concern for cost reduction being a key factor driving many of the changes witnessed in purchasing and supply. In particular, cost and efficiency factors, at least partly, led to widespread employment reduction within purchasing and supply and considerable restructuring of the function. Second, it is clear that a more professional role for purchasing has developed. This was witnessed, among other things, by the increased adoption of mission statements, formal purchasing strategies, and more sophisticated purchasing tools and techniques in place of reactive procedures. Third, there has been a change in the role of purchasing and an improvement in the internal profile of the function. Evidence in support of this finding included changes in the position of the most senior procurement manager and increased involvement of purchasing in overall company spend. Fourth, pressure to reduce external costs had also intensified. There had been an enormous increase in the outsourcing of support services, considerable improvements in supplier performance, as well as the development of more sophisticated techniques for measuring the performance of suppliers and of the purchasing department itself. A more detailed analysis of these findings is now presented.

Internal functional cost pressures

Structure of purchasing and supply

The first questions in the survey were concerned with whether there had been any changes in the structure of purchasing and supply since privatisation and their nature. Table 4.1 shows the direction of the structural changes.

Table 4.1 Direction of change in structure of the purchasing and supply function since privatisation

Change since privatisation	*No. of companies*	*%*
More centralised	12	43
More decentralised	12	43
No change	4	14
Total	28	100

Table 4.1 shows that 24 of the 28 companies have experienced a change in the structure of purchasing and supply. Therefore, only 4 organisations retained the same structure after privatisation. However, there has been no similarity of pattern, with exactly half of the companies becoming more centralised and the other half becoming more decentralised.

As Table 4.2 shows, a question on the timing of the restructuring revealed that the most popular period for restructuring purchasing was during the three years after privatisation, with 9 (32 per cent) of the companies changing during this period. Another 7 (25 per cent) experienced restructuring more than three years after privatisation. There were also 5 organisations (18 per cent) that changed before transfer of ownership. Again, there is evidence of a wide variation in responses to privatisation with some firms anticipating the change and others postponing restructuring until the effects of privatisation on business operations became clearer.

Table 4.2 Timing of changes in the structure of purchasing

Timing of change	*No. of companies*	*%*
More than 3 years before privatisation	2	7
0–3 years before privatisation	5	18
During year of privatisation	3	11
0–3 years after privatisation	9	32
More than 3 years after privatisation	7	25
No change	2	7
Total	28	100

Respondents were given the opportunity to comment on the reasons for the structural changes. Of the 12 companies that offered reasons for becoming more centralised, 6 attributed it to a recognition of the importance of purchasing and supply to the business, 2 to economies of scale, 3 to the desire to gain better control of procurement spend and 1 to 'rationalisation as part of the leaning process'. There were only 6 respondents who offered reasons for decentralisation. Of these, 3 of the cases involved restructuring of purchasing and supply as part of overall company restructuring, 2 were due to cost or headcount reduction, and 1 was due to a lack of resources leading to devolvement of spend to other parts of the business.

These answers are reminders that, although firms may restructure in similar ways, they may not do so for the same or similar reasons. Also, a significant trend that was detected among the 12 companies interviewed was initial centralisation in order to improve control of company spend, before redevolving low-value, less-strategic spend to lower levels or regional locations for reasons of efficiency and/or flexibility.

Employment in purchasing and supply

Privatisation leads to a reconsideration of staffing levels across the organisation (Parker and Martin, 1996). Respondents were asked how many people were currently working in the purchasing department, excluding clerical and support staff, and how this had changed since privatisation. They were then asked to offer reasons for any changes that they reported. The results are summarised in Table 4.3 on page 52.

There was obviously a clear trend towards employing fewer staff in the purchasing function, with over a half of respondents (15) reporting a drop in staff and just 5 showing an increase. The fall in numbers had been substantial: the average number of people employed in purchasing fell from at least 123[1] before privatisation to 79 currently. This represents a decrease of 36 per cent. It should be noted that there might be some confusion as to the exact definition of the 'purchasing department', as this can be limited to the central purchasing function or purchasing staff throughout the company. However, the

Table 4.3 Changes in the number of purchasing staff since privatisation

Direction of change	*No. of companies*
More staff	5
Less staff	15
No change	5
Insufficient information	3
Total	28

Table 4.4 Reasons for changes in the numbers employed in the purchasing department

Reasons for reduction	*No. of respondents*	*Reasons for increase*	*No. of respondents*
Devolvement (less staff at centre)	4	Recognition of strategic importance of procurement	3
Pressure on costs, headcount or bottom line	4	Increased scope of activities due to success	2
Reflects efficiency improvements	3	Centralisation (more staff at centre)	1
Company downsizing	2		
Result of technology/ automation	2		
Centralisation (less staff in total)	2		
Concentration on core activities	1		

definitions were clarified during the interviews and, in any case, the respondents used consistent definitions for 'before' and 'after', thus maintaining the validity of the results. Most respondents gave reasons for the changes in employment, and these are presented in Table 4.4 above.

The main point to note is the effect of commercial pressure, in the form of pressure on costs, headcount and the bottom line, on those companies experiencing a decrease in staff numbers. Four respondents named this as a direct influence, but factors such as downsizing, technology and efficiency improvements were all, at least partly, due to this same pressure. By contrast, the main causes of increased staffing levels were a specific reflection of the success of the purchasing function, rather than forming part of company-wide trends. Three respondents cited increased recognition of the importance of purchasing and supply within the company, and two reported an increased scope of purchasing activities due to their success. There was a general indication that the internal profile of the function had improved since privatisation in the companies experiencing an increase in staff numbers.

Professional purchasing functionalism

Privatisation might be expected to lead to a reassessment of the role of procurement within the business for reasons discussed earlier in Chapter 2. Assessing this type of change is not straightforward and certain proxy indicators must be used with care. Here, in order to discover whether the purchasing function had become more professional, respondents were asked questions about their mission statements, purchasing strategy, and the tools and techniques that they commonly use.

In terms of mission statements, the replies indicate that 20 of the 28 firms (71 per cent) were using them at the time that the research was undertaken, while only five (18 per cent) were not (three firms chose not to reply to this question). Prior to privatisation, just two organisations (7 per cent) used them, showing a stark contrast. This significant growth in the adoption of mission statements might signify that the purchasing function was becoming more strategic; on the other hand, it could simply reflect a fad for company missions in the late 1980s and early 1990s. In any case, the fact that a purchasing department has a mission statement does not necessarily alter its behaviour. It is only when the activities and role of purchasing and supply staff change in order to deliver that mission that a more strategic focus may begin to develop.

The replies to the questionnaire did not enable a decision to be made as to whether the development of mission statements was a significant strategic change or simply a passing fad. However, supplementary questions relating to the content of the mission statements revealed some common themes, summarised in Table 4.5 on page 54. These are consistent with the notion that the purchasing function was becoming more strategic. The fact that full-life value for money (assessing the value gained from a product or service over its full lifetime rather than buying on short-term considerations such as price) was now considered when purchasing a product or service, and that supply chain management techniques were being adopted where there had been none before, is suggestive that a longer-term, more proactive view was being taken. The mention of professionalisation of staff and the adoption of best practice is also consistent with a more focused approach to procurement.

Moreover, 26 of the 28 companies (93 per cent) answered that they had a formal strategy for their purchasing department (the other two firms provided no information). Before privatisation only 6 companies (21 per cent) had such a strategy and 15 (54 per cent) had none (7 companies gave no information). These answers add support to the view that the purchasing and supply function has developed a more professional focus since privatisation. Follow-up interviews in 12 of the firms further endorsed this view. In many cases, company strategy had been deliberately distilled within purchasing strategy, which had then been broken down into individual performance objectives for the staff of the purchasing department.

The answers to the question on purchasing tools and techniques suggested that a wide variety of techniques were in use. Table 4.6 on page 54 lists the

Table 4.5 The most popular themes in purchasing mission statements

Theme in purchasing mission statements	*No. of times mentioned*
Full-life value for money; lowest total cost of acquisition	4
Best practice	3
Professional training & development of staff	3
Supply chain management techniques	3
Working/partnerships with internal customers	3
Supplier reduction	2
Working with suppliers	2

Table 4.6 Procurement tools and techniques most commonly used before and after privatisation

Purchasing tools and techniques	*Before*	*After*
Writing tender specifications	13	12
Organising bids	19	18
Negotiating	17	24
Awarding contracts	23	23
Expediting	17	13
Inspection of goods on arrival	10	10
Vendor accreditation	11	20
Formal vendor selection mechanisms	9	23
Benchmarking/best practice	3	22
Purchasing portfolio analysis	3	22
Strategic source planning	3	21
Purchase price cost analysis	7	19
Strategic supplier alliances	3	17
Partnership sourcing	2	20
Network sourcing	1	11
Relational competence analysis	1	10

replies, ranging from the most reactive at the top and gradually becoming more proactive and arguably professional. The answers provided a clear distinction with very little change in the more reactive activities – from writing tender specifications to inspection of goods on arrival – but a significant increase in the use of the more proactive techniques, ranging from vendor accreditation onwards in the Table. The use of benchmarking and purchasing portfolio analysis, for example, seems to have risen from just under 11 per cent of the sample (3) before privatisation to almost 79 per cent after privatisation (22). The use of strategic supplier alliances, partnership sourcing and network sourcing had also increased substantially. In addition to suggesting a much more proactive approach to procurement since privatisation, these developments indicate a change in supplier relationships towards a more collaborative arrangement.

It is interesting that the use of negotiating, one of the more reactive techniques, showed an increase of 16 percentage points – from 60 per cent (17) to 86 per cent of the sample (24). Although the reasons for this were not evident from the questionnaire, the interview results suggested that some companies,

Table 4.7 Initiatives in purchasing and supply since privatisation

Initiatives in purchasing and supply since privatisation	*No. of times mentioned*
More alliancing; JVs; partnerships	7
More training & development of staff	5
Low-value spend: use of credit and fuel cards	4
Supplier rationalisation	4
Customer–supplier development programmes	2
Continuous improvement	2
Relationship; contract management	2
Concept of internal customers	2

particularly the utilities, did not even engage in price negotiation before privatisation. Instead, they simply accepted the prices quoted by the suppliers. This is consistent with the notion that there is much less pressure to achieve efficiency or cost targets under state ownership.

Further evidence of significant changes in the nature of purchasing and supply was apparent in answers to a question on *initiatives taken in purchasing* since privatisation. These are summarised in Table 4.7. The emphasis on training and development and the concept of continuous improvement are two initiatives which underline this, while the fact that alliances, customer–supplier development programmes and relationship management programmes have become more popular suggests that there has been a shift towards more collaboration with suppliers. A number of the organisations seem to be favouring partnership-type relationships with fewer suppliers rather than the more traditional public sector arm's length approach to contracting, where contracts are based on formal tenders and involve little interaction with suppliers. The adoption of staff credit cards for low-value spend (Table 4.7), along with methods such as purchase price cost analysis (see Table 4.6 on page 54) may suggest that controlling input costs is now more of a priority than before.

Improvements in the role and profile of purchasing and supply

Further questions on the role of purchasing and supply within the firm were asked with the intention of unearthing the extent to which the internal profile of the function had changed. If purchasing is now truly more professional and strategic, then the expectation would be that the role and profile of purchasing within the company would have altered significantly. That is, it would assume a more strategic role and generally gain more respect from the rest of the organisation, being perceived as more important.

Again, the results show a considerable transition with 25 companies (89 per cent) reporting a change in the role of purchasing. Moreover, at least half of the respondents stressed that there had been a complete transformation of the role of purchasing, in most cases from a purely administrative, 'paper-pushing' role with little kudos, to a more commercially focused, strategic and professional task.

It appears from Table 4.8 that transfer to the private sector has enabled the purchasing function to enjoy an enhanced role within the business, allowing the function to move upstream and become more recognised as of importance within the company hierarchy. This view was supported by the interview results, which suggested that it was an increased focus on profitability and commercialism throughout the organisations that had opened up this opportunity for purchasing. If the function could demonstrate and publicise significant cost savings by adopting a more commercial approach, it could begin to gain recognition from the rest of the business and gradually increase its internal profile. Success in this endeavour, however, also appears to have depended on the attitude of senior management within the organisation and on the ability and proactiveness of senior purchasing staff. It follows that by no means all purchasing functions have enjoyed equal success.

The fact that the purchasing role has, generally, become more commercially orientated is illustrated in Table 4.8 by the increased focus on financial contribution, adding value and efficiency. Also, the trend towards collaboration is again underlined by the increased emphasis on partnerships and alliances in Table 4.7 on page 55.

Having described the changes in the role of purchasing, respondents were then asked which factors had driven this change. The results are presented in Table 4.9 on page 57. These show that organisations undergoing privatisation experience fundamental changes in structure, which include changes in purchasing. Indeed, 23 companies (82 per cent of the sample or 92 per cent of the 25 companies that reported changes in the role of procurement) experienced overall restructuring around the time of privatisation. Such restructuring had important ramifications for purchasing. Moreover, the organisational change was part of an overall drive for increased efficiency and

Table 4.8 Changes in the role of purchasing since privatisation

How the role of purchasing has changed since privatisation	*No. of times mentioned*
Increased profile; moved upstream; recognised as a mainstream business function; more important role in company performance	8
More strategic	7
More focused on financial contribution to company; more emphasis on commercial element	5
Now highly skilled & professional; more sophisticated	5
More focused on adding value/extracting value	4
More focused on efficiency	3
Focused on developing partnerships & alliances/supplier relationships	3
More proactive within the company	2
Focused on better supply chain management	2
Focused on achieving world-class standards	2

commercialisation. This is reflected in the significance of the need to reduce overhead costs, with 21 of the companies experiencing change (84 per cent) mentioning this as an influential factor.

The cost factor has affected purchasing in a number of different ways, but the outcome seems generally to have been positive for the profile of the function. Although cost pressures led to reduced resources (mainly staff numbers) within purchasing in some companies, and this restricted the development of activities, many respondents felt that this had pushed them to become more efficient and effective in their task. Also, the overall focus on commercialism had opened up opportunities for purchasing, as explained above. By demonstrating major cost savings through more professional buying, one of the key objectives in a newly privatised company, purchasing could gain due recognition. In addition, a squeeze on resources throughout the organisation led to other managers looking to the purchasing function to take over the buying process, when before it had been carried out within their department. There is a virtuous circle here: if purchasing can gain recognition by publicising significant cost savings, then it becomes more popular within the organisation and gains further responsibilities. Most of the companies interviewed reported this type of reinforcing process at work.

Table 4.9 also shows the importance of new senior staff in developing the role of the purchasing and supply function in privatised firms. A new managing director and/or purchasing director played a part in at least half of the cases reporting change. In a number of the organisations interviewed, managers were deliberately recruited from outside the company and brought in as change agents i.e. specifically to drive a change programme within the organisation.

There were only three respondents reporting no change in the role of purchasing since privatisation. One of these believed that senior management's lack of understanding of the needs of purchasing was the barrier to change. In the companies reporting limited changes, a lack of professional training and

Table 4.9 Factors that have driven changes in the role of purchasing

Factors driving change in role of purchasing	*No. of times mentioned*
A fundamental review of organisational structure, including changes in purchasing	23
The need to reduce overhead costs	21
A new MD introduced changes in purchasing	12
A new head of purchasing was brought in	12
Consultants recommended changes in procurement	11
Existing head of purchasing was given more power	10
Other[a]	6

Note

a Other includes alliances with new partners, pressure to contribute to the bottom line, the need to improve continually, the proactiveness of procurement managers to bring about change, and the division of the company into separate business units.

qualifications for purchasing staff was one factor impeding a recognition of the importance of purchasing and supply. But perhaps more important was a resistance to change from purchasing staff themselves. When purchasing staff have been used to carrying out an administrative role they may be daunted by a new commercial focus. This view was reiterated during the interviews, with many respondents describing how the low level of training and generally low calibre of purchasing staff sometimes led them to resist facing up to a change in their role and responsibilities.

The internal 'profile' of purchasing relates to its general importance within the organisation and how it is perceived by other departments. For example, is it seen as a low-level support activity with little kudos attached, or as a mainstream strategic function with importance to the whole business, or somewhere in between? Two factors which might shed some light on the profile were investigated in the questionnaire, namely the *position of the most senior purchasing manager* in the company, and *purchasing's level of involvement in company spend.* Company spend was divided into total spend and its two constituents traditional spend and non-traditional spend. Traditional spend is defined as that related directly to the production of the good or service, and non-traditional as any ancillary expenditure such as consultancy, advertising, travel expenses and so on. The term 'traditional' reflects the fact that it is the former which has traditionally occupied purchasing offices.

The answers in Table 4.10 on page 59 indicate that there has been a perceived improvement in the position of the most senior purchasing manager since privatisation in almost half of the sample of companies studied. In only two cases was there an identified deterioration. The answers in Table 4.11 on page 59 show that, while some respondents were unable to divide company spend into the two areas (and so gave overall figures only) the trends are clear: 19 of the respondents (68 per cent) increased their involvement in total company spend, 11 (39 per cent) in traditional spend, and 15 (54 per cent) in non-traditional spend. The numbers experiencing a decrease in responsibility are negligible. There was also a marked trend towards head office functions (such as marketing and finance) surrendering spend to purchasing that had previously been under their control ('non-traditional'). Examples include the purchase of advertising, insurance and banking services.

The results summarised in Tables 4.10 and 4.11 confirm an 'enhanced role' for purchasing since privatisation. Possible reasons for this are the success of the department in demonstrating its ability, and the reduction of resources elsewhere in the business that has forced other parts of the company to look to purchasing as a service provider. There appears to have been more change with regard to non-traditional spend. This is partly because there was sometimes less scope for increasing involvement in traditional spend. In six firms the purchasing department already controlled 100 per cent of traditional spend before privatisation.

Table 4.10 Perceived changes in the position of the most senior purchasing manager since privatisation

Change in position	*Number*	*%*
Moved up the hierarchy	13	46
Moved down the hierarchy	2	7
No change in position	4	14
No information	9	32
Total	28	100

Table 4.11 Changes in the involvement of purchasing in company spend since privatisation

Type of spend	*Increase*	*Decrease*	*No change*	*No information*	*Total*
Total spend	19	1	5	3	28
Traditional spend	11	1	11	5	28
Non-traditional spend	15	2	3	8	28

External cost reduction and outsourcing pressures

Outsourcing

One way to reduce costs and improve the strategic role of purchasing is to increase outsourcing. Instead of supplying materials and services in-house, they can sometimes be obtained more efficiently from external suppliers. The expectation is that privatisation will have been associated with a reassessment of this decision with a view to increasing outsourcing of support services. Outsourcing is commonly associated with cost reduction (reduced transaction costs) and improved quality/delivery.

Questions were asked about outsourcing trends in each of the organisations and how closely the purchasing function was involved in making such decisions. The results are given in Tables 4.12 below and 4.13 on page 60. The first question asked whether the company had moved to more in-house production or more outsourcing of support services since privatisation.

Table 4.12 Changes in outsourcing since privatisation

Direction of change	*No. of companies*
More in-house production	1
More outsourcing	23
No change	4[a]
Total	28

Note

a This includes one respondent who claimed 'no changes yet'; the organisation concerned was undergoing privatisation at the time that the survey was being carried out.

Table 4.13 Reasons for changes in the level of outsourcing since privatisation

Reason for change	*No. of respondents*
The need to reduce costs in the company (employment costs, operating expenditure or costs generally)	18
The decision that you/other companies can produce certain goods or services more efficiently	16
Release from government intervention allowing management to make the decision	7
Other[a]	4
Need for liquidity leading to the sale of manufacturing facilities	1

Note

a 'Other' includes concentration on core businesses, focus on core competencies, the City perception that the company was overstaffed, in order to bring about culture and attitudinal changes, and a willingness to outsource only if specialist expertise exists outside of the company.

A very distinct trend was established here with 82 per cent (23) of respondents reporting an increase in outsourced activity and just one case showing more in-house production. The respondents were then asked to give reasons for the changes. The first point to note from the responses in Table 4.13 is a reiteration of the importance of cost pressures with eighteen companies naming these as a reason for a change in outsourcing. The second reason in the Table ('the decision that you/other companies can produce certain goods or services more efficiently') also suggests the importance of cost factors, though 'efficiency' can extend beyond cost to include the quality of bought-in supplies and the flexibility that outsourcing can achieve. Public sector organisations are often mandated to perform certain activities and this prevents them from outsourcing. This accounts for the seven companies who noted the release from government intervention as one influential factor. In terms of the activities outsourced, these covered a wide area of support activities with IT, catering, engineering/maintenance, cleaning and security heading the list.

A further question on outsourcing concerned whether purchasing was involved proactively, reactively or not at all in the outsourcing decisions. Proactive involvement indicates that purchasing had some influence in the decision as to whether or not to outsource an activity, or in suggesting areas that might be outsourced; whereas reactive involvement means that purchasing would only get involved once the decision had been made. In most cases, this would mean setting up and/or managing the contracts with the suppliers of the outsourced activity.

The answers suggested that 64 per cent (14) of respondents were generally involved proactively in outsourcing decisions, and another 2 had a proactive role in at least some cases. Only 3 companies excluded purchasing entirely from this important area of decision making. This is another positive sign for the internal profile of the purchasing function, illustrating that purchasing has become more involved in strategic issues in place of its traditional, bureaucratic, 'order-taker' role.

Supplier performance

In so far as privatisation leads to a search for efficiency gains, the expectation is that this will be reflected in a review of supplier performance. Respondents were asked how supplier performance had changed since privatisation in a selected number of areas. The results are summarised in Table 4.14. They show a significant improvement in supplier performance on most key criteria.

Taking cost competitiveness as an example, 18 (64 per cent) of all respondents reported a major improvement since privatisation and a further 8 noted a slight improvement. No companies reported a deterioration under this heading and, indeed, there were just 3 reports of a deterioration across all of the performance indicators. Respondents were then asked to note any other measures of supplier performance that they used, and whether performance had improved or deteriorated since privatisation. Out of the 28 respondents, 12 mentioned other measures of supplier performance in addition to those mentioned in Table 4.14, which are summarised below. The key message was 'improved supplier performance across the board'.

The answers indicate a trend towards adopting what are seen to be increasingly sophisticated supplier assessment techniques. Whereas pre-privatisation the key criterion in supplier assessment was price, all except one or two companies in the sample had moved far beyond this consideration. Many of these companies now assessed suppliers across a broad range of criteria and

Table 4.14 Changes in supplier performance since privatisation

Performance indicator	*Major improvement*	*Slight improvement*	*No change*	*Slight deterioration*	*Major deterioration*	*Total*[a]
Cost competitiveness	18	8				26
Product/service quality	10	13	1	1		25
Cycle times	8	9	7	1		25
New-product development time	6	5	12	1		24
Flexibility	10	15	1			26
On-time delivery	10	11	4			25
Access to new technology & innovation	9	8	6			23
Other	1	—				1

Note

a Some respondents did not complete the question, hence the totals do not add up to twenty-eight. This was mainly because the criteria were not appropriate to their particular company.

some had developed specific supplier appraisal programmes. Examples of criteria for assessment included: supplier proactiveness, competencies, attitude, year-on-year performance, responsiveness, ability and willingness to work *with* the customer, how the supplier can help with storage, and so on. Companies had also implemented continuous improvement procedures, programmes to develop world-class suppliers, supplier relationship assessment (i.e. measuring the performance of the relationship rather than the supplier) and quality awards for suppliers. This is a far cry from the short-term, price-based judgements that seem to have been prevalent when the firms were in the public sector.

Performance of the purchasing department

Lastly, performance measurement of the purchasing department was assessed. Questions were asked about the criteria used to measure the performance and how these had changed since privatisation. The development of some form of performance measurement since privatisation was reported by 19 (68 per cent) of the firms. Before privatisation most organisations had no purchasing performance measurement whatsoever and in most cases insufficient data were collected to enable an analysis. The handful of companies (5 in total) that did measure performance before privatisation based their analyses either on cost savings, price, and/or savings against the general rate of price inflation indicated by the retail price index (RPI). The analyses tended to be highly administrative and statistically (quantitatively) based.

Performance measurement of purchasing is now much more widespread, although it varies widely from fairly crude approaches to more 'sophisticated' techniques. There seems to be no common pattern in the methods adopted. Of the 19 companies that gave details of their systems, 14 remained largely cost based and 5 appeared to be more sophisticated, taking a much broader view of what determines success in purchasing and supply management. Examples of criteria measured in the cost-based approach included year-on-year savings, price, 'below current cost', price reduction on previous contracts, stock levels and the number of orders placed. Examples of an arguably more sophisticated approach included benchmarking the purchasing department against those of blue-chip companies on key performance criteria, and measurement through service level agreements, total contribution to profit, and a vendor-concern reporting system throughout the company.

In summary, the questionnaire and follow-up interviews confirmed that performance measurement in purchasing has developed considerably since privatisation. While the majority of systems remain largely cost based, some companies have adopted a longer-term, more broad-based approach to performance assessment.

Section 2 Questionnaire results: public sector

This section reports the questionnaire results for the four public sector organisations involved in the study, namely the Civil Aviation Authority, London Underground Ltd, The Post Office and one other organisation, which insisted upon anonymity. As with the privatised sector, details from the follow-up interviews with these organisations are sometimes included to develop points raised by the questionnaire responses, although the main case study reports for the public sector appear in Chapters 7 and 12. The results are presented here in the same format as for the privatised companies. These relate to the four key hypotheses set out in Chapter 3.

Timing of the changes

The aim of the research was to determine the nature of changes in purchasing and supply management in privatised companies. This meant that the question of the timing of the changes was straightforward when dealing with the privatised sector: it was simply since privatisation or around the time of privatisation. This was clearly a more difficult issue when dealing with the control group consisting of four organisations which had not experienced a transfer of ownership. The main objective was to study the nature of changes in these organisations over a similar period of time to that studied for the privatised group. The research dealt with this by asking whether there had been a period of significant change over the last five to ten years. The main reasons for these changes were then determined. In all four cases, there *had* been a marked period of change in purchasing and supply management with clear drivers for the change process. This is discussed in more detail later in the separate case studies.

In summary, the Civil Aviation Authority began a period of significant change in 1995, which was induced by discussions about privatising part of its operations. London Underground had seen the beginnings of a change process around 1990 when the government, having tested for and rejected privatisation, made moves to increase the efficiency and commercialisation of the company. This was combined with the 'shock therapy' of the King's Cross fire disaster of 1987[2] which forced London Underground to reassess its operational focus.

For The Post Office, consideration for privatisation also acted as a driver for change, which began in the early 1990s and accelerated in 1993. The privatisation factor was combined with Monopolies and Mergers Commission (MMC) reports criticising The Post Office (for example MMC, 1980 and 1984) and survey reports revealing that the organisation suffered from a poor public image. The main driver for change at the fourth public sector organisation was its transformation into an executive agency in 1993. For each organisation, these dates were agreed as the focus for the period of change, and the discussions and hence the results presented below were anchored around them.

Internal functional cost pressures

Structure of purchasing and supply

Table 4.15 shows that two of the organisations became more centralised and the other two decentralised. The two that centralised did so in order to gain better control of spend and develop a more coherent purchasing strategy, and the two that decentralised were aiming to increase efficiency, for example by devolving lower-value spend to non-purchasing specialists. London Underground was developing a policy of staff 'empowerment', which clearly implied decentralisation.

Table 4.15 Direction of the change in the structure of the purchasing and supply function – public sector

Change since privatisation	*No. of organisations*
More centralised	2
More decentralised	2
No change	—
Total	4

Employment in purchasing and supply

As illustrated in Table 4.16, the changes have involved a reduction in the number of purchasing staff in two of the organisations, an increase in one and no change in the fourth. The decreases took place at the Civil Aviation Authority and London Underground. This was in order to reduce costs and formed part of a policy of devolvement. The Post Office maintained the same level of purchasing employees, but had taken on an increased task, meaning that purchasing had become more efficient in terms of labour productivity. The fourth, anonymous, organisation was the only organisation to increase staffing levels and it was felt that this was a recognition by senior management of the importance of the purchasing function. Having achieved and demonstrated significant cost savings, the department was given increased resources for recruitment.

Table 4.16 Changes in the number of purchasing staff – public sector

Direction of change	*No. of organisations*
More staff	1
Fewer staff	2
No change	1
Total	4

Taking the four organisations together, the net reduction in employment is coherent with the results from the privatised sample; although it is accepted that this second group forms an extremely small sample and therefore this, and the other conclusions presented here, must be treated with caution.

Professional purchasing functionalism

As with the privatised companies, three indicators were used to test whether purchasing had become more strategic. These were the use of mission statements, formal purchasing strategies, and purchasing tools and techniques.

All four of the organisations had formal mission statements at the time of the research and two confirmed that they had had no such statements before their 'major change'. Since 1995, the Civil Aviation Authority's mission statement has involved working with customers, best practice and gaining the best value for money, and it is linked to the organisation's strategic intent. Unfortunately, the organisation provided no information about mission statements before this date. London Underground's purchasing mission statement at the time of interview involved reducing the total cost of acquisition and working with suppliers to remove unnecessary costs from the supply chain. Before, the achievement of short-term gains was the priority at London Underground with the focus on the purchase cost at the time of acquisition and rigorous negotiation with suppliers. At The Post Office, the purchasing mission statement was 'to be recognised as a world-class benchmark', and this was introduced in 1994. No mission statement existed prior to this. The key themes in the mission statement at the fourth public sector organisation were securing full-life value for money and developing partnerships with internal customers. Again, there was no earlier mission statement.

Regarding purchasing strategy, respondents were asked to describe their current strategy and show any major changes during the time period in question. Details of these strategies appear in Table 4.17 on page 66. In summary, all four organisations had a formal strategy at the time of the study. Before, only one of the four had such a strategy in place, two had no strategy, and one gave no information. The results are again coherent with those from the privatised sector. That is to say, there has been an increase in the number of organisations with formal purchasing strategies, and certainly a more proactive approach to the purchasing task now exists. Two of the respondents mentioned whole-life costing, the use of which is clear evidence of a more proactive and longer-term approach to purchasing. A longer-term approach means developing a strategy based on the benefits of sourcing a product or service over the long term, rather than on short-term gains such as price differences.

A point which arose from the interviews is that the changes tended to happen later in the public sector companies than in the privatised sector, and in some cases at a slower pace. At the Civil Aviation Authority and the anonymous organisation the strategy described was being introduced during the research period with strategic development being a very live issue in both

Table 4.17 Details of current purchasing strategy – public sector

Organisation	*Key elements of purchasing strategy*
Civil Aviation Authority	Deliver value for money while observing the legal requirements; supplier reduction; whole-life cost beginning to be considered; still focused on competition. *Changes in strategy were underway at the time of the research.*
London Underground	Since 1990, key aim has been to 'get more from less' through reducing the total cost of acquisition. This involves working more closely with suppliers in order to remove costs from the supply chain. Before, purchasing strategy was more tactical with a more aggressive stance towards suppliers evident.
The Post Office	Current strategy is a commodity-based approach involving product group teams. Before, the approach was reactive and 'day-to-day', mainly based on contribution to profit.
Anonymous organisation	Quality, policy and the task of gaining from economies of scale take place at the 'strategic centre' (head office) and all other purchasing activity takes place at the operating units. There was no strategy before executive agency status was gained.

organisations. By contrast, in all of the privatised organisations interviewed, a purchasing strategy had been in place for some time.

The respondents were also asked which purchasing tools and techniques they used and how this had changed over the given time period. They were presented with a list of these tools and techniques, which ranged from the more reactive at the top of the list to the more proactive at the bottom. The list appears in Table 4.18 on page 67, where the results are also presented.

A quick glance at Table 4.18 shows a clear trend away from what are today seen as reactive purchasing methods, towards proactive purchasing techniques among the public sector organisations. There has been no increase, and in most cases a decrease, in the use of the reactive techniques at the top of the Table, whereas there has been an increase in the use of *all* of the more proactive ones (from vendor accreditation onwards in Table 4.18). Three of the four companies now use purchasing portfolio analysis and partnership sourcing, for example, whereas none of them did so before the change period noted at the beginning of this section. The increase in the use of partnership sourcing suggests another similarity with the privatised sector results: it appears that the public sector organisations studied are also forming more collaborative relationships with suppliers.

When asked whether there had been any other initiatives in purchasing strategy, respondents offered the following. The Civil Aviation Authority were trying to adopt best-practice techniques, but this was described as 'more words than action' at the time of interview. London Underground mentioned the introduction of whole-life costing as a key initiative. The Post

Table 4.18 Procurement tools and techniques most commonly used – public sector

Purchasing tools and techniques	*Before change period*	*Since change period*
Writing tender specifications	2	1
Organising bids	2	1
Negotiating	2	1
Awarding contracts	2	1
Expediting	1	1
Inspection of goods on arrival	1	1
Vendor accreditation	0	2
Formal vendor selection mechanisms	1	2
Benchmarking/best practice	0	2
Purchasing portfolio analysis	0	3
Strategic source planning	0	2
Purchase price cost analysis	0	1
Strategic supplier alliances	0	1
Partnership sourcing	0	3
Network sourcing	0	1
Relational competence analysis	0	1

Office had introduced a supplier accreditation programme, entitled the 'First-Class Supplier Programme', and the anonymous organisation used this opportunity to underline that they were 'just beginning' to use benchmarking, strategic source planning and partnership sourcing. While these results reveal much activity in terms of developing a purchasing strategy, they also suggest that the public sector may lag behind the privatised sample as far as the stage of development is concerned. Two of the four organisations are only just beginning to adopt more proactive techniques, whereas the privatised companies had tended to adopt a more proactive strategy some time before the research began.

Improvements in the role and profile of purchasing and supply

Respondents were asked an open question about the role of purchasing, whether and how it had changed over the period in question and were asked to give reasons behind any changes reported. For this second question, a table of possible factors was provided. The results appear in Table 4.19 on page 68.

At the Civil Aviation Authority (CAA), the role has reportedly become more strategic and commercial since 1994, although there remains a procedural bias to purchasing activity. The CAA was just beginning to benchmark at the time of interview and had just adopted a vendor accreditation system. The main driver behind the changes was considered to be the possibility of privatisation, which forced the organisation to reassess its operations. This pushed the CAA towards restructuring in order to become more commercially focused. Another linked factor was the need to reduce overhead

Table 4.19 Factors that have driven changes in the role of purchasing – public sector

Factor driving change in the role of purchasing	*No. of times mentioned*
A fundamental review of organisational structure included changes in purchasing	3
The need to reduce overhead costs	3
A new head of purchasing was brought in	3
Consultants recommended changes in procurement	3
Existing head of purchasing was given more power	1
A new MD introduced changes in purchasing	1

costs, but this was said to be more because it was politically 'the done thing' than the result of real commercial pressure.

At London Underground, the role of purchasing had become more professional, and a longer-term approach to the activity had been adopted. The main drivers were the appointment of a new head of purchasing as a 'change agent' and the need to increase efficiency following a reduction in government financial support.

The Post Office has also seen a significant change in the role of purchasing: from a reactive, fragmented and poorly controlled approach to what was considered to be a highly strategic role by the respondent. It was also noted, however, that a procedural bias remained. The Post Office has developed a commodity-based approach with product group teams, quality has become more important and more information is collected, allowing for the use of tools such as purchasing portfolio analysis. The main drivers for these changes at The Post Office were those discussed at the beginning of this section. Consideration for privatisation and the public's poor perception of The Post Office pushed the organisation to introduce significant change, and this included the purchasing function. Moreover, a new head of purchasing was recruited from the private sector in 1993, who instigated changes in the role and organisation of this activity.

Before the changes at the fourth public sector organisation, purchasing appears to have been a tactical and poorly controlled activity with no real strategic direction. Since 1993, however, there has been a major increase in central authority and a dramatic increase in the scope and authority of purchasing, as the activity has been centralised. In this organisation, the introduction of executive agency status led to the need to ring-fence activities in order to increase visibility and decrease costs. This resulted in the recruitment of a new head of purchasing, who was given greater power and resources than previously to make fundamental changes.

As far as the reasons for the changes in the role of purchasing are concerned, Table 4.19 shows that similar factors were at work in most of the organisations. It is interesting to note that cost reduction was mentioned as a driver in three organisations, reminding us that cost pressures are felt in public as well as privatised bodies. These results also underline the importance of newly

Table 4.20 Changes in the position of the most senior purchasing manager – public sector

Change in position	*Number*
Moved up the hierarchy	2
Moved down the hierarchy	0
No change in position	0
Insufficient information	2
Total	4

recruited senior staff as 'change agents', with new heads of purchasing being a driving factor in three cases. Two organisations mentioned factors inhibiting the change process. These were that senior management failed to understand the needs of purchasing, and that training and qualifications of purchasing staff tended to be lacking.

The two indicators used to measure the internal profile of purchasing were the position of the most senior procurement manager and the involvement of purchasing in company spend, and Tables 4.20 and 4.21 present the results for the public sector organisations studied.

Table 4.20 shows that in two cases the position of the most senior procurement manager improved. In one of the cases which provided insufficient information, the respondent noted that the scope of responsibilities of the most senior procurement manager had increased considerably, even though the reporting line had not changed. This could also be interpreted as an improvement in the position of purchasing within the organisation.

Table 4.21 gives a clear picture of increasing involvement of purchasing in company spend, suggesting an improved internal profile for the function. All four organisations have increased their involvement in both total spend and non-traditional spend. At the CAA and The Post Office, purchasing was beginning to get involved in more non-traditional spend at the time of interview. For the CAA this included the purchase of insurance and hotels and travel, and similarly for The Post Office it involved hotels, travel and consultancy. Purchasing at the anonymous organisation was increasing its involvement in non-traditional spend through participation in cross-functional teams, and becoming more involved in capital expenditure as the scope and influence of the function increased. Although these results suggest an improved profile across the board, it must be stressed that changes

Table 4.21 Changes in the involvement of purchasing in company spend – public sector

Type of spend	*Increase*	*Decrease*	*No change*	*No information*	*Total*
Total spend	4	0	0	0	4
Traditional spend	1	0	1	2	4
Non-traditional spend	4	0	0	0	4

underway during the research period tended to lag behind the privatised companies where many such developments had already taken place.

External cost reduction and outsourcing pressures

Outsourcing

As far as the outsourcing of support services is concerned, Table 4.22 shows a similar trend to the privatised sample, with all four organisations increasing outsourcing. London Underground stressed that they had become involved in much more outsourcing in recent years. Examples of activities outsourced by the public sector organisations include energy management, executive recruitment, information technology and facilities management. When asked for reasons behind this increase, two respondents believed that this was due to efficiency factors (i.e. the decision that other companies could perform certain activities more efficiently than the organisation in question), and one noted the need to reduce employment costs within the organisation. This respondent also stressed, however, that there was no direct pressure to reduce employment costs, rather it was felt to be the right thing to do given the austere political environment at the time. This again underlines the fact that, while there exists pressure to increase efficiency in the public sector, it may not derive from commercial competitive factors. Pressure to increase efficiency tends to be less direct and appears to result in a slower and a less-marked reaction on the part of the organisation concerned than in the private sector sample.

Table 4.22 Changes in make–buy since privatisation

Direction of change	*No. of organisations*
More in-house production	0
More outsourcing	4
No change	0
Total	4

Supplier performance

Regarding changes in supplier performance, Table 4.23 on page 71 speaks for itself with improvements on all key criteria and no deterioration whatsoever. These results are coherent with those from the privatised sector, which also showed considerable and wide-ranging improvements. Interestingly, however, both the CAA and the anonymous organisation could give no indication of supplier performance at all. This means that the Table gives results for London Underground and The Post Office alone. At the time of interview, the CAA was

Table 4.23 Changes in supplier performance since privatisation – public sector

Performance indicator	*Major improvement*	*Slight improvement*	*No change*	*Slight deterioration*	*Major deterioration*	*Total*
Cost competitiveness		2				2
Product/service quality	1	1				2
Cycle times	1	1				2
New-product development time		1				1
Flexibility		2				2
On-time delivery		2				2
Access to new technology and innovation	1	1				2
Other						

in the process of introducing 'better' performance measures and incentives to encourage suppliers to improve performance. As a result, they expected improvement in the near future, but were not yet in a position to report any progress. Similarly, at the anonymous organisation, the purchasing function had focused all resources on improving internal operations and had yet to address external supplier performance at the time of the research. This was next on the agenda. The organisation expected improvements in supplier performance but was not yet in a position to report any. These results again demonstrate the lag between the public and private sectors: most of the privatised sample had already addressed supplier performance and ensured significant improvements.

Performance of the purchasing department

Turning finally to performance measurement of the purchasing department, Table 4.24 again shows similar trends to the privatised sample: a general increase in performance measurement and the development of what are considered to be more 'sophisticated' techniques. At London Underground, for example, criteria have changed to reflect the developments in purchasing strategy described earlier. Essentially this has involved a move away from a traditional, adversarial approach towards a longer-term strategy related to the nature of the product or service being sourced. Another interesting point is that changes were once again underway at the CAA during the research period. The approach to measuring performance at the fourth public sector organisation had been newly introduced since executive agency status had been achieved in 1993. The respondent was not aware of previous performance measures and it is very unlikely that there existed any comparable criteria, given the fragmented nature of purchasing activity prior to the changes described in this section.

Table 4.24 Performance measurement of the purchasing department

Organisation	*Current performance measurement*	*Previous performance measurement*
Civil Aviation Authority	Changed from cost savings to value added in the 1980s but has not changed significantly since. Performance measurement was a live issue at time of interview with new measures under development.	No information.
London Underground	Performance measurement is based on type of product e.g. strategic products might require a partnership with supplier, and so criteria to judge the performance of the partnership will be applied. For leverage products where large volumes allow preferential terms, performance measurement will be more price based.	Key measures were savings against budget and the level of competition, i.e. the proportion of spend based on competitive tender.
The Post Office	Measures include contribution to profit, internal customer satisfaction surveys and contract renewal time.	These measures were in place before, but they have become more focused with clearer targets.
Anonymous organisation	The purchasing strategic plan is broken down into individual tasks so that each purchasing employee has cost savings targets. Individual performance criteria can also include risk reduction.	No information.

Summary: the search for static and dynamic efficiency gains in privatised and public sector organisations

The aim of the questionnaire survey was to test for immediate efficiency gains in privatised and a small number of public sector organisations. In summary, the results demonstrated that the majority of the twenty-eight privatised companies in the survey were aggressively pursuing static efficiency and dynamic efficiency gains based around the four hypotheses posited on pp. 38–41, but not necessarily in the same way or using the same tools and techniques. As far as the public sector organisations studied are concerned, static and dynamic efficiency gains were also being pursued, but in a less aggressive way, and again using a variety of tools and techniques. Also, the process of searching for such gains appears to have begun more recently than in the privatised companies. These points can be illustrated more clearly with reference to the four hypotheses.

Internal functional cost pressures

Both the privatised and the public sector groups experienced considerable changes in the structure of purchasing, but with no commonality in the direction of the changes. There was also a downward trend in the number of procurement staff across both groups with cost reduction being the most significant driving factor in both. This suggests that the majority of organisations studied focused on *internal cost reduction* as a means to achieve static efficiency gains.

Professional purchasing functionalism

Both groups developed a more proactive approach to purchasing over the period in question. This is demonstrated by the increased use of mission statements, formal purchasing strategies, and purchasing tools and techniques. However, there were some differences between the privatised and public sector organisations studied, in that the former appeared to be more advanced in the development of a more strategic approach to purchasing activity. In at least two of the public sector organisations, the development of modern purchasing tools and techniques and of a formal purchasing strategy was taking place during the research period, whereas in privatised companies such developments had already been underway for some time. These results indicate that the majority of organisations were developing a more effective approach to dynamic efficiency gains, with the privatised sector introducing this approach at an earlier stage and seemingly advancing at a faster, more aggressive pace.

Improvements in the role and profile of purchasing and supply

Results suggest significant changes in the role of purchasing together with improvements in the internal profile of the function. This applies to both groups, although changes again appeared more marked in the privatised sector. Generally speaking, the role of purchasing has changed from a highly administrative to a more commercially focused task, although in two of the four public sector organisations a procedural bias remains. Improvements in the internal profile are evidenced by improvements in the position of the most senior procurement management and increases in purchasing's involvement in company spend. There were clear indications that the public sector sample lagged behind here. For example, purchasing at three of the four public sector organisations was still in the early stages of increasing its involvement in company spend, while the majority of privatised companies had already achieved gains in this area. Overall, these changes are further evidence of a desire to achieve a more professional approach to purchasing with the objective of dynamic efficiency gains.

External cost reduction and outsourcing

There was a considerable shift from internal production to external supply (outsourcing) across both groups – 82 per cent of privatised companies experienced an increase in outsourcing following transfer to the private sector and all four public sector organisations reported the same trend. As far as the reasons for outsourcing are concerned, the public sector organisations were sometimes driven by political factors with one organisation focusing on outsourcing at least partly because, as it maintained, it gained political 'brownie points', for example. In the privatised sample, commercial considerations were more often the drivers for change – this at least partially reflects the services provided by the organisations. Supplier performance also improved across both groups, but to a greater extent in the privatised sector. Two of the four public sector organisations were unable to comment on supplier performance because they did not have measures in place, whereas almost all of the privatised companies interviewed were in a position to report results because they had systems to measure the performance of suppliers. This is an example of the public sector lagging behind in the development of more advanced (performance-related) forms of purchasing management. In summary, these results support the view that a more effective approach to achieving dynamic efficiency gains has been pursued in both groups, but at an earlier stage, and in a more aggressive manner, in the privatised sector.

Taken together, these results suggest a significant improvement in static and dynamic efficiency among the organisations studied, although particularly within the privatised sample. This has been achieved through the changes described above, which relate directly to the four hypotheses set out on pages 38–41. While this finding is encouraging, there is evidence from some of the answers to our questionnaire that the purchasing function is still regarded as a reactive, administrative function in a number of the companies studied. Only in some companies is there evidence that purchasing is being taken more seriously at a *strategic* level in the business. Why should this be so, and does this situation pose a threat to the effective management of external resources?

This crucial question cannot be answered by the survey data alone. At the same time, it was realised early in the research that it was important to understand in detail why, and how, particular changes were taking place in some organisations and not in others. It was for this reason that the follow-up structured interviews were undertaken with a cross-section of the companies involved in the questionnaire survey. The interviews focused on the same four themes as the questionnaire: internal cost reduction; purchasing professionalism; the role and profile of purchasing and supply management; and outsourcing and supplier relationship management. The next three chapters report the results of these follow-up interviews. Chapter 5 deals with changes in purchasing and supply management in privatised utilities and reports on six companies; Chapter 6 deals with the changes in privatised non-utilities; and Chapter 7 looks at developments in public sector purchasing and supply management.

5 The impact of privatisation on utilities' purchasing and supply management

This chapter builds on the questionnaire results reported in Chapter 4. It reports results of interviews with procurement management in six privatised utilities in the gas, water and electricity sectors. These are British Gas, the two water supply and sewerage companies, Welsh Water and South West Water, and the electricity companies PowerGen, Scottish Hydro-Electric and NORWEB. The chapter aims to delve more deeply into the four key areas of study, for each separate company, identified earlier, namely: internal cost reduction; purchasing professionalism; the role and profile of purchasing; and outsourcing and supplier relationship management. Developments in these areas are described in the six case studies and reasons for the changes (or lack thereof) are given. This second, more detailed, level of study aims to build on the questionnaire results, to understand why some companies have developed in certain ways and others have not, and why some have advanced rapidly in the development of what many would see as a more professional approach to purchasing management, while others have been relatively stagnant.

The specific developments will be related to the three-phase learning process that we identified for the privatised companies, which was explained in Chapter 1. This model suggests the process that companies may follow when privatised, as far as their approach to purchasing management is concerned. Phase 1 involves a focus on immediate cost reduction and short-term measures aimed at lowering costs. This might involve restructuring the purchasing function in order to create a leaner organisational form and/or employment reduction in purchasing, for example. Phase 2 involves companies moving beyond this stage and developing a longer-term approach to improving the efficiency of operations, aiming to improve the competence of their existing purchasing and supply function. Developments within this stage include the recruitment of higher-calibre, more highly qualified individuals into purchasing, increased training of purchasing staff, and perhaps a reconsideration of supply strategies to ensure that value for money is being gained in the long term. Phases 1 and 2 form part of the pursuit of static efficiency and dynamic efficiency gains (improvements within and changes to the existing procurement processes). It is only in phase 3 that the company begins to search for improvements in transformational efficiency (the creation of new procurement processes or products and services). This phase is termed here the procurement competence and supply alignment phase, as introduced in Chapter 1 and as discussed again later in the book.

BRITISH GAS

The British Gas case is interesting because it shows that companies can focus on strategic realignment at the cost of a systematic operational focus on functional professionalism in purchasing and supply. While there is evidence of some increase in purchasing professionalism in each of the four hypothesised areas associated with static and dynamic efficiency gains (these relate to internal cost reduction; purchasing strategy; the role and profile of purchasing; and external cost reduction pressures, and are discussed at the beginning of Chapter 3), it is clear that the continual inability of the company to resolve its strategic focus and supply alignment has militated against the achievement of the high level of static and dynamic efficiency that might have been possible in a more settled strategic and operational environment.

Background

British Gas was the second national utility to be privatised in the United Kingdom, transferring the country's state-owned gas supplier into private hands in late 1986, in a high-profile stock exchange flotation. British Telecom (BT) had been the first utility to undergo privatisation in 1984. While the transfer of BT to the private sector is generally viewed in a positive light, that of British Gas is often quoted as an example of a badly managed privatisation, whose mistakes should be recognised and learned from. British Gas was privatised intact and retained most of its national monopoly in gas supply, leading to claims that shareholders were gaining at the expense of customers, who had no choice but to pay the prices charged. In later years, British Gas sought to justify substantial pay rises for senior management by the argument that the company now had to pay private sector salaries in order to attract and retain talented executives, but this did little to restore public confidence in the company.

The introduction of competition in gas supply began gradually but was accelerated from 1992 especially following a Monopolies and Mergers Commission enquiry (MMC, 1993). This caused serious problems for British Gas and worsened its financial results. The company's reputation was further damaged when service difficulties, associated with the company's restructuring, led to rising consumer complaints. Since privatisation, the company has been through several phases of restructuring in attempts to adapt to its changing industrial environment, all at a high cost to the company. It has also been caught out by long-term 'take and pay' gas purchase contracts from North Sea producers, signed when it was fully protected from competition.

This has resulted in British Gas having to buy more gas than it needed, and at higher prices than those prevailing in the spot market, again costing the company dearly and putting it at a severe disadvantage *vis-à-vis* competitors.

By 1997, British Gas had agreed the most fundamental restructuring to date, a demerger into two separate companies, as well as successfully renegotiating a number of the gas supply contracts. In the absence of the renegotiation, the long-term financial position of the company would have been at risk (*The Economist*, 10 February 1996). The demerger took place in February 1997 and created two new companies. Centrica plc is UK based and comprises domestic and industrial gas supply, some gas production, central heating installation and the retail division. It incorporates a new-services division, whose most recent launch was the Goldfish credit card. The other company is called BG plc. This includes Transco, the operator of the UK gas transportation pipeline and storage facilities, and a range of other businesses, some with international operations. These include exploration and production; international downstream; and technology. This half of the demerger represents the international side of the British Gas business, although UK-based Transco still represents 80 per cent of its turnover.

An assessment of British Gas's year-on-year performance is very difficult because the company has undergone such extensive restructuring since privatisation. Turnover for the year ending 31 December 1996 was £9.5bn., showing a gradual reduction since 1990 (BG plc, 1997). To be more exact, income has fallen by 9 per cent since 1993.[1] The company made a pre-tax loss of £237m. for the year ending 31 December 1996.[2] It had been trading profitably for the previous two years, but had lost £569m. in 1993. The losses in 1996 were caused largely by exceptional charges related to restructuring and associated redundancies, and the legacy of the gas supply contracts described above.

Evidence of static and dynamic efficiency gains

The structure of purchasing and supply management

The overriding influence on the structuring of purchasing at British Gas has been the extensive change in company structure since privatisation in 1986. For this reason, the overall changes will be explained alongside those in purchasing and supply, so that the development of the function can be fully understood. The key pattern for purchasing is increasing centralisation throughout the 1980s and until 1994, when the division of the UK gas business into four main strategic business units (SBUs) led to the fragmentation of central purchasing, as each SBU took responsibility for its own supplies.

Pre-privatisation and up to 1993, British Gas consisted mainly of twelve businesses based upon regions within the UK, a structure inherited from the days of state ownership. The regions were highly autonomous with powerful regional chairpersons. Each region had its own supplies and transport (S&T)

department with a S&T director who reported to the regional chair. There was always a central supplies and transport department at head office in London, but the main reporting line was to the regional chairperson, with only a 'dotted line' to the head office function.

The role of central S&T was essentially reactive and expediting. Its main task was to set procedures, national contracts and exploit economies of scale where possible, although it appeared that its influence on the regions in the latter respect was limited due to their high level of regional autonomy. Central S&T also had other responsibilities not directly related to the regions. The pipelines department, for example, responsible for the construction and maintenance of national pipelines and not attached to any region, reported directly to head office from its base in Hinckley. The exploration and production and construction departments also reported directly.

Moves towards centralisation in purchasing began during the early 1980s because of cash limits under state ownership and the increasing likelihood that the organisation would be privatised. Government was pushing the company to increase its efficiency. National purchasing contracts were increasingly put in place, beginning with those for meters and gas pipes. Between privatisation and 1993/94, the time of the major restructuring which dismantled the regional organisation, there were efficiency drives throughout the business aimed at increasing standardisation across the regions and encouraging the development and sharing of best practice. This included purchasing, and part of this was a continuation of national purchasing initiatives. Examples of products that moved to national purchasing were cars and commercial vehicles and spare parts for gas fires.

Overall, then, the trend from 1986 was to centralise purchasing where it was considered sensible and beneficial to do so. By the time of the major structural changes in the company, which began in late 1993, the centralised S&T function was much more powerful and there was more emphasis on national purchasing. Most spare parts and appliances were ordered nationally, all purchasing originated from two stores, there were national engineering stockyards, and British Gas was beginning to receive direct delivery. However, all of this changed in late 1993 when regulatory pressures, increasing competition and declining performance, led the company to restructure completely.[3] The twelve regions were disbanded and reorganised into separate business units: public gas supply, business gas, retail and service, and Transco, the gas transportation and storage business, was separated out. Each was to be completely autonomous and have its own support services, resulting in central support services being shut down. Central support had included finance, personnel, supplies and transport and IT. These were broken up and split into the SBUs with the central service eventually being closed down at the end of 1995. Each SBU was freed to create its own purchasing strategy, so that one could no longer speak of a 'British Gas purchasing strategy'.

The SBUs have taken a variety of approaches to purchasing, but the key is that the centralisation process was effectively reversed by the restructure.[4]

Some businesses maintained large stores operations in-house, others outsourced part of their distribution (e.g. delivery from their own stores to their own internal customers), while others outsourced the entire distribution network. Some maintained direct board-level representation of purchasing, but at others it declined to third-level reporting to the board. Restructuring at Transco, the UK gas transportation business, is described below as an example of the changes in purchasing and supply structure. The key message is a disparity of approaches across British Gas after 1994 and a failure to focus effectively on a systematic approach to the achievement of static and dynamic efficiency gains.

Transco – an example of reorganisation since 1994

Transco – the pipeline and storage business within British Gas and now within BG plc – adopted a matrix structure on its inception. This included a highly devolved purchasing function. This involved a very small central purchasing department at Transco Head Office in the West Midlands. The department dealt with policy issues in the main, and reported to the finance director of the business. The fact that even the IT department of Transco carried out its own procurement perhaps underlines how little involvement central purchasing had in actual spend. Purchasing was devolved to four area offices. These were responsible for local purchases covering their region, and they also took on national responsibility for certain strategic goods, such as pipeline. So, one of the four area offices would buy all of the pipe for Transco on behalf of the other offices. Allocation of national responsibilities was decided on factors such as the capabilities and contacts of the staff involved. It was, therefore, a highly reactive and opportunistic, rather than systematically focused organisational structure. It responded to internal engineering and production pressures and reacted to external supply market offerings in an unsystematic way.

Purchasing and supply professionalism

When there were twelve separate regions, up until early 1994, the strategy was to use call-off contracts nationally where appropriate, but for each separate region to purchase other goods and services themselves under separate contracts. As explained, the use of national buying and the general move towards centralisation progressed from pre-privatisation to the major change in early 1994, when the SBUs were created and went their separate ways in terms of purchasing strategy. The description of Transco above gives one example of how the businesses dealt with their own purchasing and supply management issues, and a whole array of approaches were adopted across British Gas.

British Gas International comprised the various international arms of the company plus the head office operations. The key difference here was the move towards the 'bundling' of purchasing. Before, the tendency was for 'volume contracting', meaning that the company had many separate contracts. The use of integrated contracts was increased, covering the purchase of many goods and services within one agreement, thus increasing the scope for developing more proactive relationships with suppliers as well as reducing transaction costs. This happened throughout British Gas, but was particularly apparent in divisions where purchasing tended to be of service contracts or large plant and equipment, such as in exploration and production (E&P). For example, E&P changed from having separate contracts for different aspects of rig maintenance to having a single contract with one operator who took full responsibility for rig maintenance. Overall, this reduced the number of contracts in operation, but meant that each contract was more complex, covering a broader range of products and/or services and often a longer time period. The net result was an intended reduction in transaction costs.

With fewer, more comprehensive contracts, the new approach necessitated a complex evaluation of each one, because it now covered conditions for the delivery of a greater range of products and services, often over a longer period of time. In turn, this has led to the adoption of new purchasing techniques such as 'through life analysis' (of the contract) and benchmarking. Service level agreements were also used extensively with contractors. These are seen as essential for effective control and monitoring of the project, to be regularly revisited by both sides. Although they had been used by British Gas for many years, service level agreements served a largely administrative purpose until the changes detailed above. They have since become more commercially focused, for example using metrics to measure performance, and they are viewed within British Gas (and now its successor companies) as a far more useful instrument than previously. This is clear evidence that, despite an initial lack of focus, some parts of British Gas are searching for dynamic efficiency gains – as explained earlier – but still within a relatively incoherent overall management structure.

The role and profile of purchasing

It is difficult to detail how the role and profile of purchasing have developed since privatisation within British Gas. This is because of continual restructuring throughout the organisation, coupled with the diversity of approaches to purchasing strategy since the watershed of 1993/94. It is safe to say, however, that the role has changed completely throughout the business: from a clerical to a more value-adding one, and from a low-motivation, 'paper-pusher' task, to a relatively higher-profile strategic position. Two factors have forced this change process, both of which accelerated during the 1980s: technological advances and centralisation. Put simply, the more mundane tasks were either taken over by a computer, or taken away from a local buyer and bundled into a national contract. This process obviously resulted in redundancies, but those remaining in employment now appear to enjoy a more interesting and higher-profile role within the business.

As in some of the other privatised companies discussed in this book, purchasing in the new British Gas is successfully demonstrating an ability to contribute value to the business. This has opened up new areas of involvement and improved the internal profile of the purchasing function. Other areas of the company are now more willing to involve purchasing managers earlier on, so that they can become more closely involved in decision-making processes rather than buying the goods and services only after all of the key strategic decisions within the company have been made – typical of a reactive approach to purchasing. This is further evidence of a search for dynamic efficiency gains through increased purchasing professionalism and strategic involvement.

Outsourcing and supplier relationship management

Outsourcing of support services has certainly increased since privatisation with purchasing playing an important role. Purchasing personnel are involved in most outsourcing deals. The make–buy decision is based on a matrix-type purchasing portfolio analysis methodology with internal capabilities and the strategic importance of any activity to British Gas key considerations. The decision to outsource IT to an outside contractor, Hoskyns, is probably the most complex example of outsourcing. This contract is worth many millions of pounds and purchasing management were involved throughout the entire contracting process.

The company's approach to working with contractors has moved away from what is seen as traditional and aggressive (i.e. resorting to claims on contractors for perceived contract failure) to working more closely with them. The aim is to identify and resolve problems early on in the process, in order to boost efficiency and effectiveness and avoid contract breakdown. British Gas has also increased the use of alliance relationships in major contracts. For example, E&P now look to find a lead supplier to build a rig, then get them to subcontract for its construction. In the past the tendency was to 'go it alone'. The purchasing management at British Gas International consider themselves to be at the 'leading edge' of alliancing relationships of this type. They are now working with major contracting companies to progress this further.

Supplier rationalisation has also occurred, but this has been a result of the bundling of contracts and not a deliberate policy to reduce the number of suppliers *per se*. The company recognises the need to balance supplier rationalisation with a policy of supplier development. There has been a move towards more collaboration with fewer suppliers and the company is sharing more information with suppliers. For example, a travel service contract was set up with the company Amex, which is set to run for three to five years. This is incentivised via a profit-sharing arrangement, in an open-book agreement designed to ensure that the supplier has the incentive to drive down travel costs.

Conclusions

There is clear evidence, despite the flux within which the purchasing function has had to operate since privatisation, that some areas of purchasing in British Gas have been able to achieve considerable static efficiency gains, especially of the phase-1 type; while many of the purchasing personnel within British Gas have adopted policies and practices which are clearly within phase 2 of the learning process outlined in Chapter 1. Also, it seems clear that many of the static and dynamic efficiency gains that have been achieved have probably occurred despite privatisation and not because of it. This is because many of the purchasing and supply practices currently being adopted within British Gas are commensurate with current professional views of best practice and do not appear to be unique to the specific supply management needs of the company at this time.

WELSH WATER

Welsh Water (alternatively referred to by its Welsh name, Dwr Cymru) is a useful example of a company that has been driven primarily by an operational focus on improvements in purchasing and supply functionalism. After privatisation, the search for immediate static efficiency through cost reductions did not deflect the search for more ambitious methods of achieving dynamic efficiency. On the contrary, it served to reinforce a trajectory that was already well established in the company. In the future the search for transformational efficiency through the acquisition of a new electricity distribution business, and the creation of a new company structure, may well pose some significant challenges to the company at both the strategic and operational levels.

Background

Welsh Water was privatised in 1989 along with the nine regional water supply and sewerage companies in England. Like most of its counterparts, the company has diversified away from its regulated business of water supply and waste-water disposal since its release from government ownership, moving into new geographical and product markets. These include engineering and environmental management, industrial waste-water and effluent management and infrastructure investments. The company is targeting central and southern Europe as an area for growth, and has acquired a significant shareholding in the largest water and waste-water operation in the Czech Republic. Closer to home, Welsh Water completed the acquisition of South Wales Electricity plc (SWALEC), the regional electricity distributor for South Wales, in January 1996. This resulted in the formation of a 'multi-utility', similar to NORWEB and North West Water which merged in 1995 to form United Utilities. The joint company changed its name from Welsh Water to Hyder plc in

March 1996. The information documented in this account relates mainly to the period before the merger.

Turnover at Welsh Water for the year ending 31 March 1996 reached £422.9m., an increase of 27 per cent over the five years from 1990/91 (CRI, 1997, p. 28). Pre-tax profits at current cost were £100m., down very slightly on the 1990/91 figure but including £7.5m. in exceptional charges. The general trend has been for increasing profitability since privatisation, current cost operating profit rising by 31 per cent between 1990/91 and 1995/96.

As far as changes in purchasing and supply management are concerned, it is clear that privatisation acted as a catalyst for change, accelerating a process that was already in place, rather than being the single causal factor. However, privatisation 'paved the way' for more extensive changes in that the regulated business has since become part of a group of companies, where each part brought different views about how best to organise purchasing.[5]

Evidence of static and dynamic efficiency gains

The structure of purchasing and supply management

Before privatisation, Welsh Water had a strong head office purchasing function. This formed part of a functional organisational structure. There were fairly strict procedures to be followed regarding responsibility for purchasing, which gave the central function the right to control certain areas of spend. Other parts of the corporation were 'mandated' to use corporate framework agreements for given types of goods and services. This accounted for approximately 40 per cent of total corporation expenditure on goods and services. The main focus of the head office function was corporate contracts, where framework agreements were developed whenever appropriate. Terms and conditions together with price, quality and delivery, etc., based on estimated demand were confirmed, and internal users normally ordered within the agreed terms.

Privatisation brought decentralisation to purchasing, although the extent of the restructuring was not great. The restructuring took place within three years of privatisation, or before the end of 1992. The change was from a 'devolved–controlled' structure, controlled and co-ordinated from the centre, to a 'devolved–enabled' structure, defined as autonomous purchasing units at the SBU level with a strategic central control.[6] As a result of severe cost pressures it was decided to 'empower' others in the organisation to buy lower-value, less strategic items, leaving the centre to focus on high-value products and services with more strategic importance to the business. Devolvement was to 'better-trained generalists', either lower-level purchasing staff or non-purchasing specialists, with the centre providing a support and facilitating service.

Since the late 1980s, purchasing and supply management at Welsh Water has faced a vastly increased task with no corresponding increase in resources. For example, capital investment has grown largely due to the need for improvements in the water supply and sewerage systems, required under EU Directives. All the privatised water and sewerage companies have been obliged to carry out large investment programmes. In 1989, 25 per cent of all sewage works in England and Wales had failed their legal consents. The implications of such an increase for purchasing are obvious, but at Welsh Water no extra staff could be employed to cope with the task because of continuous cost reduction drives. This forced the company to change its approach to purchasing, from a 'mandated' approach – where central purchasing controlled certain areas of spend as a matter of procedure – to what the company calls 'enablement'. This means that the central function has reduced its direct involvement in purchasing and instead acts as service to the rest of the company.

Central purchasing at Welsh Water believes that this change in approach has actually increased its involvement in company spend. This is because it now plays a facilitating role in a wider range of activities in its capacity as a service provider, rather than being involved in the various steps of a buying process. Staff numbers at the centre have remained similar, falling from seven pre-privatisation to six in 1996. Ongoing efforts to reduce costs, and more especially staffing levels, have prevented any increase. Faced with a significant increase in purchasing activity and with no prospect of additional staffing resources, it is hardly surprising that the company's approach to purchasing had to change.

Purchasing and supply professionalism

Central purchasing has now freed labour resources to concentrate on high-value goods and services and has developed an approach which will extract maximum value from the purchase of the more strategic items. Before, much time was devoted to dealing with the administrative side of purchasing, thus preventing a more strategic involvement. The key factor which instigated this change was the hike in capital expenditure, which quickly revealed that the systems in place could not cope and prompted the empowerment of lower-skilled staff.

The change in approach is reflected in the company's purchasing strategy, which now reads:

> To enable an empowered workforce to achieve commercial success through more astute and professional buying practices and forging partnerships with appropriate trading organisations.

An example of devolvement is the purchase of fencing materials. Framework agreements were arranged centrally, but now one of the local area buyers has been given responsibility for managing all of the company's requirements. As far as central purchasing is concerned, the new approach has focused on developing the use of particular purchasing tools and techniques. While the company had been using purchasing portfolio analysis as a basis for operational strategy for over ten years, it has recently begun to develop new techniques such as benchmarking, purchase price cost analysis, strategic supplier alliances and partnership sourcing. It was also developing the use of network sourcing at the time of interview. The need to do 'more with less' has also led to rationalisation of the supplier base and standardisation of products whenever possible, presumably in order to reduce transaction costs. The focus is now on reducing the 'whole-life cost' of the product or service acquired (its cost to the company over its lifetime), in contrast to pre-privatisation, when the purchase cost was the more influential factor.

The role and profile of purchasing

Broadly speaking, the role of purchasing has evolved into a policy formulation and support service task. Before, it tended to cover all aspects of purchasing and as such formed a central administrative role. A change in corporate strategy with a greater focus on profit making and, consequently, cost-cutting has helped to make the role more commercially focused, with a stronger emphasis on achieving value for money. In an interview with procurement personnel, it was stressed that there never was a 'bottomless pit' of money before privatisation, but there has been a greater focus on efficiency post-privatisation.

The two proxy indicators for the profile of purchasing – level of involvement in company spend and the position of the most senior purchasing manager – give little away in this case. As far as the position of the most senior purchasing manager in Welsh Water is concerned, little seems to have changed significantly since privatisation. This position has remained second tier, i.e. reporting to a main board director, but not actually sitting on the board. In the public sector days, the head of purchasing reported to the director of central services. Since privatisation, the reporting line has been to the finance director, who sits on the main board. Involvement in total company spend has increased from 40 per cent to 60 per cent. This, however, is because the function has changed its level of involvement in spend, as detailed above. While central purchasing is 'involved in' 60 per cent of spend, the final buy decision rests with the user department. From this evidence, it cannot be concluded that the profile of purchasing has improved significantly. Formal purchasing-qualification levels of purchasing personnel have shown very little change, while they have improved in most other organisations involved in the study. This was explained by the fact that parts of Wales are relatively poorly served for gaining the main professional qualification, CIPS.[7]

The research at Welsh Water revealed, however, that purchasing had gained greater recognition since privatisation from the rest of the organisation by demonstrating how 'good purchasing works', for example in adding value to contract negotiations. As a result of this success, purchasing was becoming more involved in new areas of company spend and the head of purchasing was being given more freedom. From this account, it would appear that the profile of purchasing has improved since privatisation. Whereas the department previously had a mandated right to be involved in certain activities, they are now earning this right through their own contribution to the company.

Outsourcing and supplier relationship management

As a whole, Welsh Water has followed a wider trend in the economy towards increased outsourcing of support services in the 1990s. This has included activities such as pipe-laying, ground and vehicle maintenance, printing and certain legal services. At the time of interview, 90 per cent of printing had been outsourced, and staffing of the legal department had been reduced from 18 to just 5. This change has been driven both by a desire to focus on 'core competencies' and a drive to reduce costs. For example, the company made a decision that it was good at designing processes, but not laying pipes, hence the contracting out of this activity. They also examined the costings which revealed that others could carry out this task more cheaply. Welsh Water employees must wear high-profile branded clothing, use vehicles and plant carrying company livery and conform to strict health and safety regulations, all at additional cost. Subcontractors can marginalise many of these obligations, allowing them to undercut the costs in Welsh Water. Purchasing's role in outsourcing has involved setting up bids and ultimately contractual arrangements, once decisions to examine outsourcing opportunities have been made elsewhere in the company.

Supplier rationalisation has been ongoing and is considered necessary by the company for two reasons: first, because of the administrative costs of supporting a large number of suppliers; second, because of increasing regulatory pressures (the company is regulated by the Office of Water Services) pushing Welsh Water into establishing a 'tighter regime' with key suppliers. Welsh Water is increasingly establishing 'partnership sourcing'-type relationships for the purchase of strategic goods and services.

As is suggested in the company's purchasing strategy given earlier, Welsh Water is tending towards more collaborative relationships with suppliers, although this is restricted largely to strategic products. The company has built an increasing number of framework agreements and agreed on standard products to be used over a number of projects. Before, products that were used in sewage treatment works within the company, for example, were not standardised. The result was that the individual project manager decided on the type of products sourced, leading to a proliferation of product types and standards throughout the company. Now, most products used in a project are standardised across the business and the project manager is obliged to conform. This change tends to reduce transaction costs and increases opportunities for leveraged buying.

Considering finally the location of suppliers, although Welsh Water has never operated a 'buy British' policy, it has, where commercially advantageous, recognised the community ethos of supporting local and regional economies. The position post-privatisation is virtually unchanged as far as geographic sourcing is concerned. The overriding factor has remained the ability to achieve best value for money, commensurate with the company's interest in the development of the local economy.

Conclusions

There is no doubt that Welsh Water is an example of a company that has always had a relatively high level of operational awareness of the need for improvements in functional professionalism. The improvements in purchasing and supply management described here were already in train well before privatisation occurred. This implies that, rather than starting the process, privatisation merely acted as a further pressure to increase the search for *efficiency* gains. The immediate focus on cost reduction through headcount limitations and the subsequent need to provide a 'leaner' organisational structure clearly contributed to the development of functional professionalism. This has been due to the need to review outsourcing decisions for a range of support products and services. This pressure contributed to the use of new and what are commonly perceived as more professionally focused purchasing tools and techniques.

In the future this improvement in functional professionalism at the operational level may be challenged, however, by the creation of the new multi-utility, Hyder. In this environment, the need to manage static and dynamic efficiency gains at the operational level in very different supply chains will be paramount. There is little doubt that Welsh Water's acquisition of SWALEC and metamorphosis into Hyder plc may have been an attempt by the company to develop an acquisition approach to transformational efficiency improvement. It remains to be seen, however, whether the acquisition of a very different operating company will provide the synergies that the combined company is hoping for.

SOUTH WEST WATER

This case demonstrates how a company that faces few competitive pressures can still achieve considerable static and dynamic efficiency gains through a focus on purchasing functional professionalism at the operational level. It also demonstrates the very important point that privatisation on its own does not improve procurement efficiency. Among other things, improvements in performance are nearly always assisted by the ability to find competent individuals, who understand what it is that is appropriate to do, given the circumstances they face. Despite the improvements made in static and dynamic efficiency terms, there was little evidence at the time of the research of transformational efficiency thinking at South West Water.

Background

South West Water is responsible for water and waste-water services in the south west of England, covering mainly Devon and Cornwall. Like Welsh Water, it was one of the ten water and sewerage authorities privatised in 1989. Today it is one of the smallest of these ten companies, with only Wessex Water behind in both turnover and employee number terms by 1994/95 (CRI, 1995). South West Water's turnover is only about one quarter of Severn Trent's, another case study from the water industry discussed on pages 142–55. The company employed just over 3,000 people in 1994, in contrast to Severn Trent's 10,600 staff (CRI, 1995).

The company has, however, grown considerably since privatisation. Turnover for 1994/95 was just over £286m., around double 1990/91 levels of £143.8m. The majority of this growth has come from within the core water supply and sewerage activities, but approximately one-third has come from 'enterprise businesses', which represent acquisitions of other activities. South West Water has diversified into construction, waste management and instrumentation equipment since 1990, in each case by acquisition (SWW plc, 1995).

Turnover for 1994/95 showed a 14 per cent increase on the previous year, indicating that a strong post-privatisation growth trend continues. Pre-tax profit for the period increased by 6 per cent over the year, to £98.7m.[8] showing a 12 per cent increase over 1990/91 profit levels.

The company has made considerable structural changes since privatisation not least in the organisation and role of the purchasing function. Several factors have been influential in driving these changes and as such deserve a brief discussion. The key factors are threefold: the recognition by senior management (many of whom have come from outside of the water industry) of the importance of purchasing and its contribution to business success; the deliberate recruitment of a purchasing professional from the private sector with a mandate and the resources to bring about considerable change; and pressures on efficiency imposed by the industry regulator, Ofwat.

Around the time of privatisation, senior management brought in consultants who suggested considerable changes in the organisation of purchasing. The consultants also recruited the new head of purchasing on behalf of the company, in early 1991. He had formerly spent three to four years as purchasing manager for Guinness plc. Senior management accepted the consultants' recommendations that purchasing should be given a higher priority in the business. This led them to allow the new purchasing manager greater power and resources to develop the function. In addition, the new manager refused to accept the position unless he could assume responsibility for capital as well as revenue expenditure. Capital expenditure accounts for well over half of company spend and in most water companies has been under the control of the engineering directorate. This was granted – although in reality it took at least four years for purchasing to gain full control – and the former Guinness purchasing manager duly joined the company. It was the combination of these two factors which led to the considerable changes detailed below.

A third impetus for change was a regulatory price review by Ofwat in 1994 which forced South West Water rapidly to increase efficiency. The review was considered to be very harsh, requiring major economies in capital and operating expenditure. Despite appealing to the Monopolies and Mergers Commission (MMC, 1995), South West Water was forced to accept the main aspects of the review including a new price cap. The company decided to tackle this by striving to be at the forefront of efficiency in all areas. A management team was set up to deal with the change, of which the head of purchasing was a member, and reductions in internal and external costs were targeted. The fact that purchasing personnel control the vast majority of external costs (unlike in many other water companies where they control just 20 per cent to 30 per cent) meant that their role in this exercise was crucial, and this has had implications for the role and the profile of this department within the organisation, which are described below.

Evidence of static and dynamic efficiency gains

The structure of purchasing and supply management

Purchasing has been centralised within South West Water since privatisation, and this has occurred alongside a radical change in the role of the purchasing department and a substantial increase in its responsibilities. Before 1989 the company was organised into six districts and only stores purchasing took place centrally, accounting for about 5 per cent of company spend and occupying two purchasing staff – one manager plus a young assistant. The remaining 95 per cent was either spent in the districts by operational staff or by the engineering department. There was no standardisation of purchasing with project directors deciding what and where to source for their specific undertakings.

In contrast, by mid-1996 there were twenty-five central purchasing staff including clerical support, with the department now responsible for over 90 per cent of total company spend. This includes capital expenditure, as explained above, which marked a major step forward for the position of purchasing within the company. Much of the change has been in line with an overall company restructuring, which has happened in stages since privatisation. The first major company reorganisation began in 1991, resulting in the initial moves towards the centralisation of purchasing. As contracts were increasingly standardised, more of company spend took place centrally and the department gradually increased its involvement in capital expenditure. The purchasing department has continued to grow in size as a result of ongoing increases in standardisation and centralisation (another company reorganisation in 1993 introduced further centralisation of purchasing) and increasing responsibilities. This considerable increase in resources has taken place against a background of overall company downsizing.

Purchasing and supply professionalism

One could not speak of a 'purchasing strategy' as such at South West Water prior to privatisation. As explained above, there was no cross-company co-ordination. Separate project managers made isolated decisions on sourcing. Central purchasing was a 'two-man band' who effectively ran the stores and accounted for a very small proportion of company spend. Engineers in the company tended to order as and when they required items and little attention was paid to gaining value for money in contracts.

There has been considerable development in procurement strategy since transfer to the private sector, largely fuelled by the need to increase efficiency. Current strategy is determined by the company's 'Strategic Business Plan', which was borne out of the harsh regulatory review. The head of procurement predicted cost savings for 1995–2000 as part of this plan and success is based on achieving these savings.[9] No formal portfolio positioning approach is used in determining strategy but there are clear 'building blocks' used to deliver the targets. These are the identification of opportunities, e.g. for standardisation or centralisation; and the use of outsourcing, market analysis and vendor qualification, tender evaluation and negotiation, vendor and supply chain management and IT systems support.

Key features of the purchasing strategy at South West Water since privatisation are increased standardisation and centralisation. For example, whereas the material for pipes used to vary across the company, there are now standard materials used for given types of pipes, thus reducing variety and increasing possibilities for leveraged buying. Central agreements with suppliers have been established for many products that are used across the business with terms agreed at company level and the users ordering within this framework. Thus, leverage opportunities – using high-volume purchasing to drive down prices – are being realised and transaction costs reduced.

These developments have taken place alongside a continued drive to increase the involvement of purchasing in company spend. Often integrated teams have been set up in order to facilitate this. For example, teams involving a project manager, an engineer and a buyer have been established on some projects to increase the understanding of each others' roles and priorities, and thus reduce conflict.

The role and profile of purchasing

With purchasing's control over total company spend rising from 5 per cent before privatisation to over 90 per cent in 1996, the conclusion must be that the scope of activities and the role and responsibilities of the department have increased dramatically. This is supported by other evidence, notably the proactive involvement of the purchasing department in outsourcing decisions and the position of the head of procurement in the company hierarchy, both revealed in interviews with the departments.

The head of purchasing is now responsible for all company spend, be it with suppliers, consultants or contractors; this totalled about £150m. in 1995 including capital expenditure. Purchasing thus controls all parts of the supply chain within the company. There are some areas of spend, particularly capital expenditure, that are subject to joint responsibility between purchasing and project managers. This accounts for the 10 per cent not 'fully controlled' by purchasing. It is felt that this joint responsibility works well with purchasing providing the commercial expertise to complement the technical know-how of the project managers.

The position of the most senior purchasing manager within the company hierarchy has improved immensely since privatisation. Previously, the purchasing manager reported to an operations manager and had just one assistant. Now, the purchasing manager reports to the engineering director and has a team of about twenty-five staff reporting to him. Although he does not sit on the board, he has close and frequent contact with the company managing director. His responsibilities have also grown to encompass materials, equipment, transport, stores and logistics.

The realisation by company senior management of the potential contribution of effective purchasing management to company performance has obviously had a major influence here. The determination of the new head of purchasing to push the function 'upstream' has been equally important. It seems that from the start, he deliberately involved himself in more complex issues such as project management to demonstrate that purchasing is about more than simply buying. He also achieved some 'early wins' which consisted mainly of cost reductions in high-profile areas, and proposed that a matrix structure for purchasing be imposed on project management. This involved framework agreements to gain both leverage and transaction cost benefits as described earlier. This would be in conjunction with integrated teams so that the full technical and commercial issues and requirements could be understood by all involved, in order that any conflict between, say, purchasing and engineering, would be minimised. The introduction of these changes has been very successful in saving the company money. This is likely to improve or at least maintain the current position of purchasing within the management hierarchy in the medium-term future.

From the above it is clear that the internal profile of purchasing has improved substantially. The fact that the size of the purchasing department has increased from *two* to twenty-five over seven years, against a backdrop of company downsizing, underlines this point. Qualification levels have also improved. In 1996 there were fifteen 'front-line' purchasing staff: of these, all were graduates and nine were due to gain MBA qualifications by the end of the academic year. This is a far cry from the two-man team before privatisation. It appears that neither had comparable qualifications.

Outsourcing and supplier relationship management

There has been a limited increase in the use of outsourcing of support services by South West Water and purchasing has been actively involved in making decisions. Examples of activities outsourced are transport and stores, catering, and construction, although some have been transferred to associated companies. Before any changes were made, the head of purchasing and the group finance director carried out a joint exercise in outsourcing, which came to form the basis of the company's approach. A decision was made not to follow blindly the 'outsourcing trend' in the wider economy, but to outsource only where 'commercially sensible'. The philosophy is that only if there exists specialist expertise outside that the company does not possess or if the market is fast moving, should an activity be seriously considered for outsourcing. This has been the case for IT services and transport and stores, which itself is increasingly IT related.

The key change in supplier relationships by the company has been the move towards 'partnerships', the aim being to build a two-way, 'even' relationship with suppliers for mutual development. This trend, however, tends to be limited to strategic products and large project work, for example with construction and consultancy companies. South West Water has a series of agreements with contractors such as Gleeson, Degremont and Purac, and consultants such as the Pell Frischmann Group, which is an associated company. The company operates on an open-book basis with these suppliers, which means that each company allows the other access to internal cost information. There are monthly performance measures and measures for continuous improvement provided by both sides. South West Water also has a partnership agreement with a company for its vehicle fleet management.

Supplier reduction has not been an overt policy, but it has resulted from the establishment of framework agreements and the policy of standardising and centralising purchasing activity. The company views this as an improvement in supply base management. At the time of the study in 1996, 90 per cent of company expenditure was with less than 30 vendors. Turning to supplier performance, there has reportedly been major improvement in all key criteria, according to the questionnaire return: cost competitiveness, quality, cycle times, new-product development time, flexibility, on-time delivery and access to new technology and innovation. Unfortunately, no more detailed information on supplier performance was made available by the company so that the questionnaire answers could be developed.

Conclusions

South West Water has not chosen to attempt to improve profitability and revenue growth by moving quickly outside its traditional supply chain and markets based mainly on providing water and sewerage services, although today it does have interests in waste management, environmental and construction businesses. This, and the fact that it is not operating in a competitive market, means that the need to innovate and discover transformational efficiency gains seems to have been given a lower priority than it might have. Despite this, it is clear that since privatisation the company has become highly focused on functional operational improvements, which are achieving substantial static and dynamic efficiency gains. The major mechanisms for this learning process have been the recruitment of a highly competent purchasing professional to head the function from outside the industry, the willingness to provide purchasing with a more important role in the business, and support for the development of the professional competence of staff in the purchasing function. South West Water is a case that demonstrates a clear understanding of how operational efficiency can be achieved in a regulated, but non-competitive, environment.

POWERGEN

The PowerGen case is instructive because it demonstrates the problems that can arise for companies that have a fixed view of strategic means, but which lose sight of strategic ends. PowerGen is a case study of a company that has become locked into a devolved (SBU) approach to operational management, focused on static efficiency cost reduction. This has led to the creation of a devolved management structure, which has made it difficult for the company to achieve purchasing professional functionalism. This practice may well have limited the full potential for dynamic efficiency gains in the long term because there is little scope for the purchasing staff to develop phase-2 learning. There is therefore, little evidence either of transformational efficiency thinking in the company.

Background

PowerGen was one of the two non-nuclear electricity generators in England and Wales to be borne out of the Central Electricity Generating Board (CEGB), the other being National Power. In preparation for the privatisation of the industry, the two new companies were created in 1989 specifically to share the fossil-fuel-generating assets of the CEGB. At the time, the nuclear assets were considered too sensitive to be privatised and so for a time remained in the public sector and were given to the company Nuclear Electric (later British Energy). PowerGen was the smaller of the two organisations, receiving 40 per cent of generating assets against National Power's 60 per cent. The companies were both privatised in March 1991. Of the two, PowerGen is generally viewed as the more forward-thinking organisation, that has faced up to the challenges of a private sector existence. As a consequence it has tended to outperform its rival on the London Stock Exchange.

Turnover for the year to 31 March 1996 stood at £2,933m. (PowerGen, 1996), showing a gradual reduction since privatisation (reducing by 5 per cent since 1991/92). This is due to new competition in the UK market in the form of independent power producers, which has been central to government policy in this industry. Deregulation has brought down barriers to entry so that the number of players has gradually increased. In 1990 there were 10 generating companies and 16 electricity suppliers, the industry having been divided at privatisation between generation distribution and supply and transmission. Now there are 56 generators and suppliers, 11 of which perform both functions. Distribution in England and Wales is controlled by 10 regional electricity companies (RECs). PowerGen has been forced either to sell or lease generating capacity to other companies in a direct attempt to increase competitive rivalry. Pre-tax profits for 1995/96 were £687m.,[10] up 26 per cent on the previous year and close to double the figure for 1991/92 (ibid.).

PowerGen's main activity is generating and selling electricity. Sales are either to RECs or direct to larger users (i.e. those consuming over 100kWh peak demand). This large-volume market has been completely deregulated and as such is fully competitive. The market for smaller users, including domestic consumers, will be fully opened to competition during 1998/99, meaning that PowerGen will have the choice of entering the domestic supply market for the first time. The company's key strategic aim is to develop as an international electricity generator, the main driver being to replace the income being lost to competition in the domestic market.[11]

Evidence of static and dynamic efficiency gains

The structure of purchasing and supply management

PowerGen's aim was to become 'lean, mean, and fast on (its) feet' in the words of Ed Wallis, the chief executive designate appointed in 1988 to create the new company and prepare it for privatisation (Wallis, 1995). This implied drastic cost reduction, in particular of fixed costs, combined with increased flexibility. The means to achieve this were devolution and downsizing on a massive scale as part of a complete restructuring of the business. From the 'top-heavy', highly centralised and bureaucratic organisation which characterised the former state-owned CEGB, the company was transformed into a divisionalised structure with independent profit centres and a small corporate headquarters for support. The largest division was UK Electricity, which included all of the power stations. Each of the power stations became a separate profit centre, operating independently and even competing against the other power stations within the company. In summary, authority and resources were devolved massively and this was accompanied by more than a 50 per cent reduction in staffing levels. These were down to just above 3,700 by 1995, while the same period had seen a doubling of profitability.

Purchasing did not escape this transformation. The central purchasing function of PowerGen was created by transferring employees directly from the Midlands regional headquarters in Coventry. The function had almost

130 staff when the company was first established and at a time when most purchasing was carried out centrally. By 1996, however, central staffing had been reduced to less than 15 with almost all purchasing activity transferred to the power stations. This illustrates the reversal from centralisation to devolution of authority and resources. During the CEGB days, the staff at the power stations simply passed their requests to one of five regional headquarters, where the purchasing section dealt with all aspects of the purchasing process and for all goods and services except fuel, which was bought centrally by a specialist fuel-purchasing department. The only task remaining for the local staff was on receipt of the goods, which they checked against a copy of the order received from head office.

By 1996, all purchasing activity within PowerGen, apart from very large contracts, had been transferred to the power stations. Again this excludes fuel which remained a specialist, centralised activity. Each unit now carries out the process independently with minimal co-operation with other power stations (they are competitors, after all) and very limited contact with central purchasing. The team at the centre has two main roles: to ensure that company purchasing practice complies with legislation, mainly the EU Procurement Directives, and to provide a purchasing service to the business units. The SBUs can choose whether to use this, purchase themselves or use an outside agency, and they are charged for the central service if they choose to make use of it.

Purchasing and supply professionalism

The CEGB was notorious as a bastion of public sector tradition and this was reflected in its approach to purchasing. Practices were highly bureaucratic and civil service-like, relationships with suppliers were often 'cosy' and neither time pressures nor value for money figured as influential factors. Culture was also engineering led: engineers were prominent in the buying decision, leading to exacting specifications and generally inflated prices as a result. This is known as 'over-engineering' or 'gold-plating'. Many products were manufactured to CEGB specifications, which encouraged long-term relationships with a stable group of suppliers that were able to meet the required specifications. This group enjoyed a guaranteed, low-price elasticity market, hence the description of the relationship as 'cosy'.

The buying procedure in the CEGB was that users (mainly power stations) informed central purchasing of their requirements, and they then negotiated corporate contracts with one supplier. One drawback of this system was the time delay: because of the large amount of paperwork involved, users often waited weeks before receiving the required products, even for relatively simple or low-value items. A more serious problem was that the system simply did not work well due to poor communication between the centre and the operating units. For example, a contract would be negotiated with one supplier to produce bearings for the whole of the CEGB. However, because the centre was not aware of the full requirements of the different power stations in terms of range, specification, etc., only a small proportion of needs were satisfied. The power stations reacted by placing individual orders themselves with different suppliers, resulting in a doubling of effort and an effective 'bucking of the system'. It is not surprising that users of this centralised structure were dissatisfied: they rarely received goods on time, and in any case they were too often unsuitable for the purpose required.

The difficulties described above, together with an increasing drive for efficiency, resulted in the gradual devolvement of purchasing to the power stations. This began in 1989 with lower-value contracts (up to £350 initially) and was gradually increased until almost everything (except fuel) was bought independently. It is impossible to make one statement describing PowerGen's current purchasing strategy because it varies so widely between the different operating units. The only common thread is the emphasis on price reduction. The company as a whole is still striving to remove any waste from its operations in terms of excess resource. This is reflected in its approach to purchasing, where PowerGen's key aim is to drive down prices. It does this via a competitive approach to the market. The changes within the former CEGB have left suppliers in a much weaker position through a significant reduction in demand and PowerGen is taking full advantage of this situation to drive hard deals.

Central purchasing's mission states its desire to 'provide a world-class, strategic and customer-focused purchasing service to maximise PowerGen's competitive advantage'. However, because competition between the power stations prevents co-operation and the central purchasing team exists mainly as a support function, it seems unlikely that one coherent approach will emerge. There is also no shared culture throughout the organisation, making any attempt at co-ordinating purchasing policy even more difficult. The company has established some task groups involving purchasing and technical staff from both the centre and the operating units, but there has been limited interest and input from the power stations. This is because many have resource restraints as a result of the large staff reductions and, in any case, collaboration with competitors has limited appeal.

Major differences in approach exist between the power stations. While the larger, newer stations are becoming more proactive, with some evidence that they are using purchasing portfolio analysis for example, the smaller units spend most of their time 'fire-fighting'. They have neither the skills nor resources to develop a more professional approach and so concentrate on acquiring the required goods on time at reasonable prices. Purchasing staff at the operating units tend to have little knowledge of practices at other power stations, or indeed at the centre.

The role and profile of purchasing

Again, general statements about changes in the role and profile of purchasing staff are difficult in this case because of the different approaches adopted by the power stations. The only safe assertion is that the role has become much more commercially orientated and much less bureaucratic. Before devolution, power station stores flagged up their needs to purchasing, whose role was to bundle them up and send them to the regional headquarters' purchasing section for central processing. After devolution, they became responsible for the majority of their business unit spend.

As far as the profile of purchasing is concerned, it appears at first sight that staff at the power stations have gained at the expense of central purchasing staff. The influence of local purchasing staff has increased in line with devolvement of spend and they have gained recognition as a result. Central purchasing, on the other hand, has suffered massive reductions in staffing levels and in their influence on purchasing. The true picture is more complicated, however. While it is true that central purchasing has suffered a loss of recognition, it does not follow that local staff have enjoyed a corresponding increase, meaning that *purchasing at the company may have lost out as a net result of devolution*. Other factors have been influential with the result once again that there is much variety between the different power stations.

Drastic and continued company downsizing has meant that the vastly increased purchasing task has not been matched by resources. One power station visited during the research project had experienced a 50 per cent cut in purchasing staffing levels since privatisation, along with an increase in generation output from the station. This restricts the capacity of purchasing to develop a more professional approach by limiting its activities to the most crucial tasks, thus preventing it from gaining recognition via this route. A general lack of training and career development for purchasing staff at the business unit level adds to this problem. Low skilled and poorly motivated staff are unlikely to gain respect from others in the organisation. In some cases, purchasing is still struggling to shake off its 'paper-pushing' image and to win recognition from a strong engineering faction within the company, which continues to view it as regrettable red tape.

The above factors vary to some extent at each power station, resulting in much disparity across the company. While there has been some improvement in the profile of local purchasing, this does not appear to counter the recognition lost at the centre.

Outsourcing and supplier relationship management

Before privatisation, and in line with public sector practice at the time, the CEGB carried out almost all activities in-house. It would build power stations with internal resources and in-house design engineers. Transfer to the private sector necessitated large cost reductions and increased flexibility and outsourcing achieved both of these. As with many other companies, PowerGen saw outsourcing as a means of achieving a rapid reduction in costs. Following privatisation, the company made its design engineers redundant and began to contract out entire turnkey operations to companies such as Siemens, the German company. PowerGen simply gave the contractor the parameters (for example whether build should be to ISO or German DIN standards) and handed over responsibility. A number of traditional suppliers to PowerGen suffered, as they were not equipped to take on major projects. Apart from large construction projects, there has been a general increase in outsourcing at the company, but again this varies by business unit, as it is here that the decision is made. Typical examples of activities outsourced to date are cleaning and maintenance, the key driver being reduction of costs.

Traditional suppliers to the CEGB enjoyed a relatively stable market and centralised, high-volume contracts, but this situation was reversed at privatisation when drastic changes were enforced on the supplier market. An example will illustrate the impact on suppliers: BEAMA, the trade association of electrical suppliers, previously negotiated centrally with the CEGB, covering supplies for all power generation and distribution. When the CEGB was dismantled, it then had to deal with the twelve RECs and the three main generators (National Power, PowerGen and Nuclear Electricity, later British Energy) for England and Wales alone. When PowerGen went on to devolve purchasing authority, it was then forced to deal separately with twenty-one power stations[12] resulting in considerably higher transaction costs and much less stability of demand.

Moreover, relationships with suppliers became more aggressive as policies aimed at cutting costs were implemented at PowerGen. In the CEGB days, lines of communication were open and suppliers often received automatic invitation to purchasing-related meetings, where internal information was freely divulged. Shortly before privatisation, it was decided that relationships were too 'cosy', resulting in PowerGen paying over the odds on contracts. More commercially minded people were brought in to drive harder deals and exploit every opportunity to cut costs, resulting in a deterioration of supplier relationships. This aggressive approach to suppliers remains central to PowerGen's approach to purchasing. There is little evidence of longer-term, more collaborative-type relationships evolving.

Conclusions

There is little doubt that the PowerGen case demonstrates the relative costs and benefits of a top-down strategic approach to business success focused primarily on static and dynamic efficiency gains. While it is clear that senior management recognised the need to change fundamentally the old CEGB mentality of the past, the chosen instrument may well have created its own rigidities. By focusing on immediate cost reduction, through a devolved SBU structure to achieve static efficiency gains, the company may have forgone a number of dynamic efficiencies that might have achieved a more integrated approach at the strategic level. More worrying, perhaps, is the constraint that this has imposed on the development of an inclusive approach to functional professionalisation in purchasing and supply management. Perhaps the most glaring example of this is the decision to use aggressive, adversarial arm's-length relationship management with virtually all suppliers, while allowing potentially critical assets like design to be outsourced to major technical suppliers. The devolution of the purchasing competence to SBUs merely serves to reinforce a lack of focus and, arguably, myopia when it comes to the longer-term role of purchasing in the strategic management of the business.

SCOTTISH HYDRO-ELECTRIC

Unlike the PowerGen case, the Scottish Hydro-Electric case demonstrates the relative benefits that can flow to companies from a focus on flexibility in the development of purchasing professionalism. Since 1991 the company has developed a two-stage approach to static and dynamic efficiency gains. In the first stage, immediate and aggressive short-term cost reduction through centralised control and diktat was introduced. After 1993, a more developed and sophisticated approach to long-term cost management, based on functional professionalism, has been put in place. There is, however, little evidence as yet of transformational efficiency thinking.

Background

Scottish Hydro-Electric was privatised via a stock exchange flotation in June 1991. The Scottish electricity industry differs from that in England and Wales in that the companies remain vertically integrated. South of the border, privatisation produced a deliberate split between the three activities of generation, transmission and distribution to the final customer with separate companies responsible for each (although this situation may change rapidly as the electricity supply market now opens up to full competition and merger and acquisition activity redefine the industry). Following privatisation, thermal generation became an initial duopoly between National Power and PowerGen, transmission remained the responsibility of the National Grid, and distribution was carried out by the twelve regional electricity companies, such as NORWEB.

In Scotland, privatisation did not result in vertical fragmentation, but instead in the creation of three vertically integrated companies, one of which was Scottish Hydro-Electric. Before flotation, Scotland was divided regionally into two public sector organisations: the North of Scotland Hydro-Electric Board (NSHEB), and the South of Scotland Electricity Board (SSEB). The NSHEB became Scottish Hydro-Electric and the SSEB was divided into Scottish Power and Scottish Nuclear. In summary then, Scottish Hydro-Electric began its privatised life as a company based in the north of Scotland, generating, transmitting and distributing electricity to the end customer. As its name suggests, it relied largely on hydro-electric power before privatisation, but subsequent supply agreements with the other two companies mean that each company now effectively generates from a range of fuels.

Scottish Hydro-Electric's head office moved from Edinburgh to Perth in 1992, shortly after privatisation. Turnover was £887m. in the year ending 31 March 1996, an increase of just over 6 per cent on 1994/95. Its pre-tax profit for the same period was £195m., up 16 per cent on the previous year (Scottish Hydro-Electric, 1996). The company's key strategic aim since privatisation has been to broaden its business base geographically by moving south of the border. It appears to have successfully moved towards this goal with 35 per cent of sales volume produced in England and Wales in 1995/96 (ibid.).

Evidence of static and dynamic efficiency gains

The structure of purchasing and supply management

The structure of the purchasing department has changed in line with the corporate structure, which has seen at least two major reorganisations since 1990. In the public sector, the company was highly devolved with autonomous operating units and little control at the centre – what is now viewed by many in the company as equivalent to a definite lack of control. At the time of flotation the company was centralised in order to improve control and co-ordination and systems were put in place over the next two to three years to achieve this. At the end of this period, the structure was once again decentralised. By this time, central control and information systems, as well as relationships between the separate functions, had improved considerably. The reason for the second restructuring was to give power to those closest to the customer, reflecting senior management's desire to make company culture more customer focused. The current structure is described by the company as 'federal', involving devolved businesses but with centralisation where it makes commercial sense; for example where there are opportunities to gain economies of scale in marketing or finance. The trend witnessed at Scottish Hydro-Electric – whereby companies centralise to gain control of the business before redevolving – was evident in a number of the other privatised companies that took part in the research.

It was this first, centralising wave of restructuring that effectively created a purchasing function at Scottish Hydro-Electric. Before privatisation, purchasing was not regarded as a specialist activity. The result was that there was no purchasing department, as such, and almost any individual employee was allowed to spend company money, although in practice it was engineers who carried out most of the purchasing. Once the engineers had secured authority to go ahead with a project, they would usually 'get on with it themselves', taking responsibility for and control of project spend, as well as every other aspect of the project. This reflects a traditional culture of engineering dominance within the company.

The arrival of a new chief executive officer (CEO) about one year before privatisation, charged with preparing the company for the private sector, began to change all of this. Advised by consultants that 10 per cent of company spend could be saved by getting a tight grip on purchasing, he appointed a head of purchasing with the remit to reduce costs and set up a centralised purchasing function to 'go in and save money'. This marks the beginning of the severe cost-cutting and 'supplier bashing' phase for purchasing, which lasted approximately from 1989 to 1992. The desired cost reductions were achieved mainly by putting intense pressure on suppliers to reduce their prices, 'price-grinding' for want of a better phrase. Central purchasing was given considerable power at this time, illustrating the significance attached to reducing the cost of bought-in spend through supplier price reduction. The rest of the business was instructed to inform purchasing if expenditure was planned, and then it was up to the department whether to intervene with the aim of cost reduction.

After the centralisation stage, in line with company devolvement and a change in purchasing strategy – from cost-focused to a longer-term approach – purchasing was decentralised. The corporate restructuring created separate strategic business units (SBUs) which operate independently with their own budgets. Senior management wanted to ring-fence activities in order that inefficiencies could be recognised quickly and the industry regulator (the Office of Electricity Regulation: Offer) wanted to compare Scottish Hydro-Electric's activities with the English electricity companies. This structuring allowed for both. So the generation business of Scottish Hydro-Electric could be compared with PowerGen and National Power, for example. 'Procurement and contracts', to give the function its correct title, operates as a service provider. Internal customers are free to choose whether to use this service or to carry out purchasing themselves; while procurement and contracts is free to sell its services externally. This means that procurement and contracts operates much like a business in itself, in that it is required to market the benefits of its service to its prospective customers. The department sees itself as a sort of internal consultancy, offering training and advisory services in purchasing as well as actually taking on the purchasing process.

The contrast with the immediate post-privatisation strategy is clear: whereas there was an effective mandate to use purchasing before with the function operating largely as an instrument for cost reduction, this mandate has now been removed and replaced by an internal market where the central purchasing function must survive on its own competitive merits.

Purchasing and supply professionalism

In line with the above structural changes, purchasing strategy has passed through three phases of development since privatisation. It began as no strategy at all, just a civil service-type formal tender process based on price. It then moved to a cost-cutting stage based on price-grinding and putting pressure on suppliers before developing into a longer-term and what some might see as a more strategic role where the focus has broadened to include much more than cost reduction. The aim of procurement and contracts is now to sell a full purchasing service to its customers, whereas previously its main *raison d'être* was hard negotiation with suppliers to drive down prices.

There have been several different drivers for change throughout the period in question. During the 1990/91 pre-privatisation stage, the main driver was 'getting ready' for flotation and the CEO's decisions in relation to this, influenced by the recommendations of consultants. For example, consultants advised that Scottish Hydro-Electric was being given a poor deal by suppliers. This was probably true considering that quotations were often accepted without question and suppliers included all sorts of terms and conditions in contracts that were favourable to them. After 1991 and transfer to the private sector, the influence of City opinion and Offer, the industry regulator, began to influence company behaviour. The City considered that the company was inefficient (along with every other privatised electricity company) and pressured Scottish Hydro-Electric to remove the 'fat' from its activities; while Offer policed prices, thus limiting income and necessitating reduced costs in order to generate the profits demanded by the City.

The cost-cutting phase had its desired effect and was probably appropriate at the time, given the situation that the company was in and the pressures upon it. However, it also seems to have led to lower quality and poorer delivery, as suppliers did everything to reduce prices. The result was generally acrimonious relations with vendors and fewer and fewer suppliers wishing to deal with the company. This was hardly a feasible strategy in the long run. Around 1992 it was decided that a longer-term approach to purchasing was needed and the structure and strategy of the function went through its second transformation. The product is what exists today.

Current strategy has moved away from a focus on hard negotiation towards developing expertise in managing the entire purchasing process and offering this as a service to internal customers. This can include anything from identification and supplier selection, to supplier development, to a full supply chain review of the business in question. None of this was done before by purchasing. There is now much more interaction with both internal customers (for example to discuss the most appropriate form of contract or supplier) and suppliers. Although purchasing has been devolved from the highly centralised structure of the cost-cutting phase, the level of centralisation is flexible and depends on the wishes of the two parties involved, i.e. the internal customer and procurement and contracts. It might be that the customer wants to hand over the entire purchasing process to the department or that it prefers to maintain control over some elements, such as supplier selection. For its part, procurement and contracts generally aims to avoid involvement in low-value spend because this is viewed as an ineffective use of its skilled resources.

By 1997, the purchasing department had completed supply chain reviews for three of the strategic business units within the company – generation, power systems and information technology. As a result of the review of power systems, procurement and contracts now employs a permanent, full-time individual working on the supply chain of this business. It can be concluded from such examples that purchasing is now viewed as a professional service at Scottish Hydro-Electric, in stark contrast to the pre-privatisation days when a purchasing strategy did not exist at all, and to the immediate post-privatisation stage where purchasing's role was confined to price-focused negotiation. The cost-cutting phase was considered as apt for the time. It was necessary to get the City 'off the company's back' and free it to begin thinking more long term. Pressure to lower costs remains, but senior management now view this over a long-term basis rather than in terms of quick-fix cost reductions, which were deemed necessary at the time of privatisation.

The role and profile of purchasing

The above discussion clearly demonstrates that the role of purchasing has been transformed since privatisation. It is also clear that the profile has improved considerably, although it would be difficult not to improve on a function that in effect did not exist!

The profile of purchasing staff illustrates these changes well. There were no specific purchasing staff in the company's public sector days, as almost anyone was allowed to buy, although it was mainly engineers that actually did so. On centralisation, seven people were recruited from within the company to form the purchasing department. These people were familiar with the buying process but had low technical ability, tending to be storepersons or administrators. The only training that they received in preparation for their new positions was in negotiation, reflecting the price-focused nature of their task. In contrast, all of the sixteen current purchasing staff have either degrees or CIPS[13] qualifications (this is now a minimum requirement), or are currently studying for them. In addition, ten of them have been recruited from outside the company.

The activity of the function has obviously increased, necessitating a doubling of staff. This is an outcome of the success of the procurement and contracts 'business' in promoting the benefits of its service within the company. It also reflects the fact that it performs a broad range of activities related to the purchasing and supply process as opposed to price negotiation alone. As far as its involvement in spend is concerned, it has never been involved in buying fuel or energy, which accounts for 50 per cent of total company input costs. Excluding fuel and energy, Scottish Hydro-Electric typically spends about £250m. annually on routine purchases of plant, equipment and consumables, and procurement and contracts control 65 per cent of this (£160m.). This is lower than during the cost-cutting stage when the mandate to use purchasing created a near 100 per cent rate of involvement in company spend.

Outsourcing and supplier relationship management

Outsourcing of support services has increased since privatisation at Scottish Hydro-Electric, largely as a means of reducing headcount in reaction to City opinion that the company was overstaffed. This has resulted in some decisions being taken arguably without adequate analysis. Two activities already outsourced are customer information systems, which is a database of customer records that has gone to Severn Trent plc (a water and sewerage company) for a five-year period, and desktop and infrastructure IT services. The company was also considering the feasibility of outsourcing fleet management and facilities management at the time of the study.

Supplier relationships have seen much change since privatisation. Beginning with a highly adversarial approach during the cost-cutting stage, which put some vendors out of business and led to others refusing to deal with the company, relationships have now become generally closer and more amicable. Scottish Hydro-Electric now tends to get involved earlier in the buying process so that the company can inform the suppliers of its exact needs. This is a far cry from selecting the lowest price tender and running with it for a year, as was the practice until the change in approach. The company now aims to manage relationships towards a 'joint vision', and focuses on processes rather than outcomes. This means that rather than looking at the end product alone, the company studies how the supplier makes the goods so that improvements can be made in quality and other relevant aspects. Supplier rationalisation has taken place gradually. It did not happen during the cost-cutting stage because more suppliers were encouraged, in order to increase competition among them and so drive down price. But it has happened as a consequence of the new strategy, as the company has begun to work more closely with fewer, more carefully selected suppliers.

Supplier selection and performance measurement have become much more sophisticated. Whereas they were previously selected on price, Scottish Hydro-Electric now considers three factors when assessing a potential supplier: their ability to supply in the short to medium term, their potential to develop and whether they can be effectively managed and controlled. The company searches for worldwide best practice in suppliers, considering financial strength, safety, environmental performance, management capabilities and cost, among other factors. Existing suppliers are also assessed on their year-on-year performance in their dealings with the company.

Management argue that supplier performance has improved across the board. This has mainly resulted from the company getting involved at an earlier stage of the buying process and fully informing the supplier of its needs, leading to the development of products and services that are of higher value to the company as a customer. An example is the purchase of computer equipment: the company assessed its needs, realised that it had no internal expertise in computing and so went out to suppliers to discuss the best solution. Scottish Hydro-Electric now buys a complete equipment, maintenance and repair service from the same supplier which is tailored to its specific needs.

Conclusions

The Scottish Hydro-Electric case demonstrates the benefits of a company adopting a flexible and 'fit for purpose' approach to strategic and operational practice in purchasing. After privatisation, static efficiency gains were achieved primarily by a heavily centralised and immediate cost-cutting approach to purchasing. This cost reduction mentality was probably appropriate at the time it was introduced, largely because of the lack of a purchasing and supply function in the past, and the attendant purchasing incompetence evident within the company at that time. By 1993, however, the company had recognised that the benefits of this short-term cost reduction approach to purchasing had been largely exhausted. The result was a more devolved approach, involving a shift from phase-1 to phase-2 thinking in terms of the schema set out in Chapter 1.

NORWEB

Like Scottish Hydro-Electric, the NORWEB case demonstrates the benefits that can flow to companies if they adopt a functional professionalism approach to achieving static and dynamic efficiency. However, this may be more problematic after the 1995 merger with North West Water, to form a new company called United Utilities, because the combined company will have to manage two very different subsidiaries operating within very different supply chains. Despite this, there is little doubt that the NORWEB case is an excellent example of a company operating at a high level of purchasing professionalism and achieving significant cost improvement.

Background

NORWEB is an electricity distribution company operating in the north west of England and was one of the twelve RECs to be privatised in December 1990. It had previously been a member of the public sector Electricity Council, along with the other eleven regional distributors and the generator, the Central Electricity Generating Board (CEGB). NORWEB supplies electricity to a population of just under five million, covering an area stretching from the conurbation of Manchester up to the Scottish border.

According to 1995/96 turnover figures, NORWEB was the third largest REC behind Eastern Electricity and Southern Electric (CRI, 1997). In that year, turnover reached £1.5bn. at the company, having risen gradually from just over £1.2bn. in 1990/91, the year of privatisation. Profit before tax stood at £295m. for 1995–96, showing a significant increase on the 1990/91 figure of £65m. (NORWEB, 1995; CRI, 1997).

NORWEB no longer exists as a separate company, having been taken over by North West Water in November 1995. The two companies have since been merged to form United Utilities, the UK's first multi-utility. The stated aim of the merger was to reduce costs through synergistic gains and improve performance by focusing on the core utilities business and selling off peripheral companies (*The Financial Times*, 29 March 1996). This text, however, will continue to refer to the company as NORWEB, as the initial research took place just before the takeover and the changes described relate to the 1990–95 period, from privatisation to the time of the takeover.

Evidence of static and dynamic efficiency gains

The structure of purchasing and supply

Following privatisation, there was a complete change of both structure and strategy in purchasing at NORWEB, in line with an overall change in company culture, from one focused on engineering excellence to a customer-service and profit-driven philosophy.

The most visible change has been in the location and organisation of the purchasing function. Since privatisation, this has moved out of head office and onto a separate and dedicated site, in an attempt to bring all elements of management of the supply chain under one roof. Purchasing was highly centralised pre-privatisation with the head office function having responsibility for 95 per cent of company spend (excluding the purchase of fuel which has always been a separate function), devolving only the very low-value items. The organisation was structured on a functional basis, so that purchasing was not involved in related activities such as warehousing.

Reorganisation was aimed at ending the functionalism by placing all activities related to management of the supply chain under one roof and improving integration within this newly created department. The new site was named the 'supply chain business' and incorporated warehousing, distribution, information technology, accounts payable and purchasing. This entire department now had overall responsibility for the same 95 per cent of company spend, devolving low-value spend to the business units or directly to the users. The internal supply chain was now much more tightly controlled. Stock items, for example, were brought together on one site, whereas previously they had been bought by different buyers with their own supplier preferences, and stored at various locations. Rationalisation of stock suppliers was expected to reduce NORWEB's own stock levels by at least 30 per cent over four years (beginning in 1993). The number of stock orders had already been reduced by 50 per cent just eighteen months into this four-year period.

The reorganisation took place in 1993, and was prompted by pressure to reduce costs throughout the company. The threat of an impending electricity price review by the industry regulator, Offer, pushed NORWEB to carry out its own analysis of costs. This revealed that the internal supply chain was very fragmented and under different managers at different times. These managers often had conflicting interests and consequently purchasing failed to maximise its contribution to the bottom line. A newly promoted purchasing manager was asked by senior management how to organise the function, and he duly proposed the establishment of the supply chain business. The plan was effectively 'sold' to senior management in cost reduction terms and by the summer of 1996 the department was in the second year of a demanding five-year cost reduction project. Within the company, privatisation is seen as responsible for bringing management of the supply chain together. It was the increased focus on profitability following the move to the private sector, and hence on cost reduction, that revealed the opportunities for improved organisation.

Purchasing and supply professionalism

The extensive structural changes outlined above were matched by those in purchasing strategy at NORWEB. From having no purchasing strategy to speak of before 1990, the company believes that it has been able to develop a proactive and systematic approach. Pre-privatisation, purchasing was a highly reactive function: buyers simply received a user requirement and 'plodded away' to do their best. Processes were well regulated and controlled, but very archaic and civil service-like. The department was perceived as an ivory tower, isolated and remote from the end-user. The current approach differs completely. Consultants were brought in to help develop a new approach, and this was introduced along with the establishment of the supply chain business and now forms the basis of purchasing philosophy at the company. The new approach is based on a purchasing-positioning matrix. Products are assessed according to the buyer's influence in the market, which depends on the number of suppliers, level of spend, etc., and the buyer's level of exposure, i.e. how important the items sourced are to the company and how many suppliers exist. The position of the product in the matrix then determines the sourcing strategy to be adopted. A more sophisticated approach has developed. In addition, the concept of 'internal customers' has been introduced with service level agreements between the supply chain business and these customers. This is largely in order to demonstrate the benefits of using the 'purchasing service', and it is a far cry from the mandatory use of the centralised purchasing function before the changes took place. This further illustrates the change in focus that has occurred: purchasing itself is now customer focused and operates like an independent business unit. It offers the service of internal supply chain management to the rest of the organisation.[14]

The development of a more proactive approach to purchasing has involved the increasing use of modern purchasing tools and techniques. While vendor accreditation has been used for some time, it is only recently that vendor selection mechanisms have become more formalised. Since privatisation, NORWEB has also become increasingly involved in strategic supplier alliances, which involves joint investment with suppliers, partnership sourcing and single sourcing. Benchmarking has also been used extensively since 1990. This has included networking with purchasing managers in other companies in order to exchange ideas, and visiting 'leading edge' purchasing companies in order to learn from their practices. NORWEB managers have visited Nissan, British Aerospace and the Central Purchasing Unit, a government organisation, as part of this exercise. There has been a number of other initiatives aimed at increasing efficiency in purchasing since privatisation, for example the introduction of credit card procurement and fuel cards in an attempt to deal with low-value, high-transaction cost items. Such initiatives were few and far between under public ownership, perhaps because efficiency was not such a priority.

The role and profile of purchasing

It is clear that purchasing's role within the organisation has developed from being largely reactive and administrative towards a more proactive task, one that is required to demonstrate that it adds value to the business. This, coupled with changes throughout the rest of the organisation, has helped to improve the internal profile of the purchasing function. Its image has changed from that of being a 'Cinderella activity' and even a 'necessary evil' that had to be used, to one 'respected for its contribution to company profits'.[15]

The considerable changes detailed above have enabled purchasing to demonstrate the benefits of using its service to the rest of the company. This, in turn, has allowed the department to become involved both in new areas of company spend – those which were traditionally the domain of specialist services such as the legal department – and in outsourcing decisions, an area of greatly increased interest since release from the public sector. In fact, the drive for efficiency across the company has helped purchasing in this respect. Other areas of the business no longer have the resources to devote to purchasing and so are increasingly calling on the supply chain business to provide the service for them.

Purchasing's involvement in buying banking services is an example of its move into 'non-traditional' areas of spend. This was previously controlled by the finance department, but the supply chain business became involved for the first time during 1995 and achieved a considerable reduction in transaction charges within a year. Purchasing has also gained access to the buying of consultancy services for the first time, a reflection of its success in other areas.

The increased involvement of purchasing in company spend demonstrates how the function is 'gaining ground' within the company by adopting a more proactive approach and by demonstrating value added to the business. It is clear that the role of purchasing has moved far beyond the 'order-placer' mentality of the pre-privatisation days.

This change is reflected in the professional and age profile of the buyers. Two years before privatisation their average age neared sixty and qualification levels were very low. By 1995, the average age had dropped to thirty-eight and qualification levels had shown a notable improvement. Buyers are more commercially aware, many have professional purchasing qualifications and senior buyers are often graduates. Those interviewed within the company (admittedly, purchasing staff) believed that purchasing's role is now more highly regarded by others within the organisation and purchasing is no longer seen as being largely a clerical activity.

Outsourcing and supplier relationship management

Outsourcing of support services has increased considerably at NORWEB, and two key reasons were given for this: the decision to focus on core competencies and the need to reduce employee numbers, due to the pressures of the regulator and from City opinion. City analysts classed all electricity companies as overadministered and undermanaged at the time of privatisation. Outsourcing has so far involved peripheral services such as cable installation, helicopter patrol and overhead line construction. Purchasing has been involved in most of the decision making. At times, the idea to outsource an activity has come from the purchasing function. At other times, suggestions have originated from elsewhere in the company and the supply chain business has been asked to assess the relative benefits of in-house versus outsourced purchasing. The trend is towards increased involvement of procurement in the make–buy decision.

As with many privatised utilities, the increase in outsourcing has helped to raise the profile of purchasing, as it is normally this function that takes responsibility for dealing with contractors. The outsourcing question was hardly considered under public ownership because the integration of the company remained unquestioned and there was not the same pressure to reduce costs.

Supplier relationships are another area witnessing change. Supplier rationalisation is a key element of the cost reduction project currently underway at the supply chain business. The target is to reduce suppliers by 40 per cent over the 3 to 5 years from 1994. By the end of year one, admittedly the easiest year, a 37 per cent reduction had already been achieved, the actual number of suppliers falling from 9,500 to 6,000.

The nature of relationships with this reduced group of suppliers is becoming more complex. Whereas the tendency before privatisation was for arm's-length, adversarial-type relationships for most purchases, the new approach takes account of the nature of the product sourced and supply market conditions in deciding on the most appropriate form of relationship. The global trend towards collaboration with suppliers is being followed, as witnessed by the increase in partnership and single sourcing, but by no means across the board. Indeed, competition is being actively encouraged in some areas: NORWEB has made a deliberate move towards functional specifications and away from ones based on detailed performance criteria, aiming to attract more potential suppliers and so increase competition among them.

The considerable changes made were paying off both in terms of cost reduction and supplier performance by early 1996. Targets for reducing costs were set at £4m. over a three- to five-year period beginning in 1994 and the supply chain business had already exceeded these just eighteen months into the project. Savings for year one were £3.4m., rising to £3.6m. for the first nine months of year two. Purchasing managers confirm that supplier performance has improved on all key criteria since privatisation. There has been a major improvement in on-time delivery and cycle times (the total time taken to complete the elements of a work cycle) and a slight improvement in cost competitiveness, quality, flexibility and access to new technology on the part of suppliers.

Conclusions

The NORWEB case is an example of a high degree of success in the recognition of what are the appropriate developments to achieve static and dynamic efficiency gains through functional professionalism. One of the key moves was the recognition of the need to place the purchasing function within an integrated supply chain management business in 1993. This demonstrates, after an initial focus on short-term cost reduction, an understanding of the need to develop a more sophisticated approach (phase-2 learning, see chapter 1) to cost improvement. This has focused on the recruitment and training of better staff and on the development of advanced processes and operational tools and techniques. This trend appears to have continued since the merger with North West Water and its purchasing function. It remains to be seen, however, whether this merger will result in a confusion of competencies. The reason this may happen is due to the fact that the new company will be managing two primary supply chains – one for electricity and one for water – each with individual cost and quality drivers.

Summary of the impact of privatisation on utilities

The interview results from the six utilities discussed in this chapter reveal that two of the companies, British Gas and PowerGen, are still primarily in phase 1 (static efficiency) of the learning process as set out in chapter 1, while the remaining four seem to have reached various stages of phase 2 (dynamic efficiency). The main reasons for the relative lack of progress at British Gas were continued corporate restructuring since privatisation, which had prevented the development of a coherent purchasing strategy, and perhaps the lack of effective competition in the gas market until relatively recently, which forced the company to search for greater efficiency improvements. British Gas was privatised in 1986 but effective competition has developed mainly since 1992. At PowerGen, extensive downsizing and the devolvement of operations caused similar problems. The aim of these structural changes was to remove waste and thus create a leaner, more efficient company. The effect on purchasing, however, may have been to hinder progress in the development of a more proactive approach, one that arguably could have made a greater contribution to the long-term success of the company through an improvement in dynamic, rather than static, efficiency, as defined in Chapter 1.

The companies that have reached a more advanced stage in the development of purchasing strategy each had certain factors in their favour. At Welsh Water, regulatory pressure forced the company to increase capital expenditure sharply. However, limited resource within the company led to the need to do 'more with less' and pushed Welsh Water to search for improvements in long-term efficiency. Similarly, South West Water faced regulatory constraints on costs and prices which forced a search for efficiency improvements. The company also benefited from a senior management team who understood the benefits of an effective purchasing strategy, and the recruitment of a highly competent head of purchasing from the private sector who was given the power and resources to make considerable changes to the function. Management at both Scottish Hydro-Electric and NORWEB also appear to have recognised that a short-term, cost-cutting approach to purchasing, consistent with a phase-1 approach to procurement, is not sustainable in the long run. This realisation, reinforced by the pressures of an increasingly competitive environment in the electricity industry, led to the development of a longer-term outlook, focused on the achievement of dynamic efficiency gains. Both companies, for example, insisted on recruiting more highly qualified purchasing staff and reassessed their purchasing processes through new relationships with suppliers, focusing on gaining long-term value for money rather than opting simply for the lowest purchase price.

Despite gains in static and dynamic efficiency in the privatised utilities, there is still little evidence of any development of an understanding of supply alignment and procurement competence (transformational efficiency) or phase-3 movements in our schema (see Figure 1.1, page 4). The best that has been achieved is the acquisition strategy developed by both Welsh Water and NORWEB. In both cases there is an objective to rationalise procurement activities in the combined businesses as part of a fundamental reappraisal of their management. But the benefits which these acquisitions may bring in terms of immediate corporate profitability could well be outweighed in the longer term. This will show if either of the companies fails to recognise the need to align strategy and operational practice with the unique and contingent circumstances operating within each of the very different primary supply chains that now pass through each company. This argument is developed further in Part IV.

6 The impact of privatisation on non-utilities' purchasing and supply management

This chapter reports interview results from two non-utility privatised companies, the Rover Group and Rolls Royce.[1] Both of these companies have traditionally operated in competitive, commercial product markets, unlike the utility companies studies in Chapter 5. The structure used in that chapter, focusing on the four key themes of internal cost reduction; purchasing professionalism; the role and profile of purchasing; and outsourcing and supplier relationship management, has been maintained for comparability. The three-phase learning process set out in Chapter 1, pp. 2–4 is also used, as a framework for plotting the development of purchasing strategy in the two companies since privatisation.

THE ROVER GROUP

The Rover case is an example of continuous improvement, as the company, first under Michael Edwardes in the 1970s, and then through Honda's prompting in the 1980s and early 1990s, began to understand the need for a rapid increase in efficiency. Rover and Honda formed a strategic alliance in the late 1970s. Increased efficiency was achieved through phase-1 immediate cost reduction at first, but subsequently has given way to a much more professional approach to purchasing practice. There is little doubt that this professionalisation has been massively increased by a strategic reappraisal of the company's position in its primary supply chains. The company's shift from a high level of vertical integration to an assembly role has contributed to the development of both static efficiency and dynamic efficiency gains, as well as some clear evidence of transformational efficiency improvement.

Background

The Rover Group was transferred out of government hands in a private sale to British Aerospace in 1988. It had spent the previous thirteen years as a public sector organisation after the government rescued the company from bankruptcy by taking a majority shareholding in 1975. By this time, it had become the country's largest vehicle manufacturer, formed by the amalgamation of several smaller producers, among them such famous names as Triumph, Austin and Morris. As it has grown, the company has been through a number of name changes: from the British Motor Company to British Leyland in the 1960s, then BL, to finally become the Rover Group in the 1980s.

The company was in severe financial difficulties by the time the government stepped in during 1975. Intensifying competition in the world car industry had exposed its many weaknesses, and market share was falling rapidly. Efforts were made to improve company performance during its public sector days, although by the time of privatisation Rover was still making a small loss. Sir Michael Edwardes, chairman of the company from 1977–82 and charged with turning it around, called it 'one of the largest public sector lame ducks of all time' (Edwardes, 1983, p. 14). Efforts to improve BL's competitiveness were often frustrated by powerful trade unions and the company became infamous for its industrial disputes during the 1970s.

Since privatisation, Rover has had a number of ownership changes and these have been important in determining overall company strategy and performance. In 1990, Honda UK and Rover acquired 20 per cent of each other's equity. Four years later, in January 1994, British Aerospace sold its majority shareholding to the German car manufacturer BMW, leading to Honda and Rover untangling their cross-shareholdings shortly afterwards. BMW owned 100 per cent of the Rover Group at the time of the research, having bought the outstanding 20 per cent from Honda.

As far as the impact of privatisation on purchasing and supply is concerned within the company, the transfer of ownership is viewed as an indirect accelerator of a change process that was already evolving, rather than a direct cause of changes. Change was accelerated via two routes. First, the British Aerospace takeover led to an immediate rationalisation of operations in order to reduce costs. Purchasing did not escape this process. Second, privatisation opened the door to change by facilitating the relationships with Honda and then BMW, both of which had far-reaching effects on purchasing strategy.

Evidence of static and dynamic efficiency gains

The structure of purchasing and supply management

Privatisation caused no great realignment of purchasing structure, however it did accelerate a centralisation process that was already underway. In 1967, when British Leyland was created by the merger of British Motor Holdings and Leyland, the structure was decentralised and fragmented. This is because the two former companies were themselves formed from the amalgamation of several smaller producers, and each of these continued to buy for their own plants. There was a supplies division based at Longbridge, the company's head office, whose task was to seek opportunities for synergy across the plants. Otherwise, the units operated autonomously. The separate purchasing functions included Rover Triumph purchasing, Jaguar purchasing and Austin Morris purchasing. There were moves to develop one coherent British Leyland purchasing strategy and some changes were made towards increased centralisation. This aim was never realised, however, because the individual companies were separated again and Jaguar was sold off in 1984.

On privatisation in 1988, purchasing was further consolidated. It was divided into two product areas and three sites. All car purchasing was divided between Longbridge and Cowley, and Land Rover purchasing took place in Solihull where this subsidiary was based. British Aerospace resisted pressure to merge Land Rover with car purchasing because it wanted to keep its options open on selling the company as an independent entity. British Aerospace gave a commitment to the government when it purchased Rover that it would not resell the company for five years. However, the long-term fit of Rover within British Aerospace was always in doubt. The parent company also introduced a policy of 'leaning' Rover shortly after taking ownership. This involved the introduction of strict financial controls and identifying and removing any waste or duplication of resource throughout the company. Purchasing was benchmarked and found to be overstaffed and Rover was thus charged with reducing headcount within the function. The management achieved this by merging part of Land Rover purchasing – facilities and general services – with that of car purchasing at Longbridge. Continued focus on cost reduction and efficiency eventually pushed Rover to consolidate purchasing on to a single site. Now all of the company's purchasing takes place at Longbridge.

Following the BMW takeover in 1994 there has been some progress towards establishing joint purchasing with the parent company. In 1995, the two purchasing divisions began working together with the aim of standardising parts and using common components and technologies for some vehicles. For example, they are developing joint electrical and electronics platforms for cars within the BMW Group, and expect to begin selecting suppliers of vehicle components on a joint basis (BMW, 1995).

Purchasing and supply professionalism

Two key factors have influenced procurement strategy at Rover since privatisation: the need to reduce costs drastically in order to become profitable and remain competitive, and the alliances with the two foreign vehicle manufacturers. This account deals mainly with the impact of the Honda alliance, although the effects of the BMW takeover were apparent in Rover purchasing by 1995, when much of the research reported here was undertaken. It should be noted that the Honda Motor Company supported Rover through licensing, supply arrangements and joint product development from 1979 to privatisation in 1988 before they took any stake in the company (Nanda and Williamson, 1995). This explains why this company's influence has been significant.

It was a central aim of British Aerospace to transform Rover into a profitable company and so the parent company quickly introduced strict performance measures, such as formal financial controls, and forced purchasing to reduce headcount once it had been calculated that the function was overstaffed. Not only did this put pressure on purchasing to consolidate its activities on to fewer sites, it forced staff to find more efficient ways of operating. Alongside this pressure, the Honda alliance had exposed Rover to an advanced approach to both internal and external resource management. In the words of one interviewee, the company borrowed Honda's ideas and 'Roverised' them.

At corporate level, the upshot of these two factors was the development of a total quality programme, which began in 1987. The programme was a form of business process re-engineering and formed part of the ongoing 'leaning' process. Having studied the invasion of the United States by Japanese car manufacturers, Rover management concluded that it had to learn Japanese lean manufacturing principles if they were to avoid a similar plight. Purchasing at Rover has a substrategy which is closely aligned to the corporate quality strategy, and the three central elements are supplier development, supplier rationalisation and total cost management. These central elements confirm that the main change in purchasing strategy is towards closer relationships with fewer suppliers (Robertson, 1995). Rover has strived to move away from its traditional arm's-length approach to suppliers, where management gave little information away, negotiated largely on price and played suppliers off against each other in the hope of making short-term cost gains.

Rover has fully embraced the idea of working with fewer, carefully selected vendors, considering the total cost of acquisition rather than the price of the product in isolation and over the short term. Whereas the company used to be secretive about product development and costs, it is now much more open and expects the same from suppliers. In the past, for example, suppliers were kept in the dark about new product launches until late in the process. Now they are shown clay models of vehicles up to five years before launch (Lamming and Cox, 1995). In the words of the managing director of Land Rover, 'Adversarial relationships with hidden agendas no longer have a role to play in the Rover supply base' (ibid., p. 64).

Before the change in approach towards more collaboration purchasing strategy was tactical and reactive, much time was spent 'fire-fighting' and dealing with problems and the attitude towards suppliers was adversarial. When the pressure was on to improve performance and financial viability to assist the transfer to the private sector, Rover reacted by pressurising suppliers into price reductions that they could ill afford. One interviewee referred to this approach as 'killing the supplier'; having conceded to Rover's demands, some suppliers then went into liquidation because they simply had no scope to reduce costs without affecting profits. A second problem arose with the arrival of the Japanese car manufacturers' production facilities in the UK. These provided a new market for traditional suppliers to Rover and, as such, presented a major threat. These two factors pushed Rover to adopt a longer-term, more collaborative approach to supplier relationships in order that key suppliers would not be lost.

The new approach requires the use of relatively complex purchasing techniques. These have been under development at Rover since the programme began. RG2000 is the company's supplier assessment programme. This covers every aspect of the vendor company and is based on self-led improvement by the supplier. The company is assessed on approximately 350 attributes, and the programme focuses on establishing a platform for improvement, rather than a simple pass or fail. Such a sophisticated system would never have been used in the days when sourcing decisions were based on price alone.

The role and profile of purchasing

The role of purchasing has generally become more professional and less administrative. This is reflected in the staff profile: while the number of purchasing staff has remained similar since privatisation, essentially clerical positions have been replaced by best-practice engineers or cost estimators. There is no hard evidence, however, that the profile of purchasing has changed significantly since privatisation. The position of the most senior purchasing manager – group purchasing director – has not changed, neither has purchasing's level of involvement in total company spend. The qualification levels of staff have improved with the majority of purchasing staff completing specialist two-year courses at local universities. This is part of Rover's policy of developing change agents within the company, and possibly the Honda and BMW alliances have had some influence here.

Outsourcing and supplier relationship management

Outsourcing has increased at Rover, although to a lesser extent than in the case of the electricity and water utilities. Rover was always a major purchaser of components for car assembly, whereas the utilities tended to be vertically integrated when under public ownership. The changes that have occurred have involved non-core activities, such as the manufacture of fastenings and cleaning services. These have resulted from a combination of Rover's focus on core competencies, the capping of investment expenditure and introduction of strict financial controls by the parent company. In some cases, Rover skirted the capping of investment expenditure by outsourcing, in order that a project could go ahead. This happened with the production of the MGF model, where the car body manufacture and assembly were outsourced. The make–buy decision was considered to be 'immature' before the BMW takeover, now it is more sophisticated. Rover management compares internal costs and capabilities to those outside the company, while also assessing which activities it needs to control. If the activity is leading edge, such as the development of ergonomic seating, it will be kept in-house, while the manufacture of standard seats will be outsourced if this can be done more efficiently externally.

It is clear that Rover has greatly increased partnership-style relationships with suppliers. Close working relationships are viewed as the best way to achieve a differential in the highly competitive car market and to keep apace with fast-moving technology, an example being the development of airbags. Rover's supplier base has reduced accordingly: from about 2,000 during the 1980s, down to 1,000 by 1990, and further reduced to approximately 700 by 1993. Of the 700, a core of 350 suppliers accounted for more than 80 per cent of Rover's £3bn. annual expenditure. Almost all components for Rover products are dual sourced, apart from commodities such as tyres, and Rover is increasingly using network sourcing with suppliers taking on responsibility for the supply of whole systems (subassemblies) rather than the separate component parts. In some cases the company has devolved responsibility for design to the suppliers. Rover will now tend to give a general specification on required performance, allowing the supplier more scope in the design process.

Rover's relationship with the supplier market has passed through three key stages. It began with a 'preferred supplier' mentality, in that the onus was on the supplier to win Rover's business and the customer was in a strong position. Then the influx of Japanese companies produced competition for suppliers forcing Rover to strive for 'preferred customer' status and weakening its position *vis-à-vis* suppliers. Most recently, the introduction of lean manufacturing and supply at the company has led to the development of more collaborative relationships with the supply market, with equality between buyer and seller and a mutually beneficial relationship, in theory at least.

Conclusions

The Rover case is intriguing because it clearly demonstrates two things about supply alignment and procurement competence. Of the group of organisations involved in this study, it seems clear that Rover is the most supply aligned and procurement competent. The two major reasons for this explain something about how supply alignment and transformational efficiency through procurement competence are achieved. First, the Rover case demonstrates that purchasing and supply functional improvement can best be achieved in the context of a strategic understanding of the appropriate position for the company to adopt in its primary supply chain. In the context of the car industry, this has meant a shift from a highly vertically integrated to an assembly and outsourcing and supplier relationship management role. Rover clearly moved, as a consequence, to a less vertically integrated operating structure over the period from the 1970s to the 1990s. Second, the increase in competition experienced by the company, that was consequent on the arrival of the Japanese car manufacturers, was perhaps the most important factor in forcing the company to change its approach to relationship management. This plus the Japanese influence through the Honda joint venture have been crucial drivers behind the development of a synchronised approach to static, dynamic and transformational efficiency. The major problem for the company today may well be that the takeover by BMW could lead the company to lose impetus in the further development of these three forms of efficiency.

ROLLS ROYCE

Unlike the Rover case, it is clear that Rolls Royce is still some way from an awareness of supply alignment and procurement competence. Despite this, it is clear that after an initial focus on immediate static efficiency through cost reduction, the company has begun to develop a more sophisticated understanding of dynamic efficiency through purchasing and supply functional professionalism.

Background

Like the Rover Group, Rolls Royce was taken into public ownership following financial collapse and reprivatised some years later. The company was taken over by the government in 1971 after going into receivership, and spent sixteen years in the public sector before being sold off by the Conservative government in May 1987. From time to time, Rolls Royce had been subsidised while under public ownership and the patience of the Thatcher government with this drain on resources wore thin. The intention to privatise the company was announced in July 1983, but did not take place until four years later. Back in 1971, the collapse led to the creation of a new company whose main activities were the manufacture of gas turbines and engines for aircraft, industrial and marine applications, but still called Rolls Royce. It was at this time that Rolls Royce Motor Cars and the oil engine division were separated. They remained in the private sector and eventually became part of Vickers plc.

Rolls Royce has traditionally been highly specialised in aero-engines, and this remained the case until 1989 when it diversified through acquisition. The target company was Northern Engineering Industries (NEI), manufacturers of industrial power equipment. The main driver for the acquisition was to increase non-aerospace interests and thus reduce risk, aerospace being a highly volatile market. By 1995, NEI accounted for 33 per cent of company turnover, the remaining 67 per cent being devoted to aerospace (Rolls Royce, 1995). The company also increased its international presence during the 1990s setting up a joint venture with BMW, as well as joint manufacturing with companies in several other European countries. NEI was subsequently sold as part of a restructuring of the business.

Company performance has been transformed since privatisation due largely to a culture change from an engineering bias towards a market-focused approach. There has also been a drastic cost reduction programme. From being bankrupt in 1971, Rolls Royce had become a ‘world class player in the fiercely competitive aero-engine market’ by 1991 (Syedain, 1991, p. 45). A new chairman was appointed two years before privatisation who began a ‘relentless drive to cut costs and win market share' (ibid.), and both objectives have been achieved. Market share in the company's most important sector – engines for civil aircraft – rose from 5 per cent in the mid-1980s to 20 per cent by 1991 and almost 30 per cent by 1995. This is an impressive achievement, given the highly contested nature of the industry. There are three main players globally: GEC, Pratt and Whitney and Rolls Royce, which is by far the smallest of these three.

Cost-cutting measures have resulted in a drastic reduction in staff numbers. The company was described as 'hideously overmanned' during the 1960s (ibid., p. 47) and indeed for much of the 1970s. Employee numbers fell, from 58,000 in the early 1980s to 39,000 by 1995; a 31 per cent reduction.

Overall, the privatisation of Rolls Royce is viewed as a success because of the turnaround in culture and performance since the transfer. Profits leaped in the four years after privatisation in 1987, and performance has remained creditable since. This, despite a severe recession in the company's main market of commercial aircraft in the early 1990s.[2]

Evidence of static and dynamic efficiency gains

The structure of purchasing and supply management

The company as a whole has been restructured twice in recent years. The first restructuring took place in the early 1980s and involved the centralisation of activities in order to reduce duplication. The second restructuring involved a business process re-engineering (BPR) project and was effected over the 1992–95 period. This split the company into separate, fully accountable business units and, devolved management responsibility.

As far as the structure of purchasing is concerned, this remained decentralised for most of the 1980s, with purchasing units on each of the company's sites which operated independently. This often resulted in several buyers dealing with the same supplier, creating duplication of effort and bypassing opportunities for leveraged spend. Towards the end of the decade, all purchasing was pulled together into one purchasing department at Rolls Royce headquarters in Derby. The department formed part of the newly created supply group, which was responsible for all manufacturing and purchasing, in other words for all supply from within and outside the company. The supply group was created in order to reduce costs through rationalisation and by gaining better deals with suppliers through leveraged buying.

During 1992/93 and as part of the BPR process, the supply group was split into two separate organisations: manufacturing and procurement, so that purchasing became a separate, but still centralised, organisation. This marked an increase in the profile of the function reflected in the creation of a director of purchasing, who sat on the main board. More recently, in early 1996, purchasing has been decentralised into a devolved–enabled structure. This latest change has created two levels of purchasing. Strategic purchasing still takes place centrally and involves the management of the overall supply chain, supplier selection and the negotiation of framework contracts. But logistics has been devolved to the strategic business units (SBUs). New SBUs were created as part of the BPR project and there are four of them, each with its own logistics group: civil aircraft, military aircraft, repair and maintenance. The rationale behind this move was two-fold. First, central purchasing needed to be freed from tactical tasks and allowed to concentrate on strategic activities. It was feared that the department would inevitably spend its time 'fire-fighting' if these activities were not removed from its remit. Second, the devolution of logistics to the businesses would give them full control of their own supply chain, which was necessary if they were to be held responsible for their own performance.

Purchasing and supply professionalism

According to one interviewee in the company, there was no purchasing strategy to speak of before privatisation, activity was fragmented and 'not focused at all' and the separate purchasing departments were essentially backroom administrative operations. Now, with the deliberate split between strategic purchasing and logistics, it is clear that a more proactive approach to purchasing is developing, although the change process has been evolutionary in nature. Indeed, it is regarded as a strategic activity that others in the company have recognised as being of fundamental importance to the bottom line. It is also felt that the key driver behind the changes in purchasing strategy was the company becoming increasingly leaner and the implications that this has had for the purchasing function.

Rolls Royce purchasing now has a formal mission statement and strategy, whereas these did not exist before because of the fragmented nature of the function. Purchasing strategy has been distilled into seven key purchasing directives:

- reduce unit costs
- satisfy the customer's requirements for service and quality
- deliver to the customer on time
- capture and develop the world's best suppliers
- minimise total operating costs
- minimise demands for company cash
- develop the quality, creativity, productivity and professional fulfilment of our people

There has also been a significant increase in the use of purchasing tools and techniques. Since privatisation, the following practices have been adopted: formal vendor selection mechanisms, benchmarking, purchasing portfolio analysis, strategic source planning, strategic supplier alliances and partnership sourcing. Rolls Royce is a member of the Society of British Aerospace

Companies (SBAC) which carries out the pooling of data for benchmarking purposes. The company is also developing further benchmarking and best-practice activity in addition to this, meaning that the use of these particular tools will grow in the future.

Two other important initiatives in strategy since privatisation are the establishment of joint ventures worldwide, the most recent example being an alliance for the manufacture and service of parts in China, and the development of 'risk and revenue sharing partnerships'. This normally involves foreign suppliers who are trying to enter the aerospace industry. The suppliers pay an 'entry fee' for getting business with Rolls Royce, invest in the necessary plant and supply the product free. In return, they receive a percentage of revenue on the sale of the final product by Rolls Royce. In this way the supplier takes a share in the revenue but also shares the risk, which is dependent upon successful sales. This is regarded by Rolls Royce as a very strong and desirable strategic relationship with the supplier.

The role and profile of purchasing

> ... if you could not do what you really wanted to do in the company you became a purchasing person. There is no question in the future that purchasing has to be a clear winner, a strategic winner for the whole business.
>
> (Quotation from a senior Rolls Royce purchasing practitioner.)

It is clear from this comment that purchasing used to be a receptacle for those who lacked the calibre to succeed elsewhere in the company. This is no longer the case and the function has gained much respect within the company in recent years. There remains a long way to go, however, and purchasing staff still feel that they are fighting a battle to increase recognition from the rest of the company.

There was a marked improvement in the profile of purchasing when the supply group was divided into two units thus creating a separate purchasing department. This is because the position of director of procurement was created for the first time, the director being a member of the Rolls Royce board. This marked a stronger recognition that purchasing makes an important contribution to the company's future. The average cost of projects within Rolls Royce is divided into 70 per cent bought-in and 30 per cent manufactured costs, meaning that effective purchasing management is a key to company success.

Whereas there used to be more than 1,000 purchasing staff scattered about the business and performing largely low-profile, administrative tasks, by the mid-1990s there were 500 at central purchasing and 300 involved in logistics within the business units. The 500 central staff were divided approximately as follows: 200 dealt with production purchasing (parts, raw materials, etc.); 200

with non-production purchasing (anything else from travel to utilities and capital equipment); and 100 were involved in a range of other activities. Many of this remaining 100 had the task of approving and certifying vendors, which had to be carried out for all tiers of suppliers to Rolls Royce. The reason for this is the safety aspect: aero-engines must be faultless. The implications are that the company employs an army of staff for approval and certification, many of whom must travel worldwide to audit the capability and facilities of suppliers and run testing laboratories for suppliers' products, all at an additional cost to the company and all under the purchasing banner. Very few of the central staff are involved in administrative work. This has been devolved to the business units.

Purchasing's involvement in company spend is 100 per cent of production purchasing and this has not changed since privatisation. For non-production, products such as insurance and financial services tend to be dealt with by others, often by the finance or personnel departments. At the time of interview, purchasing was leading an examination of areas of spend not currently under their control. The likelihood is that the function will get involved in new areas of work in the future.

Outsourcing and supplier relationship management

Outsourcing of support services has increased at Rolls Royce, although this has been more in recent years than immediately post-privatisation. Examples of activities outsourced are services such as catering, security and IT, which has gone to EDS, a business consultancy and computing company. The trend towards the outsourcing of service activities is expected to continue. The key drivers have been the need to reduce costs, a focus on core competencies and the release from government constraints. Rolls Royce was never as vertically integrated as some public corporations such as the utilities, perhaps because it began as a private sector company. This means that a trend towards outsourcing is likely to be less marked.

In order to decide on make–buy, Rolls Royce divides the components in an engine into three categories: those that must be made in-house, those that should be subject to competition between in-house and external production and those that must be outsourced. If the component is a market differentiator, for example, and Rolls Royce needs to keep the technology within the company, its production is most obviously core and remains in-house.

As far as supplier relationships are concerned, the evidence suggests that Rolls Royce has been increasingly developing partnership-type relationships. The company has adopted such practices as strategic supplier alliances, partnership sourcing and risk and revenue-sharing partnerships since privatisation. However, the nature of the industry also plays an influential role here: products supplied to Rolls Royce are often highly specialised and of high value, meaning that suppliers must invest in dedicated plant and thus increase their own risk.[3] This situation often leads to the customer becoming more closely involved with the supplier. An example of this is the risk and revenue sharing partnership described on page 121.

Another trend since privatisation has been for Rolls Royce to push more risk on to suppliers by getting them involved in research and development rather than carrying it out entirely in-house. Another form of risk reduction adopted by the company is sourcing products abroad when sterling is strong, offsetting its own inflated selling prices for exports. This is important for Rolls Royce because 75 per cent of turnover is exported. The company has also increased the amount of 'offset deals' that it is involved in. This is where, in order to gain sales in a given country, Rolls Royce is obliged to source from that country. This offset activity has increased generally in recent years and the company has had little choice but to get involved. This reflects the global nature of the aerospace industry. Nevertheless, Rolls Royce still sources almost 80 per cent of its products from UK suppliers, a surprisingly high figure. Most of these companies are quite small and some are dependent on Rolls Royce for a large proportion of their sales. This gives the company a great deal of power in the supply chain (Parker and Hartley, 1997).

Conclusions

It is clear that Rolls Royce, having been a privately owned company before its collapse and public funding, retained many of its market-focused structures and practices from its private sector days. Given that the company traditionally operated in an oligopolistic rather than a more highly competitive marketplace and benefited from cost-plus defence contracts, the tendency towards overstaffing and bureaucracy was still evident on privatisation. Because of this, the company clearly had to focus initially on internal cost reduction in order to achieve static efficiency gains. Once this was achieved, however, the company was able to refocus its strategic and operational activities. This was essential given the acquisition of NEI in 1989. Rolls Royce has had to re-engineer its structure and attempt to align the operational activities of its newly created SBUs with the search for dynamic efficiency within each one. This has caused the company to reappraise its logistics and purchasing functions, while at the same time encouraging the outsourcing of support services for immediate gains, and more collaborative supply relationships for anticipated longer-term gains. There is little doubt that in the early 1990s the company shifted from an administrative view of purchasing and supply to one based on a more sophisticated view of purchasing functional professionalism. This shift from a static to dynamic efficiency framework for purchasing coincided with the company's BPR review. This created a more SBU-focused logistics process with purchasing functional professionalism earmarked for the strategic overview of the process.

Summary of the impact of privatisation on non-utilities' purchasing

In terms of the three-phase learning process, the study results suggest that both Rover and Rolls Royce have reached phase 2 in our schema set out in Chapter 1, page 4, the professional development stage. However, Rover is notably more advanced than Rolls Royce within this second stage. Moreover, the results show that Rover has arguably developed the most advanced approach to purchasing and supply management of all the organisations that participated in our study. Factors which have favoured the acceleration of progress at Rover include a continuously and increasingly competitive environment throughout periods of both public and private ownership, severe cost constraints imposed by Rover's new owner immediately after privatisation, and the alliance with Honda and now the takeover by BMW. The alliance with Honda allowed Rover to learn from the Japanese company new and more sophisticated purchasing and supply management techniques aimed at reducing cost and improving quality.

While at least three separate factors served to push Rover towards increasingly advanced purchasing management, only one clear influence was identified at Rolls Royce, which perhaps explains the slower pace of development in the latter. The key factor here has been competition: Rolls Royce has operated in a globally competitive environment (notwithstanding defence contracts) through its periods of public and private ownership, an environment where competition has become more intense in recent years. This has meant that the company has remained market focused throughout and this seems to have given it a head start on the utilities discussed in Chapter 5, in terms of advancing purchasing management. These organisations were all monopoly suppliers before privatisation and in some cases have remained partially so, resulting in less pressure to become efficient and commercially focused, both within the purchasing function and throughout the organisation.

7 Developments in public sector procurement

Chapter 7 reports interview results from two public sector organisations: the Civil Aviation Authority (CAA) and London Underground Limited. Once again, the four key themes introduced in Chapter 3 form the structure of each separate case study and the three-phase learning process, pp. 2–4, is used to plot the position of the organisations in terms of their approach to the management of purchasing and supply.

Overall, the results in this chapter reinforce the questionnaire results reported in Chapter 4. The public sector organisations are developing in similar ways to the privatised group, but change tends to be less marked, begins at a later date and progresses at a slower pace, according to the questionnaire research. Examples from two of the key themes illustrate this point. First, as far as the development of a more professional approach to purchasing is concerned (see hypothesis 2, page 39), two out of the four organisations were still in the process of developing clear strategies, along with related purchasing tools and techniques, at the time of the research. This is evidence that these organisations are lagging behind the privatised group. Second, regarding outsourcing and supplier relationship management (hypothesis 4, page 40), only two organisations were in a position to report on supplier performance. The other two lacked adequate systems for the measurement of supplier performance and consequently were unable to give any information. This is further evidence of a lack of progress *vis-à-vis* the privatised companies studied.

The reasons for the differing levels of progress lie in the different internal and external drivers faced by the organisations. These are discussed in more detail in the separate case studies in this chapter. Towards the end of the chapter the positions of the public sector organisations in the three-phase learning process are also assessed.

THE CIVIL AVIATION AUTHORITY

The CAA case supports the view that privatised organisations tend to improve their purchasing and supply functional competence more quickly than those in the public sector. There is little doubt that the CAA is some way behind the privatised companies in this respect and there is little evidence of any real understanding of supply alignment and procurement competence in the company.

Background

The CAA is a public sector body responsible for air safety and regulation in the United Kingdom. Its activities are divided into two main areas: safety and economic regulation and air traffic control services, and the organisation is split into two corresponding divisions. The first set of activities is carried out by the safety regulation group and the economic regulation group respectively, and these two together form one 'half' of the CAA. Safety regulation includes the licensing of aviation activities through issuing private and commercial pilot licences, certifying aircraft and airports and performing medicals for commercial pilots. Economic regulation includes monitoring the financial viability of airlines, for example checking a new airline that is bidding to run a given service, and regulating charges and services at the UK's main airports.

The second responsibility, air traffic control, is carried out by NATS (National Air Traffic Services), and this is also divided into two areas. First, NATS carries out *en route* control. It is responsible for all air traffic flying across UK airspace and essentially guides aircraft across the country. Not surprisingly, it has a monopoly position here.[1] Income is generated through charges made to the airlines for occupying UK airspace and these are calculated through a pan-European group called Eurocontrol.[2] Second, NATS carries out air traffic control at UK airports, though it does not have a monopoly of this activity. The airport operators, for example the British Airports Authority (BAA), has a choice between the CAA, private sector operators or employing staff directly. The CAA has the largest market share with about twelve airports across the country, including the largest, Heathrow.

The Civil Aviation Authority was formed out of the Department of Trade and Industry as an independent entity in 1972. Up until 1976 its employees remained civil servants. The organisation was created with a view to 'covering costs' through the payment of licence fees and air traffic control charges. In general this should not be a difficult task given that the CAA enjoys the sole right to operate in the majority of its activities. It has a monopoly in its safety and economic regulation activities, and in *en route* air traffic control. The only activity subject to competition is air traffic control services at airports.

The organisation has experienced considerable change over the last twenty years, gradually becoming more independent from government. By the late 1980s the CAA was fully independent except at ministerial level. In 1976 new pay structures were introduced to replace civil service grading. Staff had previously been civil servants on secondment from the Department of Trade and Industry and they were now offered contracts to work as employees of the CAA. Throughout the 1980s the government attempted to instil a move away from a civil service culture, for example by appointing senior managers from outside the organisation as change agents. By 1989, and following a decade of privatisation activity, the Conservative government decided to review the feasibility of transferring the CAA to the private sector. The major report on this was issued during 1991. This recommended that the organisation be split up into the two major activities of regulation and air traffic control (NATS) and the latter possibly privatised. By late 1994 the decision had been taken to go ahead with the separation and throughout 1995 preparations were underway. NATS became a separate subsidiary in April 1996. As far as privatisation is concerned, sale of the regulation side of the CAA's activities has never been viewed as a viable option; it is the air traffic control side that has always been under consideration. In late 1995 the government decided that privatisation of air traffic control was not practical, largely because this would involve the creation of a private sector monopoly. However, this decision was reversed by the new Labour government, when in June 1998 it announced its intention to privatise NATS.

Evidence of static and dynamic efficiency gains

The structure of purchasing and supply management

It is the organisational changes detailed above combined with political pressure to reduce costs that have driven changes in purchasing. However, the structure of the function changed very little until the late 1980s. In 1989, the CAA began to centralise purchasing systems in order to gather more information, for example on total spend and spend per supplier, as this data had not been collected previously. Before, buyers in the separate units were more independent and information systems were not centralised. The 1989 change also ensured that buyers at all levels were directly responsible to the director of contracts and purchasing.

A major structural change in purchasing did not occur until 1995 and took place as a result of wider changes in organisational structure within the CAA. Before this time, contracts and purchasing was centralised with 85 per cent of total spend taking place at the head office in London. All contracts above £5,000 were dealt with there with low-value spend delegated to local buyers. It should be noted that £5,000 might well be considered an extremely low value to an organisation the size of the CAA, but the need for central authorisation of such levels of spending is not unusual in the public sector. By 1995, NATS was being effectively separated from the regulatory side of the business. This affected the purchasing structure on two levels. First, contracts and purchasing began to buy for NATS only, whereas previously the department acted on behalf of the whole of the CAA. In reality this made little difference because NATS accounted for over 90 per cent of total spend. Second, and more importantly, purchasing was now devolved. This was because NATS was divided into three major divisions, each assuming increased responsibility for all operations, including purchasing. The separate business units are: airports, air traffic control centres (there are three of these) and infrastructure (this includes communication and remote radar stations). The change meant that higher-value spend was devolved to the divisions, each of which had its own purchasing group. They took control of contracts of up to £30–£50,000, and the proportion of spend controlled centrally fell from 85 per cent to 50 per cent. It also required the transfer of purchasing staff from the head office in London to the business units.

Purchasing and supply professionalism

The CAA's approach to purchasing appears to have become more commercially focused and long term over recent years. However, there certainly remains a bureaucratic influence, relationships with suppliers appear to be arm's length and rather secretive and the organisation is heavily constrained by legislation.

Purchasing tools and techniques that have been adopted since late 1994 include: vendor accreditation, formal vendor selection mechanisms, strategic source planning and partnership sourcing. At the time of interview in February 1996, the CAA was attempting to develop the use of benchmarking, but it was a case, in the words of the interviewee, of 'more words than action at this stage'. Staff had visited purchasing departments at other companies and attended a number of purchasing workshops, but had not yet acted upon these. The department also planned to introduce service level agreements with internal customers, but again this had not yet taken effect.

The mission statement of contracts and purchasing is 'to work with its customers to deliver through best practice, goods and services that are the best value for money in support of the NATS Strategic Intent'. The development of purchasing strategy appears to be fairly prescriptive, with an annual purchasing plan being produced by the director of contracts and purchasing and the business unit directors, based on business plans laid down by NATS. Moreover, the department produces a document which sets out purchasing policy in detail, covering subjects such as ethics, the use of competition, supplier management, commercial disclosure, value for money as well as many others. Although this document mentions the importance of value for money and whole-life cost, it is written in a highly formal and didactic style which is typically associated with the civil service.

It is mentioned that purchasing should be 'well managed to support the objective of delivering value for money whilst observing legislative requirements' (Civil Aviation Authority, 1995, p. 1), and this underlines the influence of legislation on purchasing management. The CAA is governed by the Public Procurement Works and Supply Regulations (1994) and the Public Services Regulations (1993), the main impact being on large contracts. The regulations force the CAA to issue competitive tenders for contracts above a certain threshold, thus in many cases preventing the development of long-term supplier relationships. However it does appear, leaving aside legal requirements, that competition is the preferred relationship form within the CAA, as reflected in the statement that 'Competitive tenders shall be sought unless there are justifiable reasons to the contrary' because 'competition encourages suppliers to offer the best value for money' (ibid., p. 2). There is no mention of partnerships or collaborative supplier relationships in the CAA's document.

The role and profile of purchasing

The position within the organisation of the most senior purchasing manager, the director of contracts and purchasing, has improved as a result of the structural changes. This post has moved up the reporting line: it now reports to the chief executive of NATS who is a main board director, whereas before 1995 the reporting line was to the finance director.

Looking at procurement's involvement in organisational spend, control of traditional spend has not changed a great deal even if it has been divided up differently between central and local purchasing staff. However, contracts and purchasing is beginning to increase its involvement in non-traditional expenditure. For example, at the time of the study it had recently become involved in the purchase of travel and accommodation and had set up a one-year contract for insurance for the first time. This might be viewed as further evidence of an increase in the role of the function.

Purchasing has assumed greater responsibility for a range of goods and services, particularly high-value spend, reflecting a higher profile. Purchasing management have more control because they no longer report to the finance director, moreover there has been a formal statement from senior management that wherever contracts and purchasing can add value it should be given the opportunity to do so.

More generally, the main change in the role of purchasing is that it has become more commercially focused. Purchasing staff now tend to be specialists recruited from industry, whereas in the past they were generalist civil servants who 'moved across' to the department from elsewhere in the organisation. This was partly a reflection of the civil service culture of 'career generalists', and partly because purchasing was seen as a non-specialist, interchangeable job. This is no longer true. The CAA also invests more in the training and education of purchasing staff than was the case in the past.

Outsourcing and supplier relationship management

The 1990s have seen an increase in outsourcing of support services at the CAA, the two major activities outsourced to date being IT and facilities management. The reasons given for the increased interest in outsourcing are a focus on core competencies and because it is politically 'the done thing'. That is, the government wants to see evidence of cost-cutting and this can be achieved through headcount reduction and outsourcing. Purchasing tends to be involved reactively in the outsourcing decision. This means that once senior management have made the decision to outsource, contracts and purchasing deal with the contracting.

There is no evidence of a change in the nature of relationships with suppliers. The emphasis remains on competition and maintaining the competitive position of the organisation, for example by withholding what is considered to be sensitive information from suppliers. There is a stated aim of reducing the total number of suppliers used (Civil Aviation Authority, 1995, p. 3), but the only reference made to the development of more collaborative-type supplier relationships is a note that partnership sourcing has been adopted as a procurement technique in recent years. The fact that this evidence stands in isolation confirms that any trend towards collaboration is still very weak.

The CAA clearly lagged behind the privatised companies in terms of supplier performance at the time of the research, in early 1996. Whereas every privatised company noted improvements in at least some area of purchasing, the CAA reported no improvement to date. They did, however, expect improvement in the future. This is because the CAA is in the process of making changes in purchasing and supplier management. These include encouraging suppliers to improve performance and developing more sophisticated supplier performance measures. This in itself is suggestive that the CAA now recognises that it neither encouraged suppliers to 'do better' nor measured their performance adequately in the past.

In summary, major changes in purchasing strategy and structure were beginning during the research period, whereas in most of the privatised companies the change process had been underway for some time. There is clearly a lag in terms of the timing of change between the CAA and most of the privatised companies studied for this book, particularly regarding supplier management and performance measurement.

Conclusions

There is evidence that a more professional approach to purchasing and supply, that goes beyond simple cost reduction by competitive tendering, is being developed in the CAA. The development of greater dynamic efficiency through purchasing functional professionalism is, however, still in its infancy. This may be due to the inertia of being a near monopoly service provider or because of the restrictions imposed by national and EU procurement rules. On the other hand it may well owe something to a lack of clarity in government thinking about whether the organisation should be privatised or not. When this occurs there is bound to be uncertainty and a lack of focus in practitioner behaviour at the strategic and operational levels of the business.

LONDON UNDERGROUND LTD

Unlike in the CAA case, the London Underground example demonstrates that being in the public sector does not preclude the development of a high level of purchasing functional professionalism. Where there is a desire for cost reduction on the part of government, in addition to the existence of competent individuals responsible for purchasing, then more professional tools and techniques can be developed in the public sector. Despite this, it is evident that, whatever static or dynamic efficiency improvements this might achieve, performance will remain suboptimal in the absence of a more strategic focus or more attention to achieving transformational efficiency gains.

Background

London Underground Limited (LUL) is a subsidiary of London Transport, a public sector organisation formed by Act of Parliament in 1984 with a statutory obligation to provide transport services to London. The other major subsidiary is London Buses. However, since all bus routes had been franchised to private operators by 1995,[3] LUL easily forms the largest part of the company in terms of activity, accounting for 90 per cent of group turnover in the 1994/95 financial year (London Transport, 1994/95).

LUL owns and operates the ten underground railway lines that constitute London's metro service. In 1995, the company employed 19,000 staff and turned over approximately £1bn. (Bouverie-Brine and Macbeth, 1995). Back in 1990, the Conservative government studied the viability of privatising the company either in its entirety or through the sale of individual lines. A number of the lines actually began as private companies that were subsequently amalgamated and taken into the public sector. While the outcome was negative on both counts, the project did prompt the government to look for ways to improve the efficiency of London Underground. The aim was that it should behave as much like a commercial company as possible. This was one of the driving factors behind the major changes in the company which are described below. At the time the research was undertaken, during early 1996, LUL remained wholly owned by London Transport, and as such was firmly within the public sector.[4]

During the last few years the company has experienced a fundamental change in structure, strategy and culture with purchasing very much part of the process. Several factors combined to bring about this paradigm shift, some of which deserve a brief discussion. First, the disastrous King's Cross fire of 1987, in which over thirty people were killed in an underground station, prompted a major review of operations. The outcome was that LUL attempted to reverse its focus from an engineering-based operation, seemingly with little regard for passengers, to a market-led company where the provision of passenger service is paramount. Second, having realised that privatisation was not feasible, the government found alternative ways of making the company more commercial, part of which was the instruction to LUL to introduce a competitive tendering programme. This effectively increased the level of outsourcing at the company; overhaul work, for example, which was previously carried out in-house, has been increasingly externalised. Third and relatedly, anticipating that the government would increase pressure to outsource as a means of cost reduction, London Underground introduced its own make–buy programme (MBP) in early 1994. This project has grown considerably since its inception with the result that every activity performed by the company will eventually pass through MBP.

Fourth, LUL announced plans to develop a 'Decently Modern Metro' in the early 1990s, an ambitious and expensive project costing £6bn. over nine years. The government agreed to part-fund the project, but then halved funding during the second year. This is a problem for all organisations subject to government annual grant funding for capital expenditure, making long-term planning very difficult. The government's decision left LUL with a £2bn. shortfall in revenue. The only alternative to scrapping the project was to make up the loss through cost savings. This implied a major review of all operations.

Lastly, the government's private finance initiative (PFI) allows public sector organisations to raise money privately not via share issues but through practices such as joint investments and build–operate–transfer schemes (BOTS) with the private sector. As a result, London Underground has increased the involvement of private sector organisations in its capital programmes and will continue to do so. The largest PFI project to date involves a twenty-five-year deal with GEC-Alsthom to own and maintain trains on the Northern Line. London Underground will simply lease the trains from GEC-Alsthom paid out of revenues.

Evidence of static and dynamic efficiency gains

The structure of purchasing and supply management

The combined effects of the above, and in particular the King's Cross fire, provided a form of 'shock therapy' for the company. The result has been far-reaching changes throughout the organisation, not least in structure. A report issued in 1990 by the Monopolies and Mergers Commission found, among other things, a lack of commercial ethos and overcentralised decision making (Bouverie-Brine and Macbeth, 1995). Initially this prompted a restructuring based on business units with increased accountability. This was then followed by a new company plan, which was issued in 1991 and involved the devolution of assets to the operating divisions, changes in working practices and staff reductions. The objective was to create a leaner, more efficient organisation.

The devolution of purchasing formed part of this change and was a gradual process beginning around 1990. Before the change, the central purchasing unit employed seventy people. These were purchasing professionals and clerical staff. By 1995 this figure had been reduced to just twenty with little purchasing activity taking place centrally. The twenty staff dealt mainly with strategy and support activities. They were responsible for strategic purchasing planning, the development and setting of professional standards and monitoring compliance with them, and the creation of common systems for the devolved units. The separate business units performed their own purchasing, in line with the company philosophy of 'empowerment' of business units. In the past, purchasing authority was limited to purchasing professionals, but this had changed over the 1990–95 period. Non-purchasing professionals had been given authority to purchase if they could demonstrate commercial competence. This meant that planning and project managers, for example, had been put through an assessment exercise in order to determine their skill levels. The result was that there were 300 staff with purchasing authority, compared to about 50 previously. Again, this aligns with the empowerment philosophy.

Purchasing and supply professionalism

Company strategy has focused, in the words of an interviewee, on 'getting more from less' over the last five years. This is largely due to the shortfall on the Decently Modern Metro programme described on page 132. LUL decided that one-third of the shortfall would be generated through better supplier management and another third would be found from new technology developed in conjunction with suppliers. These developments would require fundamental changes in purchasing strategy.

The key element has been the switch to a longer-term approach to purchasing. This has manifested itself in the adoption of a whole-life cost approach to costing and the development of collaborative relationships with suppliers. Previously, London Underground followed a typically public sector approach to purchasing, which was driven primarily by the availability of funding. The organisation aimed for the lowest purchase price through the use of competitive tendering and rigorous negotiation and was driven by an opportunistic imperative. That is, staff surveyed the supply market only at the time they needed to buy and looked for the best deal. The post-1990 strategy offers quite a contrast: in this strategy, the supplier market is surveyed and purchasing decisions are made when the company is carrying out strategic planning rather than at the time they wish to buy. Not only does this imply that purchasing is moving 'upstream' within the company, by getting involved in strategic activity, but also that it can be more proactive and have more control over the supply market. For example, the longer-term approach has enabled the company to become involved in supply development. This would never have been possible with the approach to purchasing adopted before 1990, which forced LUL to accept whatever the supplier market offered.

Another characteristic of the new approach is the focus on reducing the total cost of acquisition. In seeking this, LUL works with suppliers to remove unnecessary costs in the supply chain. The company has set up joint teams with suppliers and invested in joint projects. Other purchasing techniques adopted since 1990 include vendor accreditation, benchmarking, purchasing portfolio analysis and strategic supplier alliances.

The change in approach is reflected in the criteria used to measure the performance of the purchasing function. Before 1990 the two key elements were savings against post-tender negotiation or previous purchase price and the proportion of spend that was subject to competition, the aim being to maximise the latter. Such criteria are consistent with the cost-driven and arm's-length approach to purchasing in use at the time. Now, performance measures are applied according to the type of supplier relationship involved. So, for strategic products where a partnership-type relationship is likely to be beneficial, measures are devised that truly reflect the performance of the relationship. For leveraged spend on the other hand, measures tend to remain highly price based as the constant aim is to drive down prices. London Underground has developed a matrix of performance measures to be applied under given circumstances.

The role and profile of purchasing

The fact that purchasing staff are now involved in strategic planning activities, as described above, indicates both a change in their role and an improvement in the internal profile of the purchasing function. Previously, most efforts were directed towards short-term cost-cutting and/or administrative tasks. Another factor which lends support to the argument for an improved profile of the function is the position of the most senior purchasing manager. While changes in the reporting line give little away, the scope of activities covered by the position has increased considerably. They now include activities related to the private finance initiative, such as outsourcing and facilities management, and secondary revenue. The latter refers to income generated from car parks and property rent, among other activities, which has grown considerably in recent years. Overall, purchasing staff within LUL have assumed significantly more responsibility.

As far as involvement in company spend is concerned, purchasing has always controlled 100 per cent of traditional spend. Involvement in non-traditional spend increased from 80 per cent to 95 per cent during the 1990–95 period. The only activities that were *not* now dealt with by the central department by 1996 were the purchase of property and financial and legal services.

Outsourcing and supplier relationship management

Outsourcing has increased significantly since 1990, partly driven by the introduction of the government's PFI and related cuts in state funding. At the same time as reducing grants for capital expenditure to public sector organisations, the government provided them with a means to raise finance through the private sector via the PFI. Traditionally, London Underground carried out all activities in-house from initial development to the prototype build of new assets, and then went outside of the company for their production. All overhaul work used to take place internally, which was typical for a public sector organisation at the time, and similar, for example, to the highly integrated British Rail before privatisation. By early 1996, 50 per cent of overhaul work was being carried out externally.

The example of the Northern Line, where the contractor GEC-Alsthom will be paid £600m. over twenty-five years for the provision of trains to London Underground, is the major example of an activity outsourced through the PFI. But LUL continues to search the private sector for other PFI opportunities, as a means of compensating for reductions in government finance. The purchasing function at the company plays a pivotal role in such outsourcing decisions with the make–buy programme coming under the department's remit, although the final decision on all outsourcing is still made at board level.

An initial move towards more collaboration with suppliers developed as a result of the King's Cross disaster. It became clear that London Underground required new and unfamiliar technologies related to safety and suppliers were an obvious source of these ideas and products. Another important influence was the reduction of government funding for the Decently Modern Metro project, forcing the company to make real and substantial cost reductions. Two means of achieving these were the development of strategic supplier management and innovative engineering, both of which involved working *with* the supplier to drive out costs and capture external technologies. Another cost reduction measure considered was the use of increased outsourcing.

In fact, London Underground has made a concerted and deliberate effort to switch from arm's-length to collaborative relationships. It has rationalised the supply base, employed consultants to help develop a model for supplier management, and adopted a model specifically designed to improve relationships with suppliers (Bouverie-Brine and Macbeth, 1995, p. 125). The philosophy behind increased collaboration at London Underground is as follows: where price is the only differentiator, the arm's-length approach to purchasing can still apply. However, in many business transactions there is the expectation of future transactions which, as some conclude, 'changes the game to one in which both parties can win' (ibid., p. 126). However, it is recognised that partnerships should not be considered unless there is potential for a specific business benefit.

Conclusions

There is considerable evidence of a significant improvement in the purchasing function in London Underground, particularly after the operational review of the company's activities and structures in light of the 1988 King's Cross fire. The devolution of purchasing activities and increasing government pressure to reduce costs have resulted in the development of more sophisticated purchasing and supply tools and techniques with the aim of achieving what have been termed in this book static efficiency and dynamic efficiency gains. Also, a willingness to use make–buy methodologies and to outsource on an aggressive basis are now apparent in the company. In reality this has not been undertaken by choice, but rather it has been a reaction to the systematic reduction in the government's funding of LUL. This means that, while the company has developed a level of purchasing functional professionalism that is on par with that of many of the privatised companies described elsewhere in this book, the application of this developing competence has been hamstrung by the inability of the government to define what is the strategic vision for the company. This has meant that many of the benefits of transformational efficiency gains may have been lost. There may also be evidence of the company losing control of some of its critical assets as it faces growing political demands for further efficiency gains and seeks more and more private funding and control of its operational activities.

Summary of developments in public sector purchasing and supply management

In terms of the three-phase learning process outlined earlier in Chapter 1, pp. 2–4 the interview results suggested that both public sector organisations reviewed in this chapter are developing a phase-2 approach to purchasing and supply management, where the focus is on achieving dynamic efficiency through an improvement of the *existing* purchasing function in terms of changing operational processes and procedures and developing a more professional approach to tasks. However, the organisations had not necessarily passed through phase 1 first, where the focus is on immediate cost reduction, before reaching this second stage. This contrasts with the privatised sector, which appeared to pass through these two stages sequentially. This difference in approach is consistent with other evidence reported in this book, which suggests that cost pressures are more immediate in privatised organisations and lead to more aggressive cost-cutting activities.

The CAA is clearly at the beginning of the development of dynamic efficiency through the introduction of a more professional approach to the purchasing task. For example, training for purchasing staff has been improved and new and fashionable tools and techniques for purchasing are being introduced. There is some evidence of a focus on immediate cost reduction, but this is much less intense than in privatised companies. The main driver for change at the CAA appears to have been the fact that the government has reviewed the possibility of privatising the organisation. Although this option was initially rejected, the results of the review led to significant restructuring aimed at making the organisation more commercial. The key constraint on improvement is, perhaps, the fact that the CAA is a near monopolist in its markets and this results in a lack of competitive pressure.

London Underground is the most advanced of these two public sector organisations in terms of the three-phase model in Chapter 1, pp. 2–4. It has certainly been forced to make substantial short-term cost reductions as a result of decisions made by the government and has developed its own approach to purchasing functional professionalism to achieve significant dynamic efficiency due to a series of external shocks. These include the possibility of privatisation, the King's Cross fire disaster and continuous reductions in government funding leading to a shortfall in income. This is however, hardly the most conductive environment in which to develop supply alignment and procurement competence.

Part III

Cases in strategic supply alignment and purchasing and supply professionalism

Introduction

Part III presents five chapters (8 to 12) of detailed case studies. The organisations studied were deliberately selected to represent a range of industrial sectors and, hence, competitive environments. The organisations covered are Severn Trent Water (Chapter 8), a water supply and sewerage company privatised in 1989; South West Electricity (Chapter 9), a regional electricity company privatised in 1990; British Airways (Chapter 10), the UK's largest airline, privatised in 1987; British Steel (Chapter 11), the UK's largest steel manufacturer, privatised in 1988; and The Post Office (Chapter 12), which remains wholly in the public sector and is responsible mainly for Post Office counters and the delivery of mail within the United Kingdom.

The reason for this third level of study of privatised organisations (following the questionnaire survey and the shorter case studies reported in earlier chapters) is in order to test for transformational efficiency gains. While the first two stages of research had revealed that most companies had achieved considerable improvements in static efficiency and dynamic efficiency, there was little evidence of more fundamental changes in the pursuit of transformational efficiency. As a reminder, static and dynamic efficiency gains relate to those made in phases 1 and 2 of the three-phase learning process (see page 4), i.e. a focus on immediate cost reduction and the development of a more professional approach to current operations respectively. Transformational efficiency relates to phase 3, the achievement of procurement competence and supply alignment. The aim of this chapter is to assess the extent to which the organisations concerned have moved beyond cost reduction and functional professionalism in the direction of supply alignment and procurement competence. Since the earlier chapters had revealed so little evidence of the search for transformational efficiency gains, it was decided to undertake the further five in-depth case studies reported in the following chapters. The aim was to assess the extent to which the five enterprises had begun to address the issue of transformational efficiency gains and to better understand the obstacles to achieving this phase of the three-phase model.

The five chapters are structured in the same way. The first part deals with the four central themes relating to the achievement of static and dynamic efficiency gains, as in the smaller case studies in Chapters 5 to 7. The second part broadens the study to look at aspects such as industrial and organisational structures and corporate strategy, as a means to assess the progress made towards the achievement of transformational efficiency.

8 Severn Trent Water

SEVERN TRENT

Severn Trent is a case study of the developing awareness of the strategic and operational importance of purchasing functional professionalism, without any real recognition of the potentialities that arise from an understanding of procurement competence and supply alignment. Immediately prior to, and after, privatisation the major concern of the company was with internal cost reduction and the more effective management of purchasing spend. By 1990 the company had recognised the need to focus on a more functionally professional approach to external spend, and this coincided with the development of a flirtation with supply alignment and procurement competence. The reason for this relatively hesitant understanding is the fact that the company, while privatised, has not really had to change its way of thinking radically because it retains a geographical, monopoly position within the water industry.

Changes since privatisation

Background

Severn Trent was one of the ten water supply and sewerage companies privatised in 1989, formerly the state-owned Regional Water Authorities. Its main activity remains the supply of these services to a population of over eight million people in the region of the Midlands in England, although it has diversified into several other new ventures since its move into the private sector. These include waste management, software and technologies related to water and waste management and international consultancy (Severn Trent plc, 1996).

Figures for the 1993/94 financial year show Severn Trent to be the most profitable water company of the 'big ten' former Regional Water Authorities, with operating profits increasing by 10 per cent to almost £330m., and the second largest in terms of turnover, behind Thames Water. In employee terms, Severn Trent was the largest, with 10,783 staff (CRI, 1995). By 1996, profit before tax had risen to £373m. on a turnover of almost £1.2bn., the latter having increased by 41 per cent over four years (Severn Trent plc, 1996).

In 1996, Severn Trent made a bid for South West Water (*The Financial Times*, 12 June 1996), a smaller water utility, which was referred to the Monopolies and Mergers Commission and later barred by the government. Otherwise, the stated policy of the company has been to grow via joint ventures and alliances with other utilities. Significantly, talks were underway with another water company, Anglian Water, with a view to joint purchasing, although nothing had been agreed at the time of the research in mid-1996.

Evidence of static and dynamic efficiency gains

The structure of purchasing and supply management

Company structure has changed significantly since privatisation. The company was gradually centralised at first, moving from fifteen districts down to eight and then finally to four, and purchasing followed. By the end of the centralisation process, all purchasing staff were located on one of two sites: either at the corporate headquarters at Sheldon in Birmingham or at the stores operation on a separate site, with no purchasing people in the districts. There were about 27 staff in the purchasing department, which was split into three commodity-based groups, one support and development group (called the measurement and control team) and one individual focusing on best practice. The commodity groups were divided into water treatment and waste, services and maintenance. There was also a stores operation at a separate site, which employed about another 20 staff.

The company then decentralised once again. By 1996 the company was organised into 15 districts, which were very similar to before. This decentralisation formed part of a drive to adopt a 'customer service' philosophy at Severn Trent. The company wished to be seen as part of the community that it served, rather than a distant 'Big Brother'. The reasons behind this move are discussed later. By 1996, the districts were run as separate profit centres, and worked to specific performance targets, such as those for service levels and financial returns. Purchasing, however, remained centralised.

The rest of the company was mandated to use the central purchasing department for items costing more than £5,000, although in reality this rule was not strictly adhered to. However, other departments had turned increasingly to the purchasing department for two main reasons. First, the department had been actively promoting its activities to the rest of the organisation in order to raise awareness of the services that it could provide. Second, pressure on resources had forced other areas of the company to look to purchasing to carry out the process for them, whereas beforehand they would have had enough spare resources to carry out the task themselves. Purchasing did not charge other departments for its service.

As mentioned above, the purchasing function at Severn Trent has gradually been centralised, a process which began three years prior to privatisation, around 1986. This process was still not complete by mid-1996, with further centralisation underway, the aim being to gain full central control of spend via framework agreements. Once this has been achieved some of the lower-value spend will once again be devolved from headquarters to the various districts.

Before the efforts at co-ordination began, purchasing was fragmented and disparate. It took place at over fifteen sites, most of which formed Severn Trent's districts, and there was negligible central control with no central purchasing department in existence. It was in fact an auditor at the company that proposed the changes, highlighting the cost savings to be gained through increased central control. He was subsequently given the task of reorganising purchasing and began the centralisation process.

Previously there were 170 purchasing staff scattered around the company's sites and they reported to their separate district managers. This number has now been drastically reduced and staff are based at one of two sites: the company headquarters and the stores and logistics depot. Low-value spend takes place in the districts with local staff responsible for single contracts of up to £1,000. Expenditure above this is increasingly controlled centrally through corporate contracts, although there remains some spend that continues to escape central control.

Purchasing and supply professionalism

Severn Trent's approach to purchasing has changed completely since privatisation. Previously, purchasing consisted largely of administration – the low-esteem 'paper pusher' role prevalent in many public sector organisations until recently. Buyers did not even negotiate with suppliers much of the time; instead they simply accepted quotations unquestioningly because they were under little pressure to reduce costs and their role was not viewed as commercial. Now there is much more emphasis on the commercial side, and on providing a value-adding service to the rest of the organisation. A strategy is currently under development with the first five-year plan for the purchasing department put in place in mid-1995, and the use of modern purchasing techniques has increased. The department has also adopted an 'internal customer' model. However, there remains some procedural bias in the purchasing process, i.e. an emphasis on the administrative process of buying rather than on necessarily adding value.

By mid-1996, Severn Trent had been using a purchasing portfolio matrix as the basis of purchasing strategy for about a year, although the approach had yet to be formalised. This is the first 'purchasing strategy' to speak of. The approach was discovered during buyer training with a specialist purchasing consultancy. In addition to the commodity-based teams at head office, there was also a measurement and control team. This team was charged with marketing the department and dealt with the development of strategy, among other things. The aim in the future was to develop strategy further through increased interaction between the separate teams within the purchasing department and with the user groups or internal customers.

Pressure to reduce costs has driven the change process at Severn Trent. Headcount reductions in the purchasing department were a further prompt to adopt the above matrix approach, and this has led to the devolvement of low-value spend, which has freed the centre to concentrate on strategic items of expenditure. The downside is that the cost pressures have tended to slow the progress made by the purchasing department towards a more professional approach to purchasing, simply because it lacks the appropriate staff levels and resources.

Accompanying the development of a more systematic approach to purchasing has been the adoption of a number of modern purchasing techniques. Vendor appraisal systems are now in place, although there is still some way to go in developing them. Benchmarking via company visits has also taken place and Severn Trent has also been involved in strategic supplier alliances and partnership and network sourcing. By late 1996 the company was at the stage of piloting partnership sourcing projects and network sourcing had resulted from the drive to reduce the supplier base, rather than being a policy in its own right. Purchasing cards were also being used as a means to reduce the supplier base, by dealing with just one card company, in addition to reducing transaction costs through less paperwork. A single sourcing approach had been adopted for some goods and services, for example fleet cars and catering. Severn Trent used to deal with more than four suppliers of company cars, but this had been reduced to just one. The main reason for this change is a reduction in transaction costs such as administration. It is accepted that there is a negative side to this change, mainly in the form of limited choice for the final user, but the cost savings are considered to outweigh this.

Performance measurement of the purchasing department has tended to focus on cost. Key criteria include savings against contract, one-off savings and savings against the performance price index (PPI), which is based on the average price paid for similar supplies elsewhere in the industry. Overall, corporate strategy has determined the main drivers of purchasing strategy, but the department has also set itself targets. For example, it promised to deliver £9m. of cost savings over three years, at an even rate of £3m. per annum. The department was on target to achieve this goal by mid-1996 with £6m. saved by the end of the second year. Other influences on the change process are related to issues such as personal development and customer service initiatives. The main restriction on achieving the department's aims, however, is headcount reduction in purchasing. For example, a 'recruitment freeze' was in operation for a number of months during the research period, preventing the department from taking on any staff. Even when this was lifted, budgetary constraints meant that only relatively low-grade positions were offered. These are unlikely to attract the calibre of applicant that the department requires to implement a sophisticated purchasing strategy.

The role and profile of purchasing

The purchasing department has increased the scope of its activities and has raised its profile within the organisation. Purchasing staff have effectively marketed their services by going to other departments, presenting the expertise that they can offer and demonstrating the benefits of using their service in terms of cost savings. 'Success stories', where purchasing has taken on a new area of spend and achieved significant savings, are used to promote the department and gain them entry into other areas. For example, the company achieved a saving of £3.5m. on electricity input costs as a result of central purchasing's involvement and this was publicised within the company. There is also an internal company newsletter issued by the department, which is another means to raise purchasing's profile. Progress has been helped by improved commercial training of purchasing staff and by reduced resources throughout the rest of the company, resulting in a greater recourse to the central purchasing service, as mentioned earlier. New areas of involvement for the department include expenditure on advertising, training, IT, legal services and telecommunications. Although progress has certainly been made in increasing the purchasing department's scope of activities, management feel that there remains much work to be done.

It is important to note that central purchasing has no control over capital expenditure at Severn Trent, which accounted for 60 per cent to 70 per cent of the total company spend of around £550m. in the mid-1990s. The engineering division has full responsibility for this, under a separate directorate. This has always been the case. Central purchasing controls operating expenditure only, which totals approximately £180m. per annum or 30 per cent to 40 per cent of total expenditure. Co-operation between the engineering and purchasing departments is on the increase, however. In the past, progress had been slowed by the reluctance of a traditionally strong engineering function to let others get involved in its operations. This situation has improved in recent years and has been helped by the increased profile and professionalisation of purchasing, more movement of staff between departments, increased commercial awareness among engineers, and the downsizing of the company, which has increased the strain on resources.

The position of the head of purchasing reflects the changing profile of the department. From a finance background within the company, he was recruited on the basis of his proposal to reduce costs by reorganising the purchasing function. He has achieved this narrow aim, but has also succeeded in improving the image of the department within the organisation. This success has been rewarded by his promotion to the broader role of head of logistics. This marks a further progression for the purchasing department in terms of enhancing its internal profile.

It is clear from the above that the position of the purchasing function at Severn Trent has improved since privatisation, albeit from a very low base. This has been helped by the leadership of a highly respected new head of purchasing, as well as a squeeze on resources elsewhere in the company, which has increased the need for a central purchasing service. Success has been reflected in the promotion of the head of purchasing and by the fact that purchasing was one of the few departments to 'survive' a second round of company downsizing in 1996 (i.e. it avoided the imposition of further staff reductions). Nevertheless, there remains a long way to go. For example, purchasing staff still feel that their career progression can be stifled within the company.

Professionalisation of staff has increased considerably since 1990. Until then, little or no internal training took place, and entry qualification levels were generally very low. Severn Trent began 'focus training' in purchasing during 1990–91 which involves training purchasing staff in specific areas such as negotiation, cost analysis and interpersonal skills. It also runs an internal BTec course for purchasing staff. Minimum entry qualifications are a degree or CIPS[1] qualification for contract negotiators, and Higher National Certificate (HNC) qualifications for buyers. However, there has been a limited influx of 'new blood' or younger staff, partly due to recruitment embargoes imposed on the department.

In spite of these improvements, the purchasing function is not yet considered to be an integral part of the 'strategic centre' of the company. It tends to be viewed by other managers as 80 per cent administrative support and 20 per cent a source of cost savings. An emphasis on the latter is growing. However, this cost focus offers the department a chance to increase its profile by achieving notable cost reductions in the future.

Outsourcing and supplier relationship management

As far as outsourcing of support services is concerned, Severn Trent believes that it has made a conscious effort to avoid following the outsourcing 'trend'. However, outsourcing has increased because of the drive to reduce fixed costs. This has involved printing, plumbing, facilities management and mechanical and electrical engineering, among other services. Outsourcing remains a board-level decision at the company with the purchasing department becoming involved once the decision has been made.

Purchasing is aiming to build closer relationships with a reduced supplier base, but has been constrained by both a lack of resources and the persistence of traditional attitudes within the industry. Within the industry buyers continue to work with an arm's-length mentality towards suppliers. At the time of the research there remained a strong reliance on traditional methods of tender, for example supplier standing lists when choosing suppliers for tender.

Severn Trent has piloted a partnership sourcing approach with a key supplier, and staff have been trained in supplier relationships, both suggesting that increased collaboration is the aim in the future. In reality, however, 80 per cent of contracts were still based on competitive tender in 1996 and negotiations remained largely price based.

Supplier rationalisation is central to purchasing policy and part of the overall drive to reduce costs. During the six months to April 1996, the supplier database was reduced from 13,747 to 12,991, a reduction of 756 or 5.5 per cent. This was after the removal of over 1,700 suppliers that had been identified as unused. The rationalisation process was still at an early stage, the aim being eventually to reduce the number of suppliers to 5,000.

Other work on improving supplier management has also taken place. Formal supplier appraisal has been introduced which involves many elements of performance; as has a quality award which judges aspects such as the responsiveness and attitude of vendors. Both of these initiatives indicate a move away from simple price-based purchasing towards a more sophisticated approach. Nevertheless, it is clear that the purchasing department feels frustrated in its attempts to improve supplier management, due to a lack of resources. Staff say that they are simply too busy 'fire-fighting' and dealing with less strategic issues to devote any resource to this area. Company pressures on headcount reduction have put strict limitations on recruiting extra staff.

Supplier performance has shown improvement in a number of areas and is expected to improve at a faster rate now that Severn Trent has begun to monitor performance more formally and across a broader range of criteria. Significant improvements in cost competitiveness and flexibility have been noted, as have more modest improvements in quality, on-time delivery and access to new technology and innovation – with the latter expected to improve significantly in the future as a result of the move to increased single sourcing and closer working relationships with suppliers.

Make–buy decisions in the company are made at board level with purchasing having no involvement. Once a decision has been made to outsource an activity, it is the purchasing department that will let the contract; but then it is generally the previous in-house managers of the activity that become the 'project' contract managers, to oversee the running of the outsourced activity. Decisions concerning outsourcing are mainly cost driven, illustrated by the fact that an activity is often outsourced and then the same staff are employed to carry out the task, but at cheaper rates. This also reduces headcount figures, an extremely important factor as described earlier. For example, printing was outsourced after an assessment of in-house versus outsourced activities suggested that it would be cheaper and the contract was awarded to the lowest bidder. Other activities already outsourced included maintenance and laboratories for water sampling and support activities such as pipe-laying. Until recently, Severn Trent still bought the pipe themselves, but now the suppliers have taken on this task, though the contracts remain with Severn Trent suppliers and under terms agreed by the company.

The overall effect of increased outsourcing is that it has made the company more aware of costs. The make–buy assessment exercise has pushed the company to analyse in-house costs, in some cases for the first time. However, because the company only conceives of the buying competence in administrative terms, there is a danger that it might create supply dependencies without fully realising this consequence; in the sense of becoming dependent upon particular external suppliers for supplies critical to the business. While there are some limits on which activities Severn Trent can outsource, in particular the company is obliged by law to remove waste water making the outsourcing of this activity quite unlikely, more generally increased outsourcing is expected in the future.

The nature of supplier relationships depends on two factors: the value of the goods or services to Severn Trent and the characteristics of the supplier market. If there are three to four suppliers in the market and the product is considered important to Severn Trent, then closer relationships are more likely to be developed. This is the case for pipes and fittings, for example. However, there is no formal system used to determine the desired supplier relationship for a particular product or service, and so many relationships tend to evolve in an ad hoc way.

For suppliers of strategic products such as pipes and fittings, a change in approach was underway by mid-1996. The company was planning to train six 'lead assessors' over the coming year to visit and assess suppliers according to a set of pre-determined criteria. Before this development, supplier visits were informal and there was no such structured assessment. Severn Trent now systematically measures performance on existing contracts with its top forty suppliers.

The company's current supply base includes around 13,000 companies and Severn Trent has a supplier reduction programme. However, managers in the company still have the authority to create new suppliers for contracts below £5,000 on the supplier database, and this is hindering the reduction programme. The purchasing department has tried to deal with this by issuing an approved-supplier list. Severn Trent is moving closer to suppliers, both as a deliberate policy and as a result of supplier reduction. The company's view is that it is cost-effective to do so, for two main reasons. First, on the basis that gaining more information about suppliers' costs provides the customer with a stronger negotiating position. Second, because the administrative costs of maintaining a large supplier database are high.

An overview of the three forms of efficiency gain at Severn Trent

It is clear that in 1989 the major focus at Severn Trent was on static efficiency through immediate short-term cost reduction. Since 1990 the use of external consultants to improve the level of professionalism has encouraged a focus on longer-term, dynamic efficiency considerations. A lack of resources in the purchasing function has, however, restricted the development of a longer-term focus.

Despite the evidence of performance improvement in purchasing and supply, there is only embryonic evidence of transformational efficiency through supply alignment and procurement competence thinking at Severn Trent. The major reason for this appears to be the fact that the company can make substantial and continuing profits because it operates in a relative monopoly position in its geographical marketplace and supply chain. The focus, both for the company and the regulator (Ofwat) tends, therefore, to be on static and dynamic efficiency only. In the discussion that follows, the constraints which this operating reality impose on Severn Trent's ability to develop a supply alignment and procurement competence approach are discussed.

Industrial structure

The key factors in Severn Trent's industrial environment which affect the company's behaviour, in descending order of importance, are: ownership and more specifically the threat of takeover (the capital market); the regulatory environment; the supplier market; and lastly competition and the customer base. These are each discussed in detail.

Ownership and regulation

The two main factors, the threat of takeover and regulatory pressure, have similar effects on the company and so will be discussed together. The two factors combined have resulted in a focus on static efficiency through headcount reduction throughout the company and increased attention to customer service and improving Severn Trent's external image. The threat of takeover results in constant attention to maintaining a high share price. The company effectively 'opened up' the takeover game by bidding to acquire South West Water. This has meant that Severn Trent, as the bidder, publicised details of its own financial position, strengths, weaknesses and corporate strategy as part of the bid, leaving itself open as a potential target for acquisition after its bid for South West Water failed. In spite of the perceived threat of takeover, it should be noted that a limited threat existed until December 1994 because the government retained a 'golden share' in the water companies. Since then the threat has remained attenuated because all mergers involving water companies trigger an automatic referral to the Monopolies and Mergers Commission (MMC), subject to an assets test. Also, Ofwat, the water industry regulatory body, has made known its opposition to consolidation in the industry because this would reduce the scope for 'yardstick comparisons' of performance upon which it bases its regulation of water charges and service quality.

The City compares the performance ratios of water utilities to those of the regional electricity companies, and this has often led to the conclusion that the former are overstaffed. Although the comparison is considered unfair because there are considerable differences in the nature of the two industries, it has inevitably increased pressure on the water companies to reduce headcount. In achieving this, they are able to fend off analysts' criticisms and defend their share price, thus reducing the risk of takeover. The constant attention to share price has also been influential in pushing Severn Trent to focus more on customer service. Poor customer service, in terms of poor compliance rates on quality, leakage rates, etc., leads to a bad press and criticism by Ofwat, which can result in a lower share price. Maintaining a high share price is now the key driver of the company, and a focus on customer service and generally being seen as a 'good company' are important ways to achieve this.

The two main regulatory effects on the company are pressure to increase both static and dynamic efficiency (applied mainly via the 'price cap' formula,[2] which limits prices charged by Severn Trent to its customers) and pressure to improve customer service (as the company strives to achieve specific standards for customer service set by Ofwat). It is via these mechanisms that regulatory pressure influences the company in a similar way to the threat of takeover, by pressurising the company to reduce costs and increase its focus on customer service.

The need to reduce costs to satisfy the regulator and the City has led to staff reductions throughout Severn Trent, but particularly in central support services including purchasing, accounts, systems and human resources. It has also resulted in efforts to 'multi-skill' those staff that remain so that they are able to perform a variety of tasks. Severn Trent has undoubtedly lost competencies because of the need to reduce headcount and because of the 'politically correct' way in which it has approached redundancy. Reductions in staff have been mainly through voluntary redundancy (a political move because it minimises bad press and opposition from unions and staff). However, this means that it has been mainly the older, more experienced staff that have left the company. In some cases, too much experience and knowledge have been lost, forcing Severn Trent to re-employ the same staff on a temporary basis. This sometimes costs the company because the individuals involved – established as consultants – contract with the company at high rates. Despite this, the key aim, which is to reduce headcount figures, is achieved because these people do not appear in the company's books as permanent employees. Severn Trent also avoid paying national insurance and pension contributions through this arrangement. One positive outcome for the company is that, where competencies have been permanently lost, Severn Trent has been forced to reassess its systems with a view to improving them.

A secondary effect of the pressure to reduce headcount is that the purchasing department feels under constant pressure to justify its existence, in order to avoid becoming a victim of the next round of staff reductions, or at least to minimise the effect on the department. It is partly for this reason that the department has been 'marketing' itself to the rest of the organisation via newsletters and presentations. These are used to publicise 'wins' achieved by the function, such as significant cost savings on specific contracts. In this sense, increased commercial pressure has enabled purchasing to enhance its profile within the company but precisely because Severn Trent has focused on static efficiency through significant cost savings.

The second major effect of the combined ownership and regulatory pressures on Severn Trent (an increased focus on customer service and costs) has led to many changes within the company. The main outcome is that resources have been diverted to the 'front end' of the business and away from support services such as purchasing, human resources, accounts and systems. In other words, the marketing and public relations side of the business has grown in importance and status while the rest continues to shrink. For example, the number of 'visitor centres' has been increased and significant effort has been put into reducing leakage rates with a 'leak line' established (a telephone number on which members of the public can report leaks). It is unlikely that Severn Trent would have taken such initiatives when in the public sector, largely because public image was seen as being a lower priority. This focus on customer care has also led the company to redesign its billing system in order to make the company more customer friendly. Rather than sending out final demands or 'red bills', Severn Trent now sends 'friendly reminders'!

It is this increased focus on image that has also resulted in the company setting up its supplier quality award. It is important that Severn Trent is seen to be concerned about quality and to work more closely with suppliers in order to achieve improvements. Management feel that the quality award increases the profile of the company and improves its image within the supplier market. In effect, this initiative does not just involve a focus on the end customer but on all external stakeholders, the ultimate goal being the maintenance of a high share price and a satisfied regulator. Ironically, this image-based approach to managing may well be stimulating a shift from a primarily static to a dynamic efficiency approach to purchasing, predicated on the development of new processes and ways of managing external resources.

Supplier market

The third most important influential factor in determining the company's behaviour, following ownership and regulation, is Severn Trent's supplier market. At the time of the research there had been no great change in the number of suppliers since the company was privatised. The only notable exception was the market for chemicals, an important area of external spend for Severn Trent. This market has consolidated with many smaller suppliers being taken over by larger chemical manufacturers. This had made Severn Trent slightly more vulnerable *vis-à-vis* its suppliers. The main effect was that the suppliers had become less flexible on price.

Regarding supplier selection, Severn Trent does come under some political and/or historical pressures to stay with certain suppliers who are also customers. In other words, because these companies 'buy' water and sewerage services from the company, they expect Severn Trent to buy from them as suppliers. These tend to be the larger companies within Severn Trent's region. An example of this is the choice of supplier for fleet cars, where Severn Trent had chosen a local supplier, who was also a customer, instead of alternative suppliers outside of the region.

Generally, the research found that Severn Trent is much more focused on cost savings than it was in the past and as such has become far more aggressive with suppliers in order to drive prices down. Before, prices were challenged less often and contracts were allowed to run with little question. There was much less pressure to achieve cost savings. There is clear evidence, therefore, that apart from chemicals, the structure of the supplier market is one that encourages dynamic efficiency gains through internal consolidation of spend, supply base leverage and rationalisation of existing products and services.

Competition and customers

Although competition and customers do affect the behaviour of the company, they are the least influential of the external environmental factors discussed here. As far as competition is concerned, there has been no real change since privatisation with the company maintaining its regional monopoly, and no prospect of serious competition being introduced in the foreseeable future. The main competition to speak of is indirect, and comes from large customers who are considering installing their own water processing and reclamation works as an alternative to sourcing from Severn Trent.

As far as most customers are concerned, Severn Trent has a captive customer base in that inhabitants of the company's region cannot 'buy' a water supply and sewerage service from any other supplier, simply because of the nature of the distribution system. The only competitive threat on the horizon is the current interest by the government and Ofwat in 'inset' competition. This is a process whereby a neighbouring water utility supplies a major (industrial) customer in another water company's area. So far however, there has only been one such case and this was outside Severn Trent's region.

As a result of these factors, it is clear that the company's geographic monopoly position, and the large scope for static efficiency gains from head-count reductions, and for dynamic efficiency from a more focused management of the existing supply base, has ensured that the company does not need to seek opportunities for transformational efficiency in an aggressive way. This fact is demonstrated by an analysis of the company's corporate strategy.

Corporate strategy

Severn Trent plc, the holding company, has a mission to 'be a world leader in the water business'. The company appears to be concentrating on developing its competencies in water delivery and treatment, such as the expertise of its people and technology, and moving into new geographical and product/service markets, where these competencies can be profitably applied. International development is a key growth area with Severn Trent aiming to extend its expertise abroad, particularly into less-developed countries where there is obviously scope for development in the water supply and sewerage industry. Developments in recent years include setting up a water consultancy company which operates worldwide, acquiring a waste management company called Biffa, and developing technology in specific areas related to water and waste management. The company sees its two core strengths as managing water and sewerage services through Severn Trent Water and Severn Trent Water International (the water operation and consultancy businesses), and waste management through Biffa. An example of Severn Trent utilising its assets and applying them to new markets is the subsidiary Paperflow. This is a direct mailing company and uses Severn Trent's database of eight million addresses in the Midlands, developed through its core water business, to sell other services to customers.

Severn Trent Water's mission is:

> To be the best water utility in the UK. We will be a profit orientated, customer service business, developing markets and meeting our obligations and quality and service objectives. We will develop a human resources strategy to achieve our Mission.

The company has a formal strategy to achieve its mission of which, the most important driver and reference point for employees appears to be the company's 'ten-point plan'. The main points of this plan are: grow the profits through cost management and growing income, expand the business, enhance customer service, improve the perception of Severn Trent (this involves the company's public image and its relationship with the regulator, Ofwat), manage risk, optimise physical assets, sustain product quality, sustain product availability (this relates to droughts), 'optimise our people' and align systems strategy. Purchasing strategy is aligned to corporate strategy in that the purchasing department has produced its own ten-point plan with each point directly linked to an equivalent one in the corporate plan.

Transformational efficiency at Severn Trent

It seems clear from the evidence presented in this case study that Severn Trent has some way to go in the development of supply alignment and procurement competence. This is a competence in understanding the fundamental properties of the total supply chains in which the company currently, or potentially, operates and how value appropriation is improved by effective ownership and control of supply chain resources. Like many companies, Severn Trent's strategy appears to be one that is focused on core competence thinking and headcount, cost reduction and outsourcing. There is little doubt that this approach is encouraged by the strategic drivers that impact on the company. The maintenance of a geographic monopoly position with dependent customers ensures that only the desire for static and dynamic efficiency improvements, which arise from City and regulatory pressures, have an immediate and major impact on behaviour within the company.

As a result, the company has been able to satisfy the City and the regulator by an immediate emphasis on short-term static efficiency cost reduction, and has made only halting steps in the development of a fully professional approach to purchasing and supply management. The company has clearly improved its approach to the effective management of suppliers but it appears that it still employs a mainly reactive approach. This is based on the assessment and limited development of existing supply offerings.

Severn Trent has, however, demonstrated a willingness to be innovative – by its decisions to establish an international presence and to acquire the Biffa waste management business. The Biffa acquisition and international presence appear to be based on core competence thinking. Only in the development of the Paperflow business does there appear to be any emerging understanding of the supply alignment and procurement competence thinking. This is discussed further later, in Chapter 13. In this case the company has begun to demonstrate an awareness of the opportunities that can flow from an understanding of the value that is hidden in many of the resources that the company currently owns, but which it is not currently utilising for its competitive advantage.

9 South West Electricity

SOUTH WEST ELECTRICITY

South West Electricity (SWEB) is in many ways similar to the Severn Trent case. SWEB was slow to develop a highly professional approach to the purchasing function immediately after privatisation. This case illustrates that a lack of focus can occur in privatised companies as well as in the public sector. After 1991, however, due to growing regulatory and competitive pressures, SWEB began to improve its approach to raising efficiency. This improvement – an increase in dynamic efficiency through functional professionalism – has been further enhanced with the takeover of the company by US owners in 1995.

Background

South West Electricity plc is responsible for the delivery of electricity across the south west of England. It was one of the 12 regional electricity companies (RECs) privatised in 1990. In 1995 pre-tax profit was £112m. and turnover was £875m. (SWEB, 1996), making South West Electricity one of the smallest of the 12 regional electricity companies in England and Wales. At the time of the research, 1996, SWEB operated as a group of three businesses: electricity distribution, responsible for the delivery of electricity across SWEB's network; electricity supply, responsible for the bulk purchase and supply of electricity; and related businesses, which included electricity generation, telecommunications, gas supply and electrical contracting.

SWEB followed a policy of diversification shortly before and after privatisation, but the company has since retrenched and concentrated on its core activities. The company diversified into IT, transport management and printing among other areas, but these have since been abandoned. Because the company already performed these activities in-house, it was considered logical to develop them further and sell the services in the marketplace. However, this strategy was later reconsidered and SWEB refocused on activities closer to its core activities.

The company was taken over by the Southern Company of the USA in September 1995. The new owners put in a new chief executive officer and a new board and instigated a process of major change within the company. As far as purchasing is concerned, the acquisition was highly beneficial to the function, allowing much more progress than had been possible both under public ownership and under the previous private ownership.

The search for static and dynamic efficiency gains

The structure of purchasing and supply management

The structure of purchasing was centralised around 1991 in order to gain control over all areas of spend and later partially decentralised for cost reasons. The company realised the importance of bought-in goods and services in achieving potential cost savings, leading them to centralise in order to gain control of costs, the main changes taking place in April 1991. When purchasing was centralised, systems were put in place to control the purchasing process. The purchasing manager's role changed completely at this time. The structure of area managers disappeared giving purchasing much more power at the centre, though some purchasing was later devolved in order to reduce costs. In particular, more junior employees were given the power to deal with lower-value spend. This freed more senior purchasing staff to concentrate on what were considered to be the more strategic goods and services.

Overall company structure has changed on a number of occasions with the last major change being after the takeover in 1995. The most important change, however, is that the company has become increasingly less hierarchical since privatisation. Company structure is functional, but only 'on paper'. In reality, SWEB operates more like a matrix structure. Purchasing is situated within the operations division, although it works mainly with finance and customer services.

There were 67 people employed in purchasing and inventory management within the company by mid-1996. Of these, 14 were direct buyers at various levels of seniority, and 35 were involved in stores. The majority of these as storekeepers and some involved in administration. The remaining staff provide clerical and administrative support.

Purchasing and supply professionalism

The mission statement of purchasing is: 'To support the Engineering Business, Division, Company and subsidiaries to achieve their strategic intent through extraordinary purchasing and inventory expertise'. This mission existed before privatisation, but it was not really acted upon until later. Management tended to pay lip-service to it and only recently has SWEB had the internal culture and systems to enable its effective implementation. There was considerable secrecy before, in particular, events in the boardroom often remained secret from the rest of the organisation. So even though the head of purchasing knew the mission and strategy, he could not divulge it to his team. This remained the case for a few years after privatisation. The company has now become much more open.

The 'strategic aims' of purchasing are now the following:

- improve contribution to profitability
- obtain goods and services at lowest lifetime costs and at minimum risk
- provide a cost-effective, balanced flow of materials and
- ensure that the support and guidance given constantly exceeds expectations

These aims also existed before privatisation but were somewhat academic. The content of the strategic aims was under review in mid-1996.

Purchasing at SWEB has adopted a number of tools and techniques since the early 1990s. The reasons for their increased use are the drive to reduce operating costs and remain competitive in the increasingly contested electricity industry and the need to improve customer satisfaction. The tools and techniques adopted include benchmarking, purchasing portfolio analysis, strategic source planning, purchase price cost analysis, strategic supplier alliances and partnership sourcing. Two forms of benchmarking are carried out. The first involves tracking the prices of services and equipment and comparing them to the industry average, and the second involves visiting other companies in order to observe their activities; the aim being to learn from examples of best practice and transfer them to SWEB. Finding partners for this second form of benchmarking tends to be difficult. This is especially true of finding willing partners in the electricity industry. Finding the time to carry out and assess company visits is also problematic.

The company has used the purchasing portfolio matrix informally for over a decade, but in recent years it has become more formalised. The matrix is used actively rather than passively. This means, for example, that SWEB aims to move all products out of the 'strategic critical' quartile of the matrix. For 'strategic critical' products or services there are few suppliers in the market and company expenditure is high (an example is the purchase of electricity cable). This is clearly not an ideal position because the suppliers tend to be in a powerful position *vis-à-vis* SWEB, and the impact on the bottom line is critical because expenditure is high. Generally, SWEB decides what strategy is needed to get the best business benefit from the Purchasing Portfolio Matrix for every product or service sourced. Each will be different and there will be different tools used for each, for example partnerships and alliances or short-term relationships will tend to be used where the main criteria for sourcing is price. The matrix is also used to determine different buyer competencies: an individual buying strategic critical products will need different competencies to one involved in low-value commodity items where there are many suppliers.

Partnership sourcing, network sourcing and single sourcing are all used according to market characteristics. The view taken at SWEB is that single sourcing should be used if the supplier market is highly competitive. This is because transaction costs of dealing with one supplier are much lower than running a large supplier base, and this tends to affect the benefits of competition.

Other tools and techniques in use include vendor accreditation and other supplier assessment systems, although these are only applied where it is considered cost-effective. That is to say, for 'strategic critical' products where company spend is high and there are few suppliers. SWEB has been improving its information systems on suppliers over the last few years. A major supply chain project led to the installation of a company-wide computerised supplier database in late 1997, which is fully under the control of the purchasing department. The company did have a computerised supplier database before this project, but it was not company wide and the information provided was far more basic and therefore less valuable as a tool for decision making.

The performance of the purchasing department is measured in three ways:

1. Contribution to profitability – this covers purchasing savings, added value, cost avoidance and lifetime cost savings.
2. Working capital – this measures the amount of money tied up in stock and the aim is to minimise it.
3. Material availability – this measure is self-explanatory, and is concerned with having materials available when needed. The broad aim is to maximise availability.

It can be seen that the 'working capital' and material availability measures conflict, but the aim is to strike a balance by maximising availability at the lowest cost to the company. The above measurements cover: how goods are bought, how much cost they incur to the business and how available they are.

There are a host of other measures. Purchasing also has project goals, for example deadlines for the implementation of a supply chain project and various stages within this; and goals for staff sickness, safety and overtime. For each, the company sets annual targets and measures performance on a monthly basis.

The purchasing department has been very successful in achieving its targets, although it is difficult to compare year-on-year because there has been a significant increase in the expenditure controlled by purchasing. Examples of recent performance are as follows: in 1997 costs savings were running at 8.1 per cent by May and have been improving year-on-year; working capital is continually reducing and material availability is increasing. Material availability averaged 95 per cent in 1996. The target was increased to 96 per cent for 1997 and was achieved by May of that year.

The role and profile of purchasing

Purchasing is now 'recognised as a mainstream business function with responsibility for maximising contribution to profitability from the total expenditure on bought-in goods and services' in the words of one interviewee. There was some change in the role and profile of the function following privatisation, but most change has happened following the US takeover in 1995.

The profile of the function has improved. The purchasing manager has increased the scope of goods and services under his control and purchasing has become involved in areas such as IT, legal services and advertising. It has also taken on responsibility for bought-in labour resources, such as contract workers to build electricity lines, the use of management consultants and auditors. The department will eventually be responsible for 100 per cent of company spend. This is likely to happen within two years. Involvement by the purchasing department in total company spend increased from 50 per cent before privatisation to 75 per cent afterwards, and has been moving towards 100 per cent since the US takeover. Roughly a half of total operating costs are bought-in, including works, goods and services. The company has 'shrunk back' its own activities, meaning that bought-in goods have become a relatively higher proportion of total costs. It should be noted that these figures exclude the purchase of electricity from the National Grid, which is a major expense and dealt with by a separate division.

Staffing levels in purchasing have increased from 10 before privatisation to 16 since the takeover, to cope with increased activity. The increased focus on cost has meant that purchasing staff have become involved earlier in projects, because the company has realised that this approach can help to cut costs. This also means that purchasing is becoming involved in more strategic decisions, i.e. the major decisions that are made at the early stages of projects. By contrast, in the past, it was the manager of each individual business unit that remained dominant and purchasing only became involved in the later stages of a project.

Leaving aside the purchase of electricity and wages, total company spend was around £95m. in 1996 and divided as follows:

£29m. – Goods that are consumed within the company, for example wood, glass and clothing
£31m. – Services
£10m. – Computer equipment and telecommunications
£7m. – Transport
£10m. – Consultancy (management, legal, financial and professional)
£8m. – Civil, i.e. building repairs and maintenance

There is a mandate within the company to use purchasing for all contracts above £10,000. This increased after October 1997 when the function gained control of 100 per cent of non-energy and non-labour spend. The purchasing department has adopted an 'internal customer' philosophy and carries out customer surveys within the company. The two main customers of the purchasing department are engineering followed by IT. The customer surveys are carried out in order to maintain a balance between the drive to cut costs and the need to provide a satisfactory service to the internal customer. The company's drive for cost reduction has led to purchasing gaining increased control of spend because the department has demonstrated its ability to reduce costs. However, there is no internal market in the sense that other departments are required to pay for the purchasing service performed at the centre.

SWEB has some subsidiary companies apart from the main electricity supply and distribution business. These are free to carry out their own purchasing and it was the purchasing manager's decision that they should continue to do so. Certain rules regarding issues such as ethics, the use of competition, and confidentiality are laid down centrally, but the subsidiaries are otherwise free to contract.

Generally, purchasing does not suffer from a lack of resources in the same way as at Severn Trent Water (see Chapter 8). For example, the department was reorganised in mid-1996 and the buying staff were increased by six people. It appears that no major problems were encountered in gaining permission for this increase in staffing. This perhaps reflects the higher profile of the department compared to many of the other cases reported in this volume; although it has only been since the takeover by the Southern Company of the US that purchasing has been afforded the current respect internally and resources that go with such respect.

Outsourcing and supplier relationship management

Before privatisation, utilities carried out most services themselves, for example cleaning and facilities management. Most of these services have now been outsourced at SWEB, the last major activity outsourced being IT. The reason given for this is that the central aim of a utility is to reduce costs, while working within a regulated income. SWEB like other electricity companies in England and Wales is regulated by Offer, the Office of Electricity Regulation. The income of a utility is squeezed by the regulator through price-capping, and costs tend to rise unless a conscious effort is made to control them. The drivers at SWEB are to lower cost in the short to medium term, and decisions are made by costing internal versus external activity. In practice, SWEB has concentrated upon outsourcing only support services, which suggests much less attention to a more strategic (less cost-focused) supply alignment or procurement competence.

Outsourcing decisions can come from two sources: either from central purchasing, in which case the department is involved throughout the process, or from the business that is looking at its own operations, who will then consult purchasing. Nothing is outsourced without the involvement of the head of purchasing. This is partly due to human resource implications when outsourcing. It seems that purchasing has a primary responsibility for dealing with trade unions on outsourcing matters.

Activities outsourced since privatisation include catering, cleaning services, some maintenance activities and inventory. Much of this outsourcing has been driven by City pressure to reduce costs and particularly to reduce staffing levels. However, the general view on outsourcing at the company is that it should take place only if the company cannot match what the outside world offers in terms of price and service. Even then it is crucial to understand fully the activity to be outsourced and its importance to the company.

Purchasing's involvement in the make–buy decision is proactive in that the department is involved from an early stage and throughout the project. Suggestions for outsourcing come from two sources: either the purchasing manager or the purchasing analyst sees an opportunity, or a non-purchasing manager, generally in a drive to cut costs, sees an opportunity and suggests it to purchasing.

Regarding supplier relationships more generally, SWEB has tended to increase collaborative-type relationships with suppliers in recent years. The company has been wary, however, of blindly following the trend towards this type of arrangement. The view is that because the costs of partnerships can be very high, they should not be entered into lightly. Partnerships require a change in the way that both companies operate, as well as considerable resources spent managing the relationship. By 1997, SWEB had three such partnerships: for cable, transformers and printing.

The constant aim is to restrict the number of suppliers because of the costs of maintaining a large database. Generally, SWEB is moving closer to a smaller number of suppliers. The company is constantly looking at how goods can be bundled together in order to gain more leverage.

As far as supplier performance is concerned, there appears to have been an improvement on all key criteria. In particular, there has been a *major* improvement in cost competitiveness and a *slight* improvement in other criteria, such as product and service quality; cycle times; new-product development time; flexibility; on-time delivery; and access to new technology and innovation.

An overview of the three forms of efficiency gain at SWEB

It is clear that SWEB did not really focus on the need for efficiency gains through an improvement of the functional professionalism of purchasing and supply management until around 1991. In this sense, SWEB is similar to the Severn Trent case. Unlike Severn Trent, however, the major focus after 1991 and until the US takeover of the business in 1995, was on incremental improvements in purchasing and supply functional professionalism. Apart from the abortive attempts to sell internally what it did well immediately after privatisation, there was little evidence in SWEB before 1995 of any interest in what are termed in this study transformational efficiency gains, gains which arise through a greater awareness of supply alignment and procurement competence. It is also clear, that the US takeover in 1995 has presaged a more forceful attention to the scope for efficiency improvements. This has been assisted by the planned increase in competition in the industry and a tighter regulatory structure through Offer. In 1995 the distribution price cap was tightened. All of this offers the potential for a new interest in transformational efficiency in the company, although it remains to be seen whether the company will shift its focus from operational improvements to improve static and dynamic efficiency. The structure of the industry and SWEB's corporate strategy seem to indicate that an operational rather than strategic competence focus will remain.

Industrial structure

The main external factors affecting the behaviour and performance of SWEB are: ownership, competition, regulation, suppliers and customers in that order. These are now discussed in more detail.

Ownership

The US takeover has affected SWEB considerably, leading to fundamental changes in structure, strategy and culture throughout the business. More specifically, US ownership has allowed purchasing to change its role completely and play a more central part in the company's success. The electricity industry in England and Wales has experienced a great deal of merger and acquisition activity since April 1995, when the government removed its 'golden share' which had restricted takeover bids after privatisation. This affected SWEB by redefining market structure and hence competitive rivalry.

The transfer of ownership from public to private sector may have also affected SWEB along with all other utilities. Companies, once privatised, are expected to give a better level of service than when they were in state hands. When in public ownership, customers may be more forgiving because the companies are owned by the taxpayer and because of the perception that public sector employees are badly paid. When private, they are viewed as independent organisations focused on profits. This, together with the press coverage of 'fat cat' utility directors receiving 'massive' pay increases after privatisation, has possibly led to a more demanding public and expectations of improved service levels.

Competition

The electricity industry has seen considerable deregulation and much increased competition in the 1990s, and this process is still in train. Generation is fully deregulated and supply to customers has been gradually deregulated since privatisation, starting with supplies to the largest users. There will be a fully open market in England and Wales, including supply to domestic customers, for electricity by the spring of 1999. In order to counter a loss of market share, SWEB has moved into gas supply, at first targeting its existing customer base in the south west of England.

Regulation

The regulatory environment was a live issue by mid-1997 because the Labour government had just gained power and the party's policy on regulation remained unclear. The previous Conservative government had allowed the regulatory bodies (Offer in the case of the electricity industry) to operate with high degrees of autonomy, but it was by no means clear that the new government would continue this policy. In general, regulation can be viewed as a 'game' by the company, in that the regulator aims to protect the consumer, while the company aims to make as much money as possible for its shareholders. There is an inevitable tension in regulatory systems between the regulator and the regulated and this is true of the relationship between Offer and the regional electricity companies (Parker, 1997, 1998).

Suppliers

The major effect of suppliers concerns the supply of electricity to SWEB. The price of electricity is set via the electricity 'pool' and strongly influenced by the three major generators PowerGen, National Power and Eastern Electricity (Kennedy, 1997). National Power and PowerGen have been keen to buy into the regional electricity companies to secure their markets and expand their businesses; while Eastern Electricity was originally a REC which purchased generating capacity. National Power's bid for Southern Electric (not to be confused with Southern of the US) and PowerGen's for Midlands Electricity in September 1995, were both subsequently blocked by the government on competition grounds. The 1997 general election caused uncertainty because the Labour government's policy towards the future of the electricity pool and the structure of the electricity sector were unclear. Recently, the new administration signalled its desire to separate distribution of electricity from its supply. The expected result is a further restructuring of the industry with the potential for companies such as SWEB to divest their supply or distribution business. In turn, this restructuring may well lead US companies, such as the Southern Company, to reassess their ownership of a regional electricity company. The separation of distribution and supply may make ownership less attractive, particularly when profits are already under pressure from competition and regulation.

Customers/market

Demand for electricity tends to follow general economic trends; growth rates in the UK have remained around the 2 per cent to 2.5 per cent mark during the mid-1990s. The important point for SWEB, however, is the fact that in the past it had a relatively firm customer base. The geographic monopoly of the supply of electricity to dependent customers is now threatened by competition in supply. At the same time, regional electricity companies are moving into gas supply as this market is liberalised. As a result, it is highly likely that customer focus and alignment will need to become a key competence in SWEB, as in every other power supply company in England and Wales. The need for supply alignment and procurement competence thinking will, therefore, increase as a result in the future.

Corporate strategy

As a consequence of imminent changes in the electricity market, the company's strategy can be described as very much 'in the air' at the time of writing this study, early 1998. Previously, SWEB had focused on cost consolidation and the development of the company's core competencies of supplying and distributing electricity, but the strategy for the future remains under discussion. The option of a more extensive expansion into the gas market is being debated (the gas market's deregulation will be completed in 1998) and an attempt may once again be made to integrate vertically generation and supply or generation and distribution once supply and distribution industries are separated. Uncertainty about the new Labour government's strategy towards the regulation of utilities continues to affect the company's decision-making process.

The problem that this creates for purchasing strategy is clear. The purchasing manager always tries to align the operational strategy with corporate strategy, and considers how this will affect bought-in goods. For example, the company's focus on static and dynamic efficiency has meant that purchasing must buy in extra skills more cheaply than the in-house operation. This focus on operational efficiency through outsourcing occurred with labour for the construction of overhead lines, most of which is now contracted out but which was previously carried on in-house. The problem is that, while short-term efficiency gains can be made in this way, the company may be demonstrating a lack of understanding of supply alignment and procurement competence. This is because SWEB might be guilty of outsourcing critical assets in its supply chains and creating dangerous supply dependencies.

This may create problems for the US parent company. The strategy of the Southern Company (the parent) is growth in the world power generation and distribution market by acquisition. The company has recently bought a company in China and has a strategy of being a global power company. Short-term efficiency gains at SWEB may militate against long-term profitability if key assets are not managed effectively, placing an increasing management burden on the parent company.

Transformational efficiency at SWEB

The SWEB case demonstrates the problems that can occur for privatised companies that do not immediately face effective competitive pressures after transfer of ownership. SWEB was initially guilty of a lack of focus even on static efficiency improvements in purchasing. It was not until 1991 that the company began to recognise the need for a focus on dynamic efficiency through purchasing and supply functional professionalism. After this date there was a rapid increase in the focus which the company brought to bear on functional improvement. This was due to the threat of competition which emerged during the decade, and also due to a stiffening of regulation at the same time.

By 1995, when the company was taken over, there had been a clear shift in the business towards a more aggressive approach to effective purchasing. Since then there has been even more improvement as a consequence of the decision by the new US owners to bring purchasing into the strategic core of the business, in a search for even more dynamic efficiency gains. Despite this, the company remains largely unfocused in so far as transformational efficiency is concerned. This is a legacy of the fact that real competitive pressures will not be felt in the domestic electricity supply market until 1998/9, and because of the historic legacy of having a dominant geographic position in the market with a dependent customer base. So far only larger electricity users have had a choice of supplier (since April 4, 1992 those with a larger than 100kWh peak demand). It will be interesting to see the extent to which the company will be able to transcend its current operational focus and adopt a more transformational and strategic view of procurement competence and supply alignment once the electricity market is fully liberalised.

10 British Airways

BRITISH AIRWAYS

British Airways (BA) presents an interesting case of a company that has improved its static and dynamic efficiency in internal and external operational practice. In recent years, due to a recognition of a significant shift in the competitive and regulatory environment in which it must operate, BA has been forced to search for efficiency gains of the type referred to in this study as transformational efficiency gains. The chosen route has been through alliances, first with USAir and more recently with American Airlines, and through a fundamental reappraisal of the historic boundaries of the firm. This latter approach has been based on the use of a radical outsourcing methodology drawing upon core competence thinking. As indicated in the conclusion of this book, it is clear that this methodology and way of thinking may well have contributed to BA's recent problems with its own staff. Also, it seems that the company may have some way to go in achieving supply alignment and procurement competence. A further problem may be that in searching for strategic focus the company will lose its earlier competence in static and dynamic efficiency.

Background

> As the world's leading international passenger airline, and one of the most profitable, British Airways has built its success on quality service provided by a dedicated workforce, combined with marketing, operational and financial excellence.
>
> (British Airways plc, 1994–95, p. 1)

> In the early 1980s, British Airways PLC was in a terrible state. We were overmanned, inefficient, and in deep trouble – losing £200 of taxpayers' money every minute of our existence.
>
> (Gurassa, 1995)

BA was formed in 1972 by the amalgamation of two public corporations: British European Airways (BEA) and the British Overseas Airways

Corporation (BOAC). However, this merger caused problems for many years, because two very different management cultures and operations were brought together and never fully combined until the 1980s. Performance was certainly impaired by the continued juxtaposition of two ways of working and by the failure to gain fully from the predicted economies of scale and cost savings arising from rationalisation. The company also suffered from poor labour relations and from a mistaken expansionist policy, resulting in continued high costs and low productivity.

BA was in no shape to face the 'oil shock' of 1979, which brought a doubling of the cost of aviation fuel, a reduction in passenger transport as the recession took hold, and the appreciation of sterling which raised BA's prices in foreign currency terms. The arrival of Laker Airline's service called Skytrain in 1977, quickly taking a 10 per cent market share on BA's key North Atlantic route, dealt another blow and contributed to record losses in 1981/82.

Plans to privatise BA were announced by the government in 1980, but the company's worsening financial results precluded any sale in the near future and privatisation did not take place until 1987. It was in order to get BA into a suitable shape for privatisation that Sir John King was brought in by Margaret Thatcher in 1981. A 'survival plan' was agreed in the same year, based on massive cost-cutting via reductions in capacity and employment and the disposal of non-core activities. Staff numbers decreased from 56,000 in 1980 to 36,000 by 1984; a 36 per cent reduction.

Other major changes accompanied these cuts. King appointed Colin Marshall as chief executive in 1983, following a long search for someone capable of turning BA into a market-driven company and focusing attention on delivering a quality service to the customer. It is the partnership of these two men that is credited with the creation of the 'new' BA. Other changes made included a shake-up of the existing top- and middle-management structures in an attempt to clear out the old 'engineering-driven' blood, which might resist change, training courses for staff at all levels to instil a customer-focused culture and increase motivation, the introduction of performance-related pay, and a major marketing initiative with the emphasis on branding the airline's services (Martin and Parker, 1997, ch. 9).

In 1984, BA became a public limited company in preparation for privatisation, and was finally floated on the London Stock Exchange in February 1987. Since privatisation, profits have continued to increase, often against the grain of the industry as a whole which suffered severely in the 1989–92 recession, and BA continued to gain respect as an excellent company. This is in stark contrast to the days when it was said BA stood for 'bloody awful' and its service levels were an international joke.

British Airways achieved a remarkable turnaround during the 1980s, from a loss-ridden state-owned organisation to a highly competitive global company respected worldwide for its performance. With profits and market share continuing their upward trend into the 1990s, the sale of BA is widely regarded as one of the most successful of the UK privatisation programme.

The 1981/82 losses, which, at over £500m., were the largest for the UK airline industry up to that time, prompted the government to instigate massive changes at BA which resulted in continuous performance improvements throughout the rest of the decade. By 1988, BA had reversed its fortunes by producing profits at record levels with pre-tax earnings exceeding £200m. for the first time. The company was now more profitable than any of the large international carriers, including KLM, Singapore Airlines, Cathay Pacific, United Airlines and USAir. The success continued, with BA remaining highly profitable through 1990–95, when the worst recession the industry had ever known forced many operators out of business. Aggregate losses for the international airline industry reached almost $16bn. in 1990–93, and it was not until 1994/95 that the industry as a whole managed to pull back into profit. Meanwhile, BA was way ahead with pre-tax profits at £327m. (1994/95) on a turnover of £7.2bn., showing a near three-fold increase in profitability and a 45 per cent increase in turnover during the five-year period from 1990. There was further improvement during 1995/96 with profit before tax up to a record £585m. and turnover reaching £7.8bn. (British Airways plc, 1996).

Profit margins rose from 2 per cent in 1982 to 6 per cent in 1984 and 1985 and 8 per cent in 1990 as market share was taken from other airlines. The company gained increasing respect in many areas, including quality, customer service and training. It was voted 'Best Airline in Europe and across the Atlantic' by a leading industry journal in 1991 and won numerous other awards. Despite recent industrial relations setbacks, BA continues to look ahead optimistically. On becoming chief executive in January 1996, Robert Ayling stated his aim to make it the best managed company in the UK by the year 2001.

Evidence of static and dynamic efficiency gains

The main focus of the changes introduced by Sir John (later Lord) King during the early 1980s involved transforming BA from an engineering to a market-driven organisation. Within the context of this fundamental shift, there are four key factors that have contributed to the success. These are: considerable and ongoing cost reduction; a focus on delivering excellent customer service at a premium price; the use of alliances and partnerships in order to increase market coverage; and investment in computerised reservations systems allowing BA to maximise yield on individual flights. This clearly demonstrates an understanding of how to achieve efficiency gains through internal and external cost reduction and functional professional improvement. This can be further demonstrated by analysing the search for efficiency in purchasing and supply management.

The structure of purchasing and supply management

Purchasing at BA underwent a transformation in strategy and structure during the 1980s and early 1990s. This was a very deliberate policy which began with the headhunting of a new purchasing director in 1982/83, who was given, in the words of one of the managers interviewed, the remit to 'fix it' (i.e. purchasing at BA), along with sufficient resources and power to give him a reasonable chance of success. The changes described here are not strictly those that have happened *since* privatisation. Considerable change was made in order to prepare the company for privatisation, and so the commentary here describes changes that span the period prior to, and following, transfer to the private sector in 1987.

Broadly, the new head of purchasing centralised the function. The reorganisation was announced in December 1983 and was in place by the middle of the following year. Before the change, purchasing staff worked and reported within their user departments with only a 'dotted' reporting line to the head of purchasing. So, the engineering purchasing team sat in the engineering department, the catering team in the catering department, and so on. Their roles revolved largely around support and administration and there was very little central co-ordination. Purchasing was there to serve the engineers and was often considered as little more than an order-placing or storekeeping function.

Although the new structure involved centralisation, the true picture is more complicated. The centralisation was functional rather than physical. That is, most purchasing staff continued to work within their user departments but began to report directly to a purchasing manager, creating a central mandate for the first time. This meant that they were spread around nine separate locations at Heathrow, with the purchasing group for catering continuing to be stationed at catering headquarters, as it had been in the past. Overall company restructuring continued with the establishment of new strategic business units during the 1980s based mainly on market sectors. The new structure for purchasing was aligned with a philosophy of 'customer-oriented' purchasing. The idea was that building a relationship with the internal customer was key, and this could be best achieved via close physical proximity. It was at this stage that the terminology also changed in order to reflect a new, more commercial ethos. Civil service-type terms such as 'purchasing officer' were replaced by 'buyer', 'manager', etc., and 'user departments' became 'client' or 'service departments'.

The new head of purchasing also set up a central purchasing group which worked at Heathrow. Staff here also had 'clients' throughout the business but were located in the central purchasing department for logistical reasons. Clients of this group included those for the purchase of fuel and aircraft and services such as advertising, marketing and IT.

Moreover, a new and more senior level of management was introduced. This comprised a team of general managers reporting to the head of purchasing, who had purchasing managers, chief buyers and buyers beneath them. Previously, the central organisation of purchasing was weak and there was no comparable structure. This reflects the position of purchasing as little more than a support role with no perceived need to co-ordinate centrally. Another change in structure involved the setting up of buying offices in the United

States and South East Asia. BA realised that it needed to operate and, therefore, source globally.

The organisational restructuring from the early 1980s involved over time considerable reductions in the number of purchasing staff – largely viewed internally as the removal of a wasted resource through the introduction of more efficient operations. There were over 800 purchasing staff before 1983. This figure had been reduced to below 200 by 1996, at a time when there was both an increase in purchasing's involvement in company spend and an absolute increase in spending. Part of this reduction was achieved through the devolvement of some low-value spend and some of the more tactical activity such as expediting (checking or 'chasing up' the progress of an order), to non-purchasing staff. In 1989, non-capital expenditure per head in purchasing stood at £2m. By 1993 this had increased to £3.6m., illustrating the efficiency improvements in the department.

The restructuring process formed part of a transformation in purchasing at BA. It was accompanied by the introduction of a new culture based on a more commercial approach to the task, the recruitment of high-calibre purchasing staff from outside the company, a new procurement strategy, a change in approach to the make–buy decision and a new attitude towards supplier relationships.

Purchasing and supply professionalism

The arrival of the new head of purchasing in 1982/83 signalled a radical change in purchasing strategy at BA. Admittedly, the company was starting from a very low base in that there was no purchasing strategy to speak of beforehand. Nevertheless, the rate of change was impressive and pushed BA well in advance of most other airlines in terms of its approach to purchasing, as well as shocking a supplier market that had long been used to a cosy relationship with the airline.

Before the change, purchasing activity within BA was limited largely to reactive tasks such as organising bids, awarding contracts and expediting, in line with its limited role of serving the engineers simply by making sure that the products were 'on the shelf'. Purchasing became involved late in the process 'when all the damage had been done'[1] and with the result that it had very little influence. By 1996 the following procurement techniques had been adopted: benchmarking and the aim to develop world best practice; purchasing portfolio analysis; strategic source planning; purchase price cost analysis; and strategic supplier alliances. Further initiatives included the introduction of buyer and supplier performance targets, a wholesale training and education strategy for purchasing staff, and systems developments in order to increase the efficiency of procurement tasks. BA decided against benchmarking their competitors because they were reluctant to give away sensitive information. Instead, they developed a measuring system which earmarked leading companies in purchasing outside the industry, including Nissan, IBM and

Motorola. BA has since worked with these organisations in order to develop and share best practice and to discover new techniques and systems.

The examples above are witness to the development of a much more proactive approach to purchasing. 'Current strategy revolves around a highly skilled, valued team operating "upstream" in the business and constantly looking to generate benefits from markets and suppliers. This has evolved but the vision since 1983 has been largely the same'. This description by a purchasing manager interviewed at BA demonstrates that the 'step change' around 1983 created a purchasing philosophy which remained constant in terms of the vision throughout privatisation, and is still present today.

The new head of purchasing introduced two major changes in strategy. The first was cost rather than price-focused purchasing. BA began to consider the lifetime cost of an acquisition, in terms of maintenance, spare parts, replacement cost and so on, rather than simply opting for the lowest price at the time of purchase. This had been the previous approach and the change reflects, among other things, a switch in purchasing's prime function from simply minimising price to adding value. The second was the establishment of 'appropriate' relationships with suppliers according to the product sourced. An example will best illustrate this approach: aircraft are core to BA's success and there are few suppliers able to meet the company's needs. This has resulted in BA building a strong relationship with one supplier, namely Boeing. By contrast, the market for computers is fast-moving and there are many potential suppliers; hence, BA does not tie itself to one company.

In line with corporate strategy of becoming a worldwide 'end-to-end' carrier and to increase market coverage, BA has taken shares in other airlines. These include USAir, Qantas of Australia, France's TAT European and Germany's Deutsche BA. In 1991, BA purchasing established joint purchasing with USAir and Qantas, in the search for leverage and synergistic gains. The aim is to increase buying power through volume purchasing and generally increase the efficiency of purchasing by working together.

The role and profile of purchasing

It goes without saying that the role of purchasing has changed completely. The fact that BA has been transformed from an engineering-based airline to a commercial business has resulted in a greater acceptance of the need for effective purchasing. The department's central aim is to add value, not simply to 'put the stock on the shelves' for the engineers and spend the company's money. Others in the company realise this, which has helped to improve purchasing's internal profile.

Previously, mainly low-calibre people were employed within BA in purchasing, essentially as storekeepers or order-placers. Sourcing decisions were made higher up the management and purchasers simply ordered according to instructions. The function was not held in high regard and was sometimes treated as a receptacle for staff who had not performed well elsewhere.

A central aim of the new head of purchasing was to move the function 'upstream' in terms of corporate decision making and to change its role from order-placing to a function closer to the strategic core of the business. In addition to the changes in structure and strategy discussed above, he used other means to this end. High-calibre purchasing staff were recruited from industries where purchasing had been recognised as an important function, including the automotive and aerospace sectors. Lower-calibre staff who retained a 'storekeeper' mentality were moved out of the department. This manœuvre was eased by the drastic reduction in personnel throughout the company at this time. Graduate training schemes and staff development programmes were introduced for purchasing personnel, which still exist today. Before the major changes from 1983, less than 10 per cent of purchasing staff held a degree or equivalent. By 1993, the figure was over 50 per cent of all staff (including all clerical support) and almost 80 per cent of core purchasing staff.

It is important to note that the new head of purchasing was given the resources and senior-management backing necessary to carry the changes through and to fight off any internal resistance. In some of the other companies involved in the research reported in this book, lack of such means often prevented the kind of rapid progress witnessed at BA. When recruiting new staff, for example, the salaries offered were commensurate with those of marketing personnel, thereby attracting high-quality applicants. A number of the other companies studied could not do this simply because the salary rates for purchasing staff were decided elsewhere in the company.

The extent of purchasing's involvement in company spend is a further illustration of its enhanced role. Since privatisation, its involvement in traditional spend (for example ground equipment and vehicles) has grown from 30 per cent to 100 per cent, while for non-traditional (including marketing, IT and consultancy) it has increased from zero to 95 per cent. There have been major gains for the function in all areas, including the purchase of property, marketing (advertising and sales promotion), consultancy and IT. The few areas not covered by purchasing include some legal and financial services; these remain under the control of the relevant specialised departments.

Outsourcing and supplier relationship management

Today, better cost management is ingrained in BA's way of working. This is illustrated in the company's 'Performance Improvement Programme', which produced savings of £750m. per annum between 1990 and 1994. Outsourcing has been increased as part of this policy. For example, BA now hires cargo space rather than owns it, thereby reducing overhead costs when demand is low. Other activities outsourced include aircraft cleaning, avionics maintenance, aircraft engine support, property maintenance, security and passenger catering.[2]

Purchasing staff have been 'at the vanguard' of the drive to outsource operationally, according to a senior manager. The head of purchasing was given the task of searching the market for opportunities to outsource after the review of the make–buy decision began in the 1980s. By the end of 1996, BA had reached the final stages of the project. They had explored most operational outsourcing opportunities and had begun to challenge the strategic core of operations in the business, in the sense of questioning whether traditionally core operations might be (to some degree) contracted out, even including the flying of aircraft.

In general, BA has moved closer to fewer suppliers over the last decade, although it is accepted that partnership-type relationships are only suitable for some products. Interestingly, the event of the Gulf war of 1990/91 proved a catalyst here, with BA seizing the opportunity both to work more closely with suppliers and to force down costs. With the company's revenues plunging as the conflict progressed and passengers postponed flying, especially on the North Atlantic routes, BA purchasing staff visited suppliers to explain exactly why they could not afford higher prices. This was widely accepted and led to a lower-cost base after the war. In many cases, this was the first time that BA had 'opened up' and provided internal cost information to suppliers and adopted a more collaborative approach to purchasing. The success drove the company to increase collaboration. This in turn helped to raise the credibility of purchasing within the company. The function had achieved considerable success in fending off price increases.

The length of contracts has increased as BA has developed closer links with suppliers. In the past, the vast majority lasted for one year, but this has been increased to two to three years, five in some cases and even ten years for some products. The establishment of longer-term contracts has prompted BA purchasing to plan further ahead with suppliers; while the number of suppliers has been drastically reduced, from 11,000 in 1983 to 3,100 by 1993. However, the figure is unlikely to fall significantly lower because of the nature of buying aircraft: there are many bespoke parts which are made only by a restricted number of companies.

In general, single sourcing has increased at the expense of multi- and dual sourcing, although the phrase itself requires qualification. BA single source *by aircraft*, but not as a company. For example, engines for the Boeing 747 are single sourced with Rolls Royce, but other engines are used for other aircraft. They also single source *by airport*, employing one catering company to supply Heathrow, or even *by country*. BA does not single source mainframe computers because of the perceived risk. Instead they dual source from IBM and one other supplier.

An overview of the three forms of efficiency gain at BA

It is clear from this initial discussion that due to the introduction of key personnel at the strategic and operational levels after 1981, BA was able to reduce significantly the internal and external costs of transactions. In the purchasing and supply area there is little doubt that the aggressive cost management focus introduced by the head of purchasing led to a more effective management of external resources. This is consistent with the view that significant performance improvement occurs when companies shift from a short-term, internal cost management focus, to a more professional approach based on functional improvement. BA is an excellent example of this and, because of the 'buy-in' of professional expertise at the very top of the company, the management of external resources improved rapidly and significantly after 1983. By 1987 it is clear that BA had developed an interest in what are termed in this book as dynamic and static efficiencies in purchasing. More recently, the company has sought what are closer to being transformational efficiency gains. This is indicated by the commencement of a further major outsourcing review, which has begun to challenge some of the historical core operational roles in the company. It is also clear that this search is being driven by significant anticipated changes in the regulatory environment within which BA operates. To understand the driver of change in BA's historic way of thinking, and why it is seeking transformational efficiency, the industrial context within which the company exists must be understood.

Industrial structure

In this section the key elements in BA's industrial environment which appear to shape and influence its behaviour are discussed. The most important factor seems to be the regulatory environment, which is the major driver behind the company's global strategy. Other key factors that impact on the company's search for efficiency are: increasing competition, distribution issues related to BA's premium brand, ownership in the form of the takeover threat, and the nature of supplier markets. These are now discussed in detail.

Regulation

BA considers itself to be heavily constrained by regulation, which takes two major forms. These are governmental and technical, the former being influential in the past through the restriction of competition. Governmental regulation often takes the form of bilateral aviation agreements made between the governments of two countries. These are very powerful in preventing BA from becoming a truly global company, as they restrict the routes that BA is permitted to fly. There are the regulatory deals between the United Kingdom and the USA for example, which BA must conform to. The transatlantic routes and the American market are very important to the company, and so it follows that these rules can have a major impact on strategy. The proposed alliance between BA and American Airlines announced in June 1996 (*The Financial Times*, 11 July 1996) provides a timely example of the regulatory influence. BA must satisfy US anti-trust laws, UK Fair Trading law and EU Treaty of Rome competition regulations before the alliance can be finalised.

There is an added twist in that the interests of the regulatory bodies can be at variance. In recent years the EU has promoted competition among European airlines, the UK government defends the British case, and so on.

The 1980s saw some deregulation in the United States, although the deregulation programme only involved domestic airlines. Restrictions on foreign ownership of US airlines remain. BA, or indeed any foreign company, is limited to a 25 per cent stake in a US airline. This limit on foreign ownership applies in many countries, often stemming from the legacy of airlines as 'flagship' industries. This is a major reason why BA and other airlines have expanded through alliances rather than acquisitions in recent years. The proposed alliance with American Airlines involves no equity stake. The fundamental challenge facing BA, however, and why there has been a search for transformational efficiency recently, is the deregulation of the European airline market by the European Commission. The EU transport ministers agreed on a deregulation package in December 1989 and in 1992 a new agreement dealing with fares, market access and licensing was introduced. The right of an EU airline to operate on a domestic route in another EU country and certain other previously restricted routes (provide 'cabotage services') was introduced in April 1997. To compete in this new, less-regulated environment it is clear that BA will have to challenge its existing operational practices and find alternative means to reduce costs.

Technical regulation, for example through the Civil Aviation Authority in the UK, appears to be relatively less of a problem for BA. Its major influence is through increased costs to the airline in meeting safety standards. For example, regulations require full traceability of the parts of an aircraft throughout its life and this adds cost through the supply chain for both BA and its suppliers. Equally, this also raises the barriers to entry in the industry.

Competition

This is the second most important influence on BA. Competition has increased enormously in recent years, and has come from three sources, as discussed below. Although BA has never held a monopoly position even in the UK domestic market, the company did enjoy protection as a nationalised, flagship industry that was not allowed to go bankrupt. This, of course, no longer applies. Changes in the competitive environment are, of course, closely related to changes in regulation and more specifically deregulation.

An increasingly important source of competition comes from a group of airlines that a manager at BA named 'revived new entrants'. These are the old public airlines that are now becoming much more efficient. The trend for privatising airlines has spread worldwide and the companies involved are forced to increase efficiency as they prepare for private sector existence and increased competition. Examples include Lufthansa, KLM, Air France and the Japanese operators. Most major non-American airlines were formerly in the public sector. Another competitive threat is the genuine new entrants, including Virgin and Valuejet. These companies are not burdened with the history of heavily centralised and bureaucratic structures, unlike many of the established airlines. They also tend to operate with lower fixed costs, as they act more like 'virtual airlines'. That is, rather than owning aircraft and related services, they may lease them flexibly depending on levels of demand. These airlines pose a genuine threat, but it is likely that they will have to establish a more solid structure (and thus increase fixed costs) if they are to grow significantly. In addition, a shortage of landing slots at major airports in the US and Europe, in particular, mean that new operators can find it difficult to expand their operations. Landing slots are generally subject to 'grandfather rights', favouring the older, established airlines.[3]

Distribution of BA's product

The third competitive threat is related to the distribution of BA's product. BA sells a premium product at a relatively high price and has enjoyed continued success based on this approach. However, there are worldwide media networks currently under development which threaten this position. The networks will enable the public to purchase air travel 'on-line', and this threatens to devalue the BA brand and turn it into a commodity along with every other airline ticket. This threat is forcing BA to realise that one of its core competencies must be the management of its premium brand image.

There are two further influential factors which are related to BA's market. The first is growing customer expectations. Customers continually want better service for a lower price and this has led to the company being squeezed on both the cost and revenue side. BA has been cutting costs rigorously over the past two decades and technological advances have made this task easier. However, management seem to believe that most major technological breakthroughs have now been made and that future advances will tend to be more incremental in nature. Cost reductions will be gradual and mainly through increased productivity, while customers continually demand a better service. It is in order to tackle this problem that recent and well-publicised cost reduction plans were put forward by BA senior management, including less favourable working arrangements for cabin staff (*The Financial Times*, 18 September 1996).

The second market-related factor is geographical. The biggest economic growth area in the future is likely to be the Pacific Rim. However, BA has little presence here, having tended to concentrate activities on the other side of the world. In 1997 the company was continuing to search for an alliance with a major North Pacific Rim airline as a means of increasing its share of this market.

Ownership

The fourth most important factor affecting BA's behaviour relates to the ownership of the company. BA no longer has any government protection, although there is a ceiling on foreign ownership, as there is with most major airlines worldwide. The threat of takeover is still taken seriously, however, especially when BA is cash rich. The company has various measures to deal with this. The development of alliances with other airlines has made use of some of the cash and thus reduced the threat, and BA has made a very conscious effort to be 'shareholder-friendly', convincing owners that the management team is making optimal use of shareholder funds.

Supplier market

The supplier market is arguably the least important environmental factor affecting BA. This divides into two main areas: the aerospace market and everything else. The first is characterised by an old-fashioned attitude to customer–supplier relationships, based largely on the fact that suppliers used to enjoy a largely guaranteed market in the defence industry. The end of the cold war has shaken up the market and pushed some suppliers to increase efficiency, but most appear to be quite slow-moving. For example, whereas elsewhere suppliers are continuously improving and reducing costs, aerospace suppliers still tend to expect annual price increases. They are also protected somewhat by regulation. For example, suppliers might argue that they are prevented from making changes to products (perhaps to achieve cost reductions) by technical regulations, leaving the buyer with less power to force down the purchase price through specification changes. Nevertheless, there has been some change.

Customers are also prevented from developing closer working relationships with suppliers by US and EU anti-trust laws designed to prevent collaboration which might lead to monopoly abuse, even though the nature of the products, for example the sheer scale of expenditure on the development of aero-engines and aircraft, may favour this form of relationship. Suppliers often form consortia to develop generic specifications for new products in a form of horizontal collaboration, and the airlines will have some involvement as the final customers. Most of the aerospace suppliers are American, and include GEC, Pratt and Whitney, Boeing and Hamilton Standard. The UK company Rolls Royce is another key supplier. Products sourced from these companies include engines, avionics equipment, hydraulic units and fixtures and fittings.

In dealing with the supply of all non-aerospace goods and services, BA tends to have limited buying power because it buys a great variety of products from different sources, preventing the company from gaining leverage benefits through volume purchasing. There may also be an attitude on the part of suppliers that they are selling to a large, rich company.

Organisational structure

BA's organisational structure was broadly functional until 1990. This was followed by a period of claimed delayering and 'empowerment' during the

1990–93 period, but much of this proved to be rhetoric only and very little change seems to have taken place. In 1996, Robert Ayling, a former City of London lawyer, became chief executive and he set about restructuring the company, creating a new organisation (*The Economist*, 19 July 1997). The aim behind the restructuring was to base the company around a time-line (short, medium and long term) and to focus activities on the search for greater efficiency gains. Three divisions were created: strategic (long term), commercial (medium term) and operations (short term). At first, purchasing was part of operations as a profit development centre. It has since been moved to corporate resources, which comes under the strategic division. This is considered a change for the better by the purchasing department, because the strategic division takes a longer-term perspective.

All staff in the purchasing department work for the purchasing director. Physically, however, they work with their internal customers wherever this is possible. They form an integral part of their customer's team, but they are not normally represented on the organisational chart of that customer. There are 160 purchasing staff worldwide; this includes buyers, managers and administrative staff, but excludes stores. Concerning the profile of the department, it is safe to say that there has been considerable improvement over the last decade. However, there remains much diversity across the company: the function appears to be viewed as strategic by some management and reactive by others.

Corporate strategy

BA's strategy is to become a dominant player in every market that it chooses to operate within, to become a global player and to be seen as such. There are six key airline markets in the world: Europe–USA, USA–Asia, Asia–Europe, and within the USA, Europe and Asia. BA wants to be in all of these, but can only do so through alliances, partially because of regulation which prevents acquisitions. Nationalism is also an important factor preventing takeovers because airlines tend to have strong loyalties in their nations of origin. Takeover bids tend to arouse strong public emotions leading to local political opposition.

BA sees its key selling point as its customer service and it intends to continue to focus on this in the future. The company will also continue to focus strongly on its core assets, which have been listed by Robert Ayling as: its strong position at Heathrow in terms of the landing slots that it holds; its fleet of aircraft; its network of flying rights; and its worldwide sales force in the form of BA travel agents.

Purchasing strategy is linked closely to corporate planning. The company has a three-year business planning process as well as annual budgets and purchasing tends to focus strongly on the former. Within corporate capital planning, the outcome determines purchasing activity, for example when the company will be buying new aircraft. The fact that purchasing now forms part of the strategy division means that it is more closely involved in strategic decisions. The department has recently worked with the chief operating officer in assessing the potential for outsourcing UK ground fleet services, for example. The company's ambitious 'Business Efficiency Plan' (BEP), which aims to remove £1bn. from costs between September 1996 and September 1999 (*The Financial Times*, 18 September 1996), involves extensive assessment of the make–buy decision. The purchasing function at BA has always been proactively involved in this area, and so will be very busy over this period.

The major problem with this strategic focus, however, appears to be the fact that it relies excessively on core competence thinking, which, it has been argued, is a static and reactive view of business strategy (Cox, 1997a). This, it has been argued elsewhere, is a partial view of make–buy decision making (Lonsdale and Cox, 1998; Cox and Lonsdale, 1998). To understand the problem with BA's search for efficiency through a focus on outsourcing, the key elements of its approach are discussed below.

Outsourcing and supplier alignment at British Airways

BA has outsourced extensively since privatisation. The trend has diminished over the last four to five years, but make–buy has recently come back into focus with the announcement of its BEP. Some of the projected cost savings will be generated through the outsourcing of BA activities. It does not necessarily follow that decisions will be made on cost alone, as the company is attempting to take a holistic view within the plan. However, the reality in the past has been that, due to a lack of suitable decision-making tools, managers have tended to fall back on an assessment of market cost when deciding on outsourcing issues. In mid-1996, when the research was being undertaken, ground fleet services were under consideration for outsourcing. In this case, decisions were being made on a broad range of factors and *not* price alone, in line with the aims of the BEP. When making these decisions, the purchasing function works with the relevant departments and pushes them to make objective decisions and consider more issues than cost, using the methodologies that were put in place in the company in the 1980s.

Decisions about outsourcing and supplier relationships are based on a portfolio approach which takes account of the criticality and cost of the product or service in question, as in Figure 10.1 on page 181. Criticality refers to how critical the product or service is to BA. There are no hard and fast rules in the use of this technique, rather it is used as guidance for buyers. It is recognised that relationships change over time as they are affected by factors such as personality and the political and economic climate, meaning that formal, rigid approaches can be inappropriate. This portfolio approach is also used to categorise suppliers, in terms of how critical they are to BA and how much business they do with the company.

A second technique used by the company involves relationship assessment, although this is generally limited to the company's most important suppliers. Each buyer assesses between two and six of the most important suppliers. This is a two-way relationship, so that the supplier can also carry out an assessment

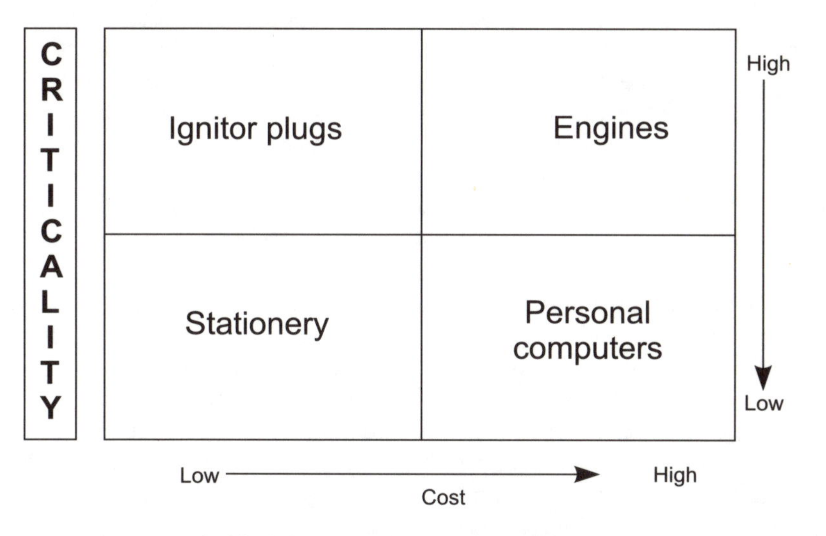

Figure 10.1 An example of a BA purchasing portfolio matrix.

of BA. These two initiatives, portfolio positioning and relationship assessment, have been introduced because the traditional methods of procurement were considered, in the words of an interviewee in purchasing, to be 'too hand to mouth, or reactive'.

1. Ignitor plugs are crucial to start the aircraft, but low in value. BA will make efforts to ensure that supplies will not dry up, for example by ensuring that the vendors are not on the verge of bankruptcy, but they will pay little more attention than this.
2. Aero-engines are clearly critical and of high value, leading BA to develop close links with suppliers. GEC, for example, supplies engines for the Boeing 777. The company also has a ten-year contract to run an engine overhaul plant on behalf of BA, located in South Wales, which BA used to own itself. GEC is therefore closely tied to its customer.
3. Stationery is low-value spend and of low criticality. The main aim here is to subcontract so that the activity takes up minimal managerial time. BA had outsourced stationery supply to the company 'Niceday' and paid them a monthly fee at the time of the research.
4. Personal computers are not crucial to BA's success, but they amount to significant spend. There are also many potential suppliers. BA treats this product as a commodity and bases strategy on driving down prices through comparing between different suppliers, not through developing long-term relationships with individual companies.

BA tends to get very close to its major suppliers, but also maintains competition among them. It does this by talking to a number of suppliers, for example Boeing and Airbus, and asking for proposals from them. This market is unusual because suppliers develop entire aircraft for their customers, requiring customers to be involved at a very early stage in the product development. BA management inform suppliers of their requirements in very broad terms, for example that they expect to be carrying a given number of passengers at a given time in the future, and ask them for proposals. A choice of supplier will be made based on an analysis of these forecast requirements, with price being just one of many criteria, and BA will work closely with the selected supplier over a number of years during the product's development and launch.

While purchasing has been responsible for the vast majority of the company's operational spend, it does not appear to have played a major role in the new BEP in relation to the outsourcing of further core operational activities. The operational areas *not* covered by the department are fuel, which is bought by the operations division, overflying and landing charges, which are paid to organisations such as the Civil Aviation Authority, hotel accommodation for flight crews and commission and discount payments to travel agents. While operational responsibility has increased considerably since privatisation, there is still an essentially reactive focus and evidence of a lack of proactive procurement competence in the function, and in the company. This creates problems at the strategic and operational level as the need to find a 'synchronised approach' to strategy and operations increases (Cox, 1998a).

In assessing supplier performance, BA has no formal list of criteria concerning selection or congruence, however it does consider a wide range of elements. These can include cost performance, quality, service performance and management commitment, and these four categories are broken down into more detailed criteria. The level of supplier assessment varies according to the product, with the more strategic suppliers subject to a more rigorous process. BA does not waste time assessing a monopoly or dominant supplier as there is little choice of source.

This thinking demonstrates the lack of a clear understanding of how procurement competence can be used as a strategic tool to achieve transformational efficiency gains. The focus on core competence thinking and the penchant for using volume of spend as a tool with which to beat suppliers underscores the relative lack of sophistication on the part of BA at the strategic and operational levels in its management of supply. A better approach might be to understand how the company can use leverage by focusing on appropriateness in supply management (Cox, 1997b).

Transformational efficiency at BA

Despite the evidence that there is a lack of clear focus on supply alignment and procurement competence at strategic and operational levels, as far as the privatisation cases in this study are concerned, BA remains a relatively focused company. Immediately prior to, and after, privatisation the company demonstrated an ability to focus on internal and external cost reduction and process improvement at the operational level. This led, initially, to a search for what are appropriately perceived as static efficiency and dynamic efficiency gains through cost-cutting and, given the low level of historic competence in the company, these were achieved rapidly and have been maintained. In the 1990s the threat of a less benign regulatory and competitive environment has forced the company to seek out further efficiency gains more akin to transformational efficiencies through the development of mergers and/or alliances and through the use of core competence thinking and outsourcing. The fact that the company has adopted a 'time-based' organisational structure to implement this approach is evidence that it (or its advisors) may not fully understand, however, the nature of a supply alignment and procurement competence approach to business management. This is discussed further in chapter 13.

11 British Steel

BRITISH STEEL

This British Steel case study provides the clearest evidence that privatisation is not always necessary for significant performance improvements to be achieved in purchasing and supply management in state-owned enterprises. British Steel improved its level of purchasing and supply functional professionalism while still in the public sector. By 1988, when the company was privatised, there was already a cost reduction focus prominent throughout the business and an attachment to core competence and outsourcing thinking as the most appropriate mechanism to achieve efficiency gains. It would appear, however, that notwithstanding the high level of dynamic and static efficiency being achieved through functional professionalism in purchasing and supply, there has been little pressure to achieve transformational efficiency through an understanding of supply alignment and procurement competence. This is clearly a function of the maturity and national concentration of the steel industry globally, which sometimes creates restricted competition in supply at the national, if not at the regional or global, levels.

Background

British Steel is the major UK producer and distributor of steel. The company was created in 1967 as a state organisation called the British Steel Corporation (BSC) after the nationalisation of a number of private sector steel producers. The Iron and Steel Act brought into public ownership about 90 per cent of Britain's steelmaking capacity. Nationalisation was considered good for British steelmaking because it allowed the reshaping of the industry from a fragmented collection of smaller-scale producers, who had suffered from perceived underinvestment for some years, into one integrated company with the potential to reap the benefits of economies of scale. The company would also benefit from public funding for investment, allowing it to modernise and catch up with other countries which had developed competitive bulk steelmaking plants. During the early 1970s the British Steel Corporation followed a major expansion and modernisation strategy aimed at developing a more compact organisation with modernised, competitive plant.

World economic conditions worked against the corporation. Dramatic increases in world energy prices in the mid-1970s, combined with sharp falls in demand for British steel, caused serious problems for BSC. With over-capacity in steel production, the corporation began the closure of plants from 1975 as it plunged into loss. Following the 'second oil price shock' in the late-1970s, losses worsened. Between 1979 and 1985 deficits totalled £2.5bn. Considerable reductions in capacity were made by 1980, but more cuts were required because the company was still uncompetitive on a price and quality basis. A corporate plan in 1980 aimed to improve costs and efficiency and achieve further headcount reduction. The objective was to 'regain a competitive position as a supplier to a world market heavily over-supplied' (British Steel, 1995).

The resulting major restructuring of the business led to a gradual but significant improvement in the company's competitive position, achieved by factors such as reduced energy consumption through conservation measures, much lower staffing levels, the negotiation of lower energy prices, plant-level wage-bargaining related to local productivity and improvements in other operations in order to increase profitability. The government imposed strict financial targets on the company in order to force efficiency improvements and in 1980 a new chairman, Ian MacGregor, was appointed, charged with introducing new commercialism into what was widely perceived to be a dying giant.

The turnaround from the early 1980s was substantial, and by 1988 the company had become one of the world's lowest cost, and profitable steel producers in Europe (Aylen, 1994; Parker and Wu, 1998). From making losses of £1bn. on £3bn. of turnover in 1980/81, the company went on to produce pre-tax profits of £733m. by 1989/90. By this time, the corporation was performing well in a highly competitive global industry. Privatisation took place via a stock exchange flotation in December 1988. Financial and economic performance since has fluctuated with the company suffering losses in 1992 and 1993 due to a world recession, reduced demand and low steel prices, before recovering. There is evidence of some relative loss of international competitiveness during the late 1980s and early 1990s (Parker and Wu, 1998).

The privatised British Steel is still by far the largest steel producer in the UK with a 58 per cent market share in 1995/96. Turnover for the same period was just over £7bn. producing record pre-tax profits of £1.1bn. The company has grown internationally since privatisation with manufacturing operations in Europe, the USA and beyond. However, its largest manufacturing base remains the UK with 70 per cent of turnover produced here in five major steelmaking sites based in England and Wales. British Steel employed around 40,000 staff in early 1996. This is in contrast to a workforce of 176,200 in 1980 and 268,500 in 1967 (British Steel, 1995). The company's main markets are construction, the automotive industry and packaging (British Steel, 1995/96).

British Steel's activities focus closely on steel processing and some distribution. It either supplies direct to the customer or to stockholding companies, although the company does much of its own stockholding. It has some stockholding in northern Europe, and a small amount in North America, but the rest is in the United Kingdom. British Steel also began steelmaking in the United States in 1996 and the company has plans to expand into the Far East and India, as these are growing markets in contrast to Europe and the USA.

In terms of British Steel's approach to purchasing and supply management, in summary purchasing changed very little on privatisation. Most change took place before the transfer of ownership, along with the transformation of the rest of the company during the early to mid-1980s. British Steel had to reduce its capacity in order to survive after the failure of its grandiose expansion plans in the early 1970s. This created incentives for the company to focus on efficiency and best practice, perhaps more so than in the electricity and water utilities, studied as part of the research and reviewed in earlier chapters. Purchasing has changed, but it has been a gradual evolution over many years and has not been attributable to privatisation, *per se*. It can be argued, however, that the changes reviewed below were part of a wider restructuring at British Steel which rendered the company fit for transfer to the private sector in 1988.

The search for static and dynamic efficiency gains

The structure of purchasing and supply management

In line with the general lack of change in the company's approach to purchasing and supply management, the structure of the purchasing function showed no change on privatisation. Structure remained somewhere between 'devolved–controlled' (controlled and co-ordinated from the centre) and 'devolved–enabled' (autonomous purchasing units with a strategic centre). The number of purchasing staff employed by the company has reduced slightly since privatisation due to increasing efficiency, but within British Steel that is not seen as being directly attributable to privatisation. By 1997 there were approximately 20 staff located at headquarters in London which dealt with strategic spend, and another 250 or so are based at the five steel-making sites scattered around the UK. This figure includes stores managers but not stores operatives.

The central purchasing group is called 'supplies and transport' (S&T) and is part of what British Steel calls its 'shared resources'. This simply means a resource at the disposal of the rest of the company. Another example of a shared resource is the company's technology centres. There are three research laboratories located at different locations around the UK, but at the disposal of the whole company. Central S&T is based at company headquarters in London, but this is fortuitous as it is not considered to be a head office function. The main reason for its location is that central S&T is responsible for buying strategic products many of which are sourced internationally and it is convenient for foreign suppliers to visit London. Other functions located at the London head office include: accounts, finance, legal, a small personnel function, the company secretary and secretariat and the company board. (This information relates to the structure at the time the main research was undertaken in 1996/97.)

Central S&T consists of the small purchasing team of twenty staff who concentrate on the following strategic goods: iron ore, coal and associated shipping (called 'inbound logistics') and energy in the form of electricity, gas and oil, which is a huge spend in any steelmaking company. Purchasing of all other goods and services takes place at the works with the purchase of some items 'networked' through a series of lead buying sites. The main businesses each have small supply teams with their own manager and they buy everything for that site, ranging from high-value contracts down to low-value items such as safety boots. In 1997 there were six purchasing teams, one at each of the major works and one at headquarters. The 'networked spend' was co-ordinated at separate lead sites and one lead site bought a certain product on behalf of the whole company, in order to maximise leverage opportunities and reduce transaction costs. So the purchase of refractories for the whole company took place in Scunthorpe, paint for the whole company in North Wales, and the purchase of scrap in Rotherham. The plan is to increase co-ordination in the future to increase leverage over suppliers where currently similar products are bought at different sites. The purchasing manager at each site has functional responsibility to the director of S&T but line responsibility to the director of the works.

Purchasing and supply professionalism

Strategy is based on a purchasing portfolio matrix similar to that found for many of the other cases studied, the two key factors being supply risk and value of spend. 'Strategic' goods are those with high supply risk and high-value, 'transaction goods' are those with low supply risk and low-value. Strategic goods account for 65 per cent of total spend and include items such as iron ore, coal and gas. Transaction goods account for just 7 per cent of spend and include proprietary stores and spare parts. British Steel was using this matrix approach to purchasing before privatisation, but it is only recently that it has been formalised. The company plans to continue to use this approach in the future, but the aim will be to focus on specific areas of the matrix and carry out drives to improve efficiency in these areas. The general opinion within the procurement function is that British Steel has reached very efficient levels in high-value strategic spend, but needs to do more work on low-value items. In the words of an interviewee, purchasing strategy is based on 'an overall drive for ever increasing efficiency and lower costs'.

Purchasing makes use of a broad range of 'tools and techniques', all as required. The company buys a large range of products, from coal to safety helmets, and selects the techniques appropriate to the product in question. There is a drive to decrease the number of suppliers and simplify the buying process, particularly for low-value items. Benchmarking is used quite extensively and the company plans to increase its use further in the future. British Steel compares itself with other steel companies on its efficiency in purchasing different products by assessing world prices and prices paid for common goods. The company wants to extend this to benchmark its operations with companies in different industries. For example, by comparing the efficiency of its road transport against companies in different industries. British Steel is confident that within the steel industry it is efficient in transporting, but does not know how well it fares against other industrial sectors. Benchmarking other sectors might reveal methods to improve efficiency that had not been previously encountered in the steel industry.

The company has increased its use of more collaborative relationships with suppliers having instigated them by approaching certain suppliers. However, the company tends not to become involved in single sourcing on the grounds that this would put the company at risk *vis-à-vis* suppliers (on the dangers of single sourcing see, for example, Parker and Hartley, 1997).

As far as vendor accreditation is concerned, British Steel uses the ISO 9000 quality system. It does set higher standards than this for a small number of critical goods and will carry out its own complex quality audit in such cases. ISO 9000 covers most suppliers, although some suppliers of low-value items are not assessed as this is not considered cost-effective. British Steel has three computerised supplier databases, all of which are controlled by purchasing. At the time of interview they were on three separate mainframes and central purchasing management were working on their consolidation and developing a management information system.

Much of what British Steel buys is internationally competitive, meaning that the company is forced to buy at the same price as its competitors, and so it cannot easily gain an advantage over them by employing a superior buying strategy. All it can do is make sure that it does not pay over the odds and fare worse than the competition, which clearly restricts the scope of its purchasing strategy. The company has made some gains from the deregulation of the UK gas and electricity markets, however, and now pays much less than some of its Continental European rivals for energy inputs.

Added to this, steel is essentially a commodity and it is difficult to differentiate the product to gain competitive advantage. The main way that British Steel attempts to differentiate itself is by offering an extremely wide range of goods of high quality. Also, since the 1980s the company has tried to reduce its reliance on bulk steelmaking (a commodity business) in favour of specialised steel products. Competition leads to a constant pressure to drive down costs as the major source of competitive advantage. British Steel focuses on both short-term costs and on gaining better value in the longer term, in terms of both purchasing and operations. A further source of cost reduction is to use fewer of the goods and services bought. British Steel is tackling this by increasing the amount of product recycled and has striven to reduce scrap levels in production.

Apart from the use of budgetary criteria, performance measurement of purchasing appears to be quite informal. The function reports monthly to the company's executive board regarding performance on high-value items. There is no other formal reporting system nor any form of customer surveys, as seen in several case studies reported in this book. However, purchasing does have a monthly meeting with its 'customers' in the works in order to review performance. The company has very tight controls on budget and headcount, both centrally and at the works level, resulting in a tight control on activity. Another measurement of the performance of purchasing is the benchmarking process described above.

Although purchasing management were unable to provide specific evidence that they had been successful in their activities, the fact that British Steel as a company is constantly driving down costs is indirect evidence. Of the company's costs, 51 per cent is on bought-in goods. British Steel now focuses on the *value in use* of a product rather than price alone and develops a strategy around this. For example, when buying refractories, the company used to pay a supplier for a quantity of a refractory. Now it often pays per tonne of steel that goes through the refractory, a form of payment by results. This means that British Steel pays as it gains value from the product. For technical products, the company states that it will always look for value for money rather than necessarily buying the cheapest item.

The role and profile of purchasing

British Steel's total annual expenditure on supplies amounted to around £2.1bn. in 1996 and managers at the centre and works level were responsible for at least 95 per cent of this spend. There has been no change in the responsibility of purchasing for company spend since privatisation. The areas not covered by purchasing tend to be either minor or specialist goods and services. These include books and periodicals for the company library, the spend of the corporate relations department on items such as advertising and insurance and banking which are controlled by the finance department. The degree of control that purchasing has over the buying process varies with the product. Normally, the user specifies the requirement (or grade if it is a raw material) and purchasing management select the supplier. This is the case for the purchase of coal: the internal user specifies the grade and it is up to purchasing to find the best deal among a number of mines worldwide that offer the particular grade in question. For iron ore, however, there may be very few suppliers of a given grade, leaving purchasing little choice in supplier selection.

The purchasing function at British Steel does not appear to suffer the lack of kudos witnessed in some companies. It is viewed as an integral part of the strategic centre of the company by senior management. This is probably due to the company's enormous expenditure on raw materials, meaning that the activities of the function have a major impact on company performance. Purchasing staff have become more professional in that they are now more highly qualified than in the 1970s and 1980s, though this has been an evolutionary process rather than an outcome of privatisation.

Outsourcing and supplier relationship management

British Steel considers that it has been at the leading edge of outsourcing for a number of years and that other companies tend to look to the company as an example of good practice. Because the company focused on its core steel production some years ago, many peripheral services have already been outsourced. British Steel made massive losses in the early 1980s and pulled itself out of trouble by concentrating on 'what it was good at' or, its 'core competencies' in steelmaking. Hence the early start in outsourcing 'non-core' activities. Such activities have been gradually outsourced.

In the past, outsourcing decisions were sometimes based on short-term cost-focused gains to help get the company out of its deep financial crisis. However, management claim that this is no longer the case and a much longer-term view is now taken when making any decisions concerning whether or not to outsource. British Steel has outsourced £350m. of activity over ten years and the IT contract alone, which was contracted during 1997, involved a similar sum. The company has considered selling off facilities management at the head office building in London, but decided against it. This is given as evidence by management that it has not been following a 'fashion' or 'fad' for outsourcing in an unquestioning manner. Two other areas were being considered as possibilities for extending outsourcing in 1997: site services, which is the process of moving material around the company's steelworks, and ships. Whereas British Steel used to own eight ships, the plan was to sell two of these and lease one bigger ship instead. These two areas are already partially contracted out.

Purchasing is heavily involved in outsourcing. Ideas can come from any source, but the central department is always involved in contracting at an early stage. The idea to contract IT, for example, came from the technical director but the supplies director became involved early in the project. When asked about the advantages and disadvantages of outsourcing, one purchasing manager considered the disadvantages to be 'very few', and saw three main advantages. First, it reduces the diversion from central management tasks; second, it allows a dedicated expert to be applied to the task; and third it brings in long-term expertise from outside the company to the advantage of British Steel.

Although outsourcing has increased at British Steel, this is not considered to be the result of privatisation. It is because the company made a decision in the 1980s to focus on its 'core competencies' and to retreat from peripheral activities. It is also because British Steel is constantly looking for opportunities to outsource as a means to reduce costs. Examples of contracted-out activities include the treatment of slag, window-cleaning and security. Whereas British Steel used to treat the slag itself, recover the iron for its own use and sell off the unwanted part, the company now pays a contractor to perform the service. All window-cleaning used to be carried out in-house. This is now outsourced by site, so that each site selects its own contractor. British Steel was in the process of outsourcing IT in 1997, and this was completed by early 1998.

The nature of supplier relationships varies with that of the product. The general trend at British Steel has been an increase in partnership-type relationships as described earlier. Relationships with raw materials suppliers are very close to ensure long-term supply. British Steel vets these suppliers for financial stability, environmental credentials and on a number of other criteria. The company tries to steer clear of using new companies as suppliers without thorough testing of the product and evaluation of the company because it is considered that a new company might pose a threat to security of supply. The view is that a newly established company is at a greater risk of going bankrupt or of other supply failures. Longer-term relationships are the norm for site services: the supplier will invest capital in equipment dedicated to British Steel and located at one of its sites and in return the latter will award them a long-term contract.

Purchasing management claims that there has been a general improvement in supplier performance over the years, although it is difficult to specify exactly which criteria have improved because such a wide range of products is sourced. British Steel has no single system to measure the performance of suppliers. The reason given for this is that the key criteria will differ for each type of supplier (for example price, delivery or quality), making any single system difficult to operate and of limited value. There are some measures in place, but they vary widely. However, in the future, the company intends to increase the measurement of key suppliers through the use of more sophisticated IT systems.

An overview of the three forms of efficiency gain at British Steel

British Steel adopted an operational focus on immediate short-term static efficiency gains from the early 1980s. This was a reaction to the massive financial losses and consequent plant closures and redundancies at that time. By privatisation, British Steel had already moved from a relatively low level of functional professional competence, through a process of initial internal cost reduction, to developing a relatively high level of functional purchasing professionalism. It is clear that privatisation was not the major catalyst of performance improvement; instead survival was the major factor that focused the company at the operational level. Despite this, the current tools and techniques used in supply management appear to be essentially professional forms of reactive purchasing. The reasons for this may be due to the continuing market dominance of the company in the UK steel industry. The structure of the industry is described below.

Industrial structure

The key external factors affecting the behaviour of the company are: first competition, then regulation, the supplier market, technology and, last, ownership.

Competition

Steelmaking is a globally competitive industry with very few barriers to competition remaining other than scale and consumer inertia. British Steel has never had a monopoly of the steel market even when under public ownership because of other and expanding world steel producers. International competition has always been intense. However, the company has benefited from a very strong position in its home market, maintaining a 58 per cent market share in 1995/96. The company's main competitors have traditionally been in Europe and the USA, though since the 1960s there has been growing competition especially from East Asia and Latin America. By 1997, British Steel was the third or fourth largest steel producer in the world but only had a 4 per cent market share. The world's biggest companies were:

1 Nippon Steel – Japan
2 Posco – Korea
3 Usinor-Sacilor – France

Thyssen of Germany is also a key player in Europe, but smaller than those listed above. France, Germany and the UK each have one dominant steel company, but this is not the case in the USA where the industry is more fragmented.

Since the 1960s, countries have been removing tariffs and other import controls, partially under the pressure of 'free trade' agreements such as GATT (General Agreement on Tariffs and Trade) and now the WTO (World Trade Organisation). The global steel industry is mainly open to competition, although there remains some regulation and government subsidisation of suppliers which restrict trade. For example, government 'anti-dumping' legislation creates some barriers especially from time to time in the USA. There are less state subsidies than in the past, when iron and steel was viewed as a nationally strategic industry and was afforded considerable protection, but there remain a few state companies that are subsidised from time to time, including those in Ireland and Italy.

Regulation

British Steel does not operate in a regulated industry in the same way as water or electricity, where the regulatory bodies Ofwat and Offer respectively can have a major impact on the behaviour of companies. The main effect of regulation in the steel industry is in relation to environmental legislation. The UK government's initiatives have included pushing the company down a route that it was already on in terms of recycling the use of scrap so as to avoid the new landfill tax. The government has asked industries to set up recycling groups which it monitors and British Steel is involved in these. This issue is particularly important to the company as it buys £200m. of scrap annually, which accounts for over 8 per cent of total bought-in goods and services.

Supplier market

There has been some increase in concentration of the supplier market as companies have grown in size, for example engineering companies have grown through acquisitions and mergers, but this has had no great effect on British Steel as a customer. Often mergers have proved beneficial because the suppliers became financially more stable. The company is aware that the market could consolidate to the extent that the suppliers become stronger and raise prices, but believes that this is not an immediate threat.

Technology

Technological developments are affecting the industry because new processes are allowing smaller-scale production of steel. This lowers entry barriers and allows more potential competitors, as seen, for example, in the 'mini-mill' developments in the USA. Technological change threatens to remove a traditional form of protection in the steel industry in the form of barriers to entry caused by economies of scale.

More generally, technology does affect the industry; but it is less important than in relatively new industries such as computing, where one technological advance might have the power to reshape the market. The steel industry is very mature, meaning that the major technological breakthroughs are likely to have already been made and any new developments are likely to be incremental. This means that steel companies need to keep abreast of technology rather than fighting to be 'at the leading edge'. Also, the industry is very open in terms of information and technological developments are well publicised. The benefits of technological change are therefore generally shared rather than monopolised by one producer.

Ownership

British Steel's shares are traded in the stock market and, therefore, a takeover threat exists, but it has proved less intense than for many of the privatised utilities, especially in the electricity sector. Many of the utilities were cash rich and relatively inefficient when privatised and maintained for a time some form of monopoly. This made them highly attractive to potential predators because there were clearly profits to be 'squeezed out' of the companies. British Steel, by contrast, is judged to be a relatively efficient company, in a competitive market. There is less scope for improving operations and increasing profits. In any case, takeovers are infrequent among the world's big steelmakers, partly because they are so big.

British Steel was protected for a five-year period following privatisation by a government 'golden share' in the company. The 'golden share' was removed in 1993.

Corporate strategy

Strategy since the early 1980s has been to focus on British Steel's core competence in steelmaking. This is in contrast to many of the company's major competitors who have diversified in order to reduce dependence on steel. The company has also integrated forward into steel distribution in order to secure market share, for example through the acquisition of a large UK stockholding company called Walkers, and through the establishment of its own distributors. The company has also focused strongly on continual cost reduction. This is not surprising given the competitive environment and the high level of production capacity in the global steel industry.

Another part of corporate strategy has been international expansion. British Steel has recently increased its shareholding in a Swedish company, Arvesta (to 51 per cent), and increased its presence in the North American market. It is now looking to move into the Far East and India, where the market for steel products is growing.

Purchasing strategy has been closely aligned to corporate strategy. For example, in anticipation of British Steel expanding into the Far East, the company sent a purchasing manager to the region to locate potential suppliers and begin to establish relationships with them.

Transformational efficiency at British Steel

It is clear from the British Steel case that the company may have great difficulty in achieving transformational efficiency gains in the future. The major reason for this is the maturity of the industry with existing technology already well understood by most major competitors and the relative dominance of the UK marketplace by the company. Although the company experiences real competitive pressures, the fact that there are substantial scale and logistical economies in its favour militates against the full rigours of a perfectly competitive market. This provides British Steel with a double-edged sword. On the one hand, the need after 1981 to survive a disastrous corporate performance in the public sector ensured that rapid improvements in operational efficiency, based on static and dynamic efficiency, had to be achieved. In this sense, the development of a relatively high level of functional professionalism in purchasing and supply management was to be expected. This clearly occurred before privatisation in 1988.

On the other hand, from 1988, it is evident that the double-edged nature of British Steel's position has come into play. Being the dominant player in the UK market, and having, as a result, a high volume of spend, the approach to efficiency improvement has relied heavily on a reactive (if a highly professional) approach to supply management.

12 The Post Office

THE POST OFFICE

The Post Office case demonstrates that organisations that do not have the same competitive or shareholder pressures that arise in the private sector can still achieve significant improvements in static and dynamic efficiency gains while in the public sector. This is due to the surrogate competitive pressure imposed by the threat of privatisation, the competitive pressures operating in parcel deliveries, and due to a tightening of the financial framework within which The Post Office operates. As a result, this organisation has demonstrated a willingness to embrace efficiency gains throughout the 1980s. Since 1993, however, the recruitment of a head of purchasing from the private sector has stimulated an increasing level of functional professionalism in purchasing and improved what has been termed in this study, dynamic efficiency (see Chapter 1, page 2). Interestingly, despite being in the public sector, The Post Office has demonstrated an understanding of transformational efficiency by the ability to recognise the value of its site-specific assets in the 1990s.

Background

The Post Office is a public sector corporation whose activities are divided into four main areas. These have been structured into four businesses and comprise the following: Royal Mail, which is responsible for the delivery of mail and packages within the UK and overseas; Parcelforce, which delivers time-critical parcels nationally and internationally; Post Office Counters Ltd, which is the network of almost 20,000 post offices throughout the UK, comprising Europe's largest retail chain; and Subscription Services Ltd, responsible for administering television licences and certain other sales operations. While Post Office Counters has traditionally dealt with state-related transactions such as benefits and pension payments, it has recently branched out into new areas such as travel insurance and foreign currency.

The Post Office was moved from control by a government department and established as a public corporation in 1969. At this time, its staff ceased to be civil servants and instead assumed the role of employees of a state corporation.

Privatisation of The Post Office has appeared on the political agenda a number of times in recent years, particularly during the last Conservative term of office (Parker, 1995), but with the recent election of a Labour government this prospect has receded. Two key issues have prevented the organisation from transfer to the private sector. These are the uniform national service obligation and uniform national pricing. The Post Office is legally obliged to provide a uniform service to all areas of the UK, irrespective of whether it is cost-effective to do so. So for example, Royal Mail is required to deliver mail nationally and Parcelforce has the same obligation for parcels. If these organisations were privatised and these obligations removed, they might well choose not to offer delivery services to those areas where transportation costs are especially high, such as rural areas or the Highlands and Islands of Scotland. The 'Counters Issue' is an illustration of this problem. This refers to the fact that, in rural areas particularly, the 'local' Post Office might be the only shop serving the community, but remains because of the obligation to provide a uniform national service. If the organisation were privatised, the local Post Office might face closure, as a commercial focus might begin to override the public service ethos currently in place. This objection was particularly powerful during the years of Conservative rule because many Conservative MPs represented rural constituencies.

The second issue of uniform national pricing also impacts on rural areas. While the Royal Mail charges the same price for a letter to travel across London as it does to travel from John O'Groats to Land's End, when the latter clearly costs more to transport, this would not be the case necessarily if the company were privatised and competition was introduced. It is probable that other companies would enter the market and charge prices that reflect costs more accurately, differentiating between lower- and higher-cost delivery locations and undermining current cross-subsidisation. In general, this would mean that rural areas would suffer because of the greater delivery costs involved per letter. Another possible reason for The Post Office remaining in the public sector is that it generates cash flow to the Treasury, resting largely on the Royal Mail's statutory monopoly in letter delivery costing less than £1.

In 1995/96 the turnover of The Post Office was £6.2bn. and pre-tax profits were £422m. The corporation employed 190,000 people (The Post Office, 1996). Being a public sector organisation, its targets are set by the government. There are three annual financial targets which the government sets – the external financing limit (EFL), return on capital employed (ROCE) and real unit cost reduction (RUC). The last two are internal financial measures relating to profitability and efficiency. The EFL determines the extent to which a public sector organisation can borrow to fund revenue losses and capital projects and is set by the Treasury each year, as part of its exercise in controlling the public sector borrowing requirement. The EFL for The Post Office has been negative in recent years, meaning that the organisation must make a net payment to the Treasury.

During the early 1990s, a number of factors combined to push The Post Office towards restructuring. These included the effect of increasing demands from the government in the form of the EFL. This factor led The Post Office to review its operations in order to become more commercial and efficient. The fact that its key European competitors were also becoming more commercialised was an added impetus for change. The Dutch and German post offices have been particularly active in developing a more commercial approach to their business. The privatised Dutch post office has bought the parcel delivery company TNT, and the public sector German post office has bought a share in DHL, another parcel deliverer. The Dutch post office was floated on the Amsterdam Stock Exchange in 1994 and has become a major player in 'remailing' (the bulk shipment of mail to a foreign postal administration). Remailing activities are a way of circumventing regulations which favour national post offices, as in the UK.

As far as purchasing is concerned, these external factors have resulted in some major changes. However, it was back in 1982 when the most significant change in purchasing took place. As a result of the pending privatisation of British Telecom, which had previously been a part of The Post Office, the latter created its own purchasing function for the first time. Once this function had been established, the rest of the 1980s saw considerable change as management strove to develop and improve the function so that it served the rest of The Post Office more effectively. Another major change in purchasing occurred in 1993 with the appointment of a new head of purchasing and logistics services (P&LS). The appointment was made from the private sector, which was in line with The Post Office's belief in learning from outside, both by appointing senior management from private industry and by studying best practice and adopting it within the Post Office.

Evidence of static and dynamic efficiency gains

The structure of purchasing and supply management

The structure of purchasing and supply at The Post Office has not changed significantly since the inception of the function in 1982, the only change being a slight decentralisation of activities. In 1982, the newly created purchasing function was highly centralised. By the late 1980s, as the activities of the department grew, management realised that more resource was needed at regional level for divisional requirements and so some decentralisation occurred. This structure has been maintained since, with no notable structural change in 1993 with the arrival of the new head of P&LS.

After 1993, the company began to gather more information on spend enabling more informed decision making. Decisions were made centrally regarding exactly where in the organisation goods should be bought and stored. For example, strategic products such as freight services, space on trains or aircraft, were bought centrally; and low-value spend such as stationery was devolved. Stationery used to be bought and stocked centrally with added warehousing costs. This was devolved and purchasing cards are being used to buy stationery. Purchasing cards were introduced by financial companies and are now used by an increasing number of organisations as a cost-effective way of dealing with low-value spend. The Post Office uses Amex and Visa purchasing cards and the system works as follows. A number of nominated cardholders are appointed in the company. These staff are authorised to use their cards for expenditure on items up to a limit (at The Post Office it was £500 in early 1998). A monthly invoice is then sent by the card operator to The Post Office and the balance is cleared each month. The main benefit of using cards is the reduction in transaction costs, as separate purchase orders and invoices are avoided.

The proportion of total Post Office expenditure dealt with centrally has not changed radically in recent years. Of bought-in spend, 50 per cent was controlled centrally in 1997, up from 30 per cent three years previously. This is partly because The Post Office saw that other companies held more control of spend at the centre and so adopted this policy, and partly for EU compliance reasons, explained below. In 1997 central purchasing controlled the entire buying process for strategic goods, whereas local buying teams acted largely autonomously for the lower-value spend. Each of the businesses had its own head of purchasing located at its own separate head office. Central P&LS worked closely with the local heads of purchasing.

Purchasing and supply professionalism

The new head of purchasing made three main changes on his arrival, introducing a new purchasing strategy based on the concept of product group teams (PGTs), a new vendor appraisal system entitled the 'First-Class Supplier Programme', and a supply chain review programme. These are now explained in more detail.

Cross-functional product group teams

The aim of this new strategy was to aggregate spend across the The Post Office in order to gain better control and unearth opportunities for leveraged spend. The Post Office had previously tended to operate in functional and business silos, resulting in such opportunities being missed. The new PGTs were based on a commodity approach to purchasing with each team focused on a distinct group of products or services. The teams themselves comprised both purchasing staff and senior individuals from elsewhere in the organisation, generally from areas that used the products or services in question. This was intended to give the 'internal customer' a forum for representation.

In 1996 there were nine teams in total, based around the nine product groups: professional services; buildings; freight services; automation; uniforms; vehicles; IT services; facilities services; and print and value items (including stamps). (The number of PGTs had been reduced to five by January 1998.) For freight purchasing, for example, the relevant team identified opportunities where Royal Mail and Parcelforce could negotiate a joint contract with British Airways in order to get a better deal. Representatives from these two businesses and from purchasing formed part of the project team to find innovative solutions and implement them.

'First-Class Supplier Programme'

The Post Office already employed a supplier accreditation programme, but the new head of purchasing made a deliberate effort to give it a higher profile through the introduction of the 'First-Class Supplier Programme'. He did this by persuading the chief executive to support an annual prize-giving ceremony for suppliers at a prestigious location, such as Olympia, with the chairman presenting the prizes to the winners. More generally, the aim of this programme was to accredit every supplier to The Post Office and to reduce the supplier base to a maximum of 1,000 key producers. By 1996, however, the organisation still had a list of 30,000 suppliers on its purchase ledger.

Supply chain review programme

As its name suggests, this programme was set up to study the entire Post Office supply chain, including both primary and secondary supply chains. This project was known as the 'Supply Chain Diagnostic' within the organisation, and consultants were appointed specifically to develop the programme. One of the streams in the supply chain review programme concentrated on developing an integrated cross-company supplier database, so that better information could be gathered about total Post Office spend. The Post Office had computerised supplier databases beforehand, but the effectiveness was reduced because each business had its own system, and even separate geographical regions of the same business had different systems.

The main drivers behind the project to install a computerised database were increased commercial leverage and the need for EU compliance, an issue which came very much to the fore in the mid-1990s. Under EU procurement directives, if company spend is over a certain limit on given goods or services, the contracts must be advertised in the *European Journal* publication. The Post Office was concerned that it might be breaking these rules simply because it had inadequate information systems internally to monitor procurement.

In addition to these three major changes, purchasing at The Post Office has adopted a number of tools and techniques to support purchasing strategy, for example purchasing portfolio analysis and benchmarking. The Post Office has been involved in benchmarking exercises with Michigan State University in the United States. Visits have also been made to other companies with the aim of transplanting best practice in purchasing to The Post Office.

Examples of companies visited are Whitbread, SmithKline Beecham, Rover and Nissan.

Alongside the new strategy, a new 'vision' was coined by the executive team in 1994, namely 'To be recognised as a worldclass benchmark for Purchasing & Logistics Services'. The corresponding mission statement included the following objectives:

- Focusing totally on the customer with the aim to be the preferred supplier to all our customers.
- Developing first-class suppliers.
- Ensuring there is a clear understanding of goals and each individual's contribution.
- Being forward looking and innovative.
- Having open and honest communication at all levels.
- Encouraging cross-business, cross-functional team working.
- Ensuring value for money through efficient and effective working.
- Encouraging continuous improvement with in-process measurements as a key stimulator of improvement activity.
- Ensuring that all managers adopt the leadership charter principles and act as the key drivers to achieve the vision.
- Creating a work environment which recognises the commitment of all employees to customer satisfaction.

The role and profile of purchasing

The annual spend on bought-in-goods of The Post Office was approximately £1.5bn. in the mid-1990s. Of this, £800m. to £900m. was considered to be 'controlled', a figure which was much lower before the changes described above were introduced. 'Controlled' means that the organisation now has systems in place to gather data on spend and exactly where it takes place. These have been introduced in the last few years. Generally, the purchasing department appears to be increasing its control over company spend, taking on non-traditional areas, for example, such as hotels, travel and consultancy. Purchasing is now 'getting a greater understanding of what can be achieved', in the words of one purchasing manager. In other words, having begun to gather more information on and control over spend, the corporation is beginning to realise the benefits to be gained from a more proactive procurement strategy.

Total Post Office sales are £6bn., meaning that the cost of bought-in goods accounts for approximately 25 per cent (at £1.5bn.). This is a relatively low proportion when compared to the average manufacturing company, and is explained by the very high ratio of staff costs to total costs in The Post Office generally. P&LS was responsible for all external spend at policy level, but not at the practical level. Of the £1.5bn., about £0.3bn. involves the purchase of buildings and is controlled elsewhere. This leaves £1.2bn. of spend, of which about half is bought centrally by P&LS, and half is spent within the businesses.

In 1996 the main groups of products bought centrally by The Post Office were the following:

- Professional services
- Buildings
- Freight services
- Automation
- Uniforms
- Vehicles
- IT services
- Facilities services
- Print
- Value stock (including stamps)

If an increasing control of total expenditure by the purchasing function equates to an improved internal profile, it is safe to assume that there has been some improvement in internal profile at The Post Office. The other indicator of internal profile, the position of the most senior purchasing manager, lends some support to this view. The newly appointed head of purchasing was entitled 'director and general manager of purchasing and logistics services'. Although there was no change in the reporting line, the title of the position changed from 'director of purchasing'. The new title implied a status equivalent to the director and general manager of a Royal Mail division (there are nine of these divisions in total), which is perceived within The Post Office as a higher level than the position of 'director of purchasing'.

Outsourcing and supplier relationship management

It appears that the continuation of a high level of vertical integration and the rejection by government of privatisation have tended to restrict the development of a clear strategy favouring outsourcing. There is a thriving internal market between the separate business units of The Post Office, and in 1996 the corporation still had its own catering and engineering operations, often the first victims of outsourcing. However, The Post Office sold 49 per cent of its catering operations to Granada in April 1998. It also owned its own transport fleet with 28,000 vehicles. It used to own over 320 workshops for the vehicles, a figure recently reduced to something over 200. The Post Office also maintained its own fuel tanks in the big workshops, where fuel was bought competitively in large tanker loads. It also continued to operate its own warehousing operation, which was run by Parcelforce on behalf of the rest of the organisation.

The Post Office has not needed to seek government permission to outsource, partly because this aligns with the previous government's aims to transfer public sector activities to the private sector. However, by 1996 the only major example of a decision to outsource was the joint venture being set up to manage the IT system with a private sector company. In the past, all IT management was carried out in-house. The Post Office will now own 49 per cent of the new venture. The driver behind the project was a major review of IT throughout the organisation. Another area under consideration for outsourcing was motor transport, although no decision had yet been made.

The Post Office is slowly moving away from vertical integration, but it should be stressed that the trend is much more gradual than in many private sector companies. Legal constraints on its activities have a major part to play here. Also, the need for government endorsement of management strategy inevitably slows down strategy implementation. Moreover, the organisation is not under the same competitive pressures as many private sector companies to drive down costs. This enables The Post Office to take longer to arrive at radical decisions, such as those concerning make–buy. The Post Office management has taken the less radical option of cutting the cost of performing the activity itself.

An overview of the three forms of efficiency gain at The Post Office

The Post Office case demonstrates that, while public ownership can militate against the development of static and dynamic efficiency, it need not do so. Furthermore, with the correct surrogate measures to encourage efficiency thinking it may be possible for public bodies to achieve significant improvements in such efficiency. Despite these embryonic developments it is clear that the role of competent managers is also crucially important. The introduction of proactive managers from the private sector was clearly important in the understanding of the leverage opportunities that existed to deliver new products and services to existing customers through The Post Office's existing site-specific assets. Furthermore, the introduction of a competent purchasing professional in 1993 significantly improved dynamic efficiency through the development of a more professional purchasing function. Despite this, it can be argued that the current level of awareness of supply alignment and procurement competence is still low at The Post Office.

Industrial structure

The following external factors affect the behaviour and performance of The Post Office: regulation (specifically EU directives); competition; the market (via internationalisation); the supplier market and ownership. This last factor, however, is volatile and could become extremely important if the government took a decision to promote privatisation or to become more involved in the management of The Post Office.

Regulation

The regulatory environment has an important impact on The Post Office because of EU regulations. As explained earlier, these have provided incentives for the organisation to install uniform IT systems across the group, to enable collection of information on aggregate spend so as to comply with tender rules. In this sense, regulation has made The Post Office adopt a more sophisticated approach to the management of purchasing, assuming that the information gathered has been used as a basis for improved decision making. The same EU regulations have also hindered the development of partnership-type supplier relationships.

The other key influence is government involvement. In particular, the government agrees to the pricing of stamps, a major source of income with the Royal Mail and by far the largest part of The Post Office, and the government sets the corporation's external financing limit which determines, among other things, capital spend. As explained earlier, external financing limits have been negative in recent years, requiring The Post Office to make net payments to the Treasury. The payments have also been increasing, putting greater demands on the finances of The Post Office. The main effect on the corporation has been cuts in investment programmes. For example, proposed projects to improve technology and develop the product portfolio have had to be curtailed.

Competition

The second external factor, competition, has grown in most areas of The Post Office's activities, in the form of private sector parcel carriers such as TNT and Federal Express, guaranteed (premium) mail delivery services, retail chains, 'remailing' and banks offering rival services to those of Post Office Counters. The Royal Mail has, however, maintained its monopoly of letter delivery priced below £1.

Market

The third factor, the market, is changing in that international opportunities are increasing as the global market for mail and parcel services is liberalised. Within Europe, the EU Commission is pressing for more competition and in some countries (e.g. Holland) post offices have been privatised. This is seen by Post Office management as a threat to the domestic market, in particular through bulk remailing services. Moreover, technological developments including faxes, telecommunications, video conferencing and the Internet pose a longer-term threat to communications through the postal system.

Supplier market

The fourth most important external factor is the supplier market. It is impossible to make a single statement regarding overall trends in The Post Office's supplier market, simply because so many products are bought. A key influence, however, is technology. Increasing volumes of mail and international developments have provided incentives for the corporation to work closely with some suppliers in the development of new equipment. For example, The Post Office has been working with international suppliers to develop integrated mail processors. This pressure has become more intense in recent years as national borders have begun to fall and international competition in mail and parcel delivery services has intensified.

Ownership

The influence of ownership is at present arguably the least important external factor. While senior management appears to have no expectation that the organisation will be privatised in the near future, it does want the government to allow The Post Office to be run as a commercial organisation. This means that The Post Office would have the freedom to enter joint ventures, for example.

From the evidence presented above, it appears that external pressure on The Post Office is possibly less intense than in many privatised companies. It is not subject to headcount reduction pressures from the City, for example, although there are government targets set for real unit cost reduction and return on capital employed. It is perhaps a reflection of this difference in external pressure that the organisation has been able to maintain a policy of no compulsory redundancies, meaning that any reduction in staff has been by natural wastage. At the same time, 'no redundancy' programmes make sense where they form part of an agreed policy of downsizing with the trade unions and sufficient voluntary leavers can be found. No or limited compulsory redundancy programmes have also operated in a number of privatised companies which have achieved large reductions in numbers employed, such as BT and British Gas and some of the other utilities.

Organisational structure

The Post Office moved towards separate businesses (Royal Mail, Parcelforce, Post Office Counters and Subscription Services) from the 1980s. This created free-standing units, so that the profit- and loss-making areas could be identified. Company structure was still based on the four businesses in 1996, but a matrix structure had been introduced. The central purchasing function, based at Swindon and London, was renamed purchasing and logistics services (P&LS) in 1993. This was subsequently reorganised in October 1996 and divided into three separate elements:

1 Purchasing services: this formed part of Royal Mail, but served the whole organisation. This included the purchasing director plus seven commercial managers who each supported a product group team. There was also a separate team focused on business excellence.

2 Logistics: this became part of Parcelforce, but it still supplied the Royal Mail and Post Office Counters Ltd through the internal market.
3 Secure stock: this was moved to Post Office Counters Ltd (concerned with post office counter services), but again it served the whole organisation.

Focusing on purchasing services, in 1996 there were about 90 staff working at the central offices in Swindon. Of this number, about 75 were buyers at different levels; 5 worked in the business excellence department which was small; and 10 worked in contract administration, dealing with compliance issues across the group. There were another 20 staff working on the supply chain development programme, mentioned earlier. Apart from the central operations, the Royal Mail was divided into 9 regions and Post Office Counters comprised of 7. In both businesses, each separate region had one purchasing and materials manager, who tended to have a small team of one or two staff. In all, there were about 200 full-time staff working in purchasing at The Post Office.

Corporate strategy

In 1996 The Post Office had three stated key strategic objectives: international expansion, the achievement of competitive costs and competitiveness through people.

International expansion

Growing internationalism in this industry is seen as both a threat and an opportunity for The Post Office, and the organisation is moving in order to make the most of market opportunities abroad, aiming at the US market among others. It has targeted large US companies that send a lot of mail to the UK. The Post Office offers to collect their mail from them and deliver it in bulk to the UK, where it uses its own distribution network. There are no restrictions on the delivery of international mail, unlike within the domestic market where The Post Office maintains its monopoly on most letter deliveries. The Post Office is also setting up alliances with private sector postal companies in Europe. Again it has targeted 'large mailers', but this time to collect their mail within the UK and send it direct to a partner postal organisation with an established distribution network in its own country. The partner postal organisation does the same in reverse.

The strategy of growth by internationalisation concerns Royal Mail primarily, although Parcelforce has also been expanding its international business. Parcelforce built a national and international hub at Coventry Airport in 1997 to further its strategy of developing its international business. The activities of Post Office Counters are limited to the UK.

Competitive costs

In line with the corporate objective of achieving competitive costs, purchasing has adopted new approaches to cost reduction, the aim being to move beyond 'supplier bashing' (short-term, price-based relationships with suppliers) in the realisation that there are more effective and longer-term methods of cost control. Two examples of the changing approach are 'challenging functionality' and business travel, as illustrated below.

- Challenging functionality: an example of the implementation of this approach is 'day one involvement'. This means that purchasing staff work cross-functionally with technical and operating units to find innovative solutions to existing problems, and to develop new products and services for the marketplace.
- Business travel: this project involved £25m. of annual spend. In the past, the purchase of business travel had been fragmented and ad hoc. There had been 'best buy' recommendations from agents and suppliers, but these had not been strictly adhered to. Under reorganisation, the entire spend is to be placed with one managing agent. The expectation is much better terms through leveraged spend and more professional buying.

Competitiveness through people

Salaries and related social insurance and pension costs account for around 70 per cent of Post Office costs. The Post Office is a highly labour-intensive organisation. One consequence is that it sees itself as very much a 'people business'. Another consequence is that purchasing services pays considerable attention to supply items related to employees, such as uniforms and bicycles, because of the importance of 'people satisfaction' to the organisation.

Other corporate objectives

The Post Office finds it difficult to grow by acquisition because its activities are constrained by government regulation and political opposition to increasing state encroachment on the private sector. However, there is a strategy of new-product development, particularly in Post Office Counters. Counters has recently begun to sell holiday insurance, life assurance and theatre tickets, and has set up as a network of bureaux de change. These new ventures had to be cleared with the government before they were introduced.

Transformational efficiency at The Post Office

The Post Office offers some evidence of a search for, what were termed in the introduction to this book (see Chapter 1, pp. 3–4) transformational efficiency improvements in its strategic and operational activities. This has been seen in the way in which it has actively begun to market a range of products and services through the Post Office Counters business, and also to seek out US companies for proactive mail service delivery. Despite this, there are a number of constraints which tend to force the company to focus more on static and dynamic efficiency gains. The Post Office operates in a regulated and relatively monopolistic business environment, especially for letter delivery, if less so for parcels and Post Office counter services. Given this environment, the effective pressure for continuous innovation to delight and keep customers comes mainly from three forces. These are the threat of privatisation, the willingness of the government to reduce subsidies or impose more demanding financial operating targets, and the willingness of personnel within the business to innovate. It is the latter which achieves transformational, rather than simply static and dynamic efficiencies.

Despite the recent improvement in functional professionalisation, there is still considerable evidence of a lack of a proper understanding of how supply alignment and procurement competence thinking can assist innovation in The Post Office. Yet the development of an awareness of some of the customer leverage opportunities through Post Office Counters Ltd is evidence that even public sector organisations can develop this type of thinking.

Part IV

Future options for supply alignment and procurement competence in privatised companies

13 Beyond purchasing professionalism

On business strategy, supply alignment and procurement competence

In this final chapter, a number of conclusions are presented about the capacity of the privatised and public sector organisations analysed to achieve static efficiency, dynamic efficiency and transformational efficiency gains from a focus on effective supply management. This is linked to the three-phase learning process methodology that was outlined in Chapter 1, pp. 2–4. This three-phase learning process was seen to involve an initial operational focus on cost reduction (phase 1), followed by the professionalisation of the purchasing and supply management function (phase 2), culminating in supply alignment and procurement competence (phase 3). While the methodology for the research reported in this book did not assume that there was any inevitability about whether or not privatised companies would adopt all, or any, of these phases, it was directed towards understanding whether or not they did do so, and what difficulties they experienced in trying to move from one phase to another. In essence, the operating assumption behind the research was that privatised companies would find it relatively easier to achieve static and dynamic efficiency (phases 1 and 2) than transformational efficiency gains (phase 3).

The initial research assumption underpinning this study has been more than adequately supported by the evidence presented here. This final chapter summarises these findings, and indicates that the majority of privatised companies (as well as most of the public companies adopted as a small control group for the study) have clearly recognised the need to achieve static and dynamic efficiency gains. The evidence for this conclusion is presented in three sections below. In the first of these sections, the four primary hypotheses related to static and dynamic efficiency gains, through a focus on cost reduction (phase 1) and the development of a more professional functional approach to purchasing and supply management (phase 2), are reiterated. In the second section, the general findings related to these four hypotheses that were supported by the questionnaire survey of twenty-eight privatised companies (Chapter 4), are outlined. In the third section, some general conclusions about the scope for, and scale of, professional improvements in purchasing and supply functional activity in eight of the privatised, and in two of the public sector, organisations in the study are presented. These ten organisations formed our initial case studies (Chapters 5 to 7).

Having discussed the scale of, and scope for, the achievement of static and dynamic efficiency gains, in a fourth section the capacity of newly privatised companies (and those public bodies remaining in the public sector) to obtain transformational efficiency gains is discussed. This is achieved by summarising the degree to which our five chosen in-depth case study organisations (Chapters 8 to 12) have moved beyond purchasing and supply functional professionalism to supply alignment and procurement competence (phase 3). In a final section, because there is evidence that few of the privatised companies have fully recognised the potential strategic and operational benefits of adopting a properly supply aligned and procurement competence approach, some clues as to how this might be developed are provided.

Four hypotheses about static and dynamic efficiency in purchasing and supply management

The research undertaken as part of this study was predicated on four key hypotheses. Each of these hypotheses was informed by a theoretical recognition that privatisation ought to lead to an immediate search for static and then, more gradually, dynamic efficiency in former publicly owned companies (Chapter 2). This implied that a two-stage learning process would occur. In the first stage, there would be a search for immediate cost reduction, especially related to internal operations through headcount reductions (phase 1). In a second stage, a more professional approach to the existing purchasing and supply management function would occur in well-managed companies involving new products and processes (phase 2). These two stages can be defined hypothetically as follows:

1. The purchasing and supply function will come under immediate pressure to reduce internal operating costs (phase 1).
2. A more professional approach to purchasing and supply will develop at the functional level (phase 2).
3. There will be a change in the role and profile of purchasing and supply management (phase 2).
4. There will be pressure to reduce the costs of internal and external spend (phase 2).

These four hypotheses, which test for immediate static and dynamic efficiency gains, were analysed through a questionnaire survey of twenty-eight recently privatised companies, with subsequent interview follow-up in twelve of the participating companies and three public bodies to obtain greater detail about the scope for, and scale of, this more professional approach to the purchasing and supply function. This was also undertaken in order to understand why implementation may or may not be more or less difficult in particular public and private organisations. The general survey findings are summarised below, while the more specific findings from the case studies are presented in a subsequent section.

The survey findings in general

The results from the survey questionnaire demonstrated that the majority of the privatised companies in the survey were aggressively pursuing static and dynamic efficiency gains based around the four hypotheses above, but not necessarily always in the same way or using the same tools and techniques. Taking each of the four hypotheses in turn, the following general conclusions can be made.

Internal functional cost pressures (phase 1)

While there is no doubt that the majority of the respondents have experienced significant changes in the structure of the purchasing and supply function, there is no communality in what has been done. For example, 43 per cent of respondents have experienced moves to centralisation, with an equal number (43 per cent) decentralising. Interestingly enough, 14 per cent of respondents had experienced no organisational change at all. Despite this, well over half of all respondents reported that there had been a considerable reduction in the number of personnel in the purchasing function. Furthermore, although the timing varied, this was one of the first changes undertaken when the company eventually decided to develop a focus on supply issues. The primary reason given for this trend was the pressure from within the company to reduce costs through a reduction in headcount and an improvement in the purchasing function's productivity. This indicates that, as expected, a majority of the privatised companies studied have focused initially on internal cost reduction as the most effective way to achieve static efficiency gains after privatisation.

Professional purchasing functionalism (phase 2)

The survey results demonstrate that, after the initial focus on internal cost reduction, there is normally a considerable increase in the development of a more professional focus within the purchasing functions of privatised companies. This conclusion is based, for instance, on the finding that only 7 per cent of respondents used purchasing mission statements prior to privatisation, whereas 71 per cent were using them afterwards. Similarly, while only 21 per cent of respondents had a formal strategy for purchasing before privatisation, 93 per cent had one post-privatisation. A significant majority of respondents also indicated that they had moved from the use of fairly simple and reactive purchasing tools and techniques to the adoption of more proactive methodologies, such as purchasing portfolio analysis, supplier alliances and partnership and network sourcing. These are all indicators of a more professional approach to the management of existing products, services and supply market offerings. This way of thinking, while still essentially reactive, is, however, clearly commensurate with a more effective approach to static and dynamic efficiency gains.

Improvements in the role and profile of purchasing and supply (phase 2)

As privatisation is established, there is considerable evidence of a significant improvement in the internal role and profile of purchasing as a function, although this is clearly not true for all of the companies studied. This is indicated by the fact that 89 per cent of respondents from within purchasing claimed a significant change in their role from a purely administrative to a more commercially focused one after privatisation had occurred. In part, this enhanced profile was due to the fact that in around a half of the companies studied, a new managing director and/or a new purchasing director/manager had been brought in, with a very different view of the strategic importance of purchasing to the business. This improved position for purchasing in the organisational hierarchy is further indicated by the fact that of the companies studied, over half reported an improvement in the hierarchical position of the head of purchasing. Furthermore, there is considerable evidence of an increase in the control of the purchasing function over the totality of external spend within the privatised companies studied. Among respondents, 68 per cent indicated that purchasing managers had improved their control over total spend including traditional inputs, as well as non-traditional general expenditure, in their companies. This is further evidence of a desire to achieve a more professional approach to purchasing, again consistent with the attainment of dynamic efficiency gains.

Cost reduction and make–buy pressures (phase 2)

A further factor that can have a considerable potential impact on the functional importance of the purchasing in a company, is the shift from in-house production to external supply (outsourcing). In 82 per cent of the companies studied, there was an increase in outsourcing activity after privatisation. Furthermore, 64 per cent of respondents claimed that they were now involved proactively in these types of decisions. This still means that 36 per cent of purchasing departments are only reactively involved in this key purchasing and supply decision-making process – so there is still a considerable way to go for some purchasing functions. Despite this, in the key area of external resource management for existing supply relationships, there is clear evidence that the majority of purchasing departments have adopted a far more professional approach to performance measurement. This is indicated by the fact that 64 per cent of respondents reported significant improvements in cost competitiveness from their suppliers. This was explained as due to a shift from the historic attachment to price as the basis of supplier selection and assessment to an increasing attachment to cost, quality and innovation criteria. This desire to develop a more professional approach to supplier performance measurement was paralleled internally, with 68 per cent of respondents reporting a significant change and improvement in the techniques used to measure the purchasing function's own cost management performance.

General conclusions

While it would be a mistake to conclude from all of this that every one of the companies privatised in the UK in the last decade has experienced a considerable improvement in the way in which the purchasing and supply function is managed, there is at least some evidence of significant change. In well over 50 per cent of the respondent companies there would appear to have been a significant improvement in static and dynamic efficiency, as defined for this study, as a result of a transformation in the functional importance of purchasing and supply. This change, when it has occurred, appears to have resulted in significant changes in the purchasing and supply role across the board in the four areas theoretically hypothesised at the beginning of the study.

Despite this generally encouraging finding, a word of caution is in order. There is considerable evidence that the purchasing function is still regarded very much as a reactive, administrative and expediting function in many of the privatised companies studied. Only in some companies is there evidence that the purchasing function is being taken more seriously at a strategic level in the business. Why should this be so? And, is it a cause for concern for the effective management of companies in the private sector?

Since these questions cannot be answered by reference only to survey data, it was recognised at an early stage in our research that it would be important to understand in detail how, and why, particular changes were taking place in some privatised companies, and why they were not occurring in others. Only by this method was it felt that it would be possible to understand whether or not the purchasing and supply function ought to be taken more seriously at the strategic, rather than at the operational, level by all companies after privatisation. The fifteen case studies in this book (briefly summarised below), tried to answer these questions, which are primarily linked to the potential for substantial static and dynamic efficiency gains, to be made from a fundamental reappraisal of the purchasing and supply function in particular privatised companies and public sector organisations. Some general points are also made, whenever appropriate, about the evidence of the development of transformational efficiency gains through the phase-3 learning in each of the cases. Phase-3 learning is about supply alignment and procurement competence.

The scale and scope for static and dynamic efficiency gains from purchasing and supply functional professionalism

The fifteen case studies undertaken in this research project (twelve involving privatised companies) demonstrate that privatisation does have a considerable potential to improve the static *and* dynamic efficiency of purchasing and supply management through functional professionalism. Despite this general conclusion, it is worth remembering, however, that just because a company has been privatised does not ensure that there will be an inevitable improvement in corporate learning and behaviour about the scope for, and scale of static *and* dynamic efficiency gains through phase-1 and phase-2 learning. Life is far more complex than this. The new freedoms to manage a business commercially that privatisation brings about must be mediated by, and through, the actions of individuals. This means that, while privatisation may provide the opportunity for a more professional functional approach to purchasing and supply, it is not inevitable that this will occur.

As the case studies reveal, there is evidence that a move towards purchasing and supply functional professionalism can occur in the public sector, as well as in newly privatised companies. Indeed, some of the public sector agencies studied here have developed equally as aggressive an approach to functional professionalism (and in some cases even more so) than many of the privatised companies that feature in this book. It would appear, therefore, that a significant intervening variable in the development of purchasing and supply functional professionalism might very well be the fact that *there is a general increase in competence within the purchasing and supply profession as a whole.* When this occurs, as appears to have been the case in the UK in recent years, then there is scope for public agencies also to improve the way that the purchasing and supply function is managed.

Privatisation clearly provides a more congenial environment for the professionalisation of the purchasing and supply function but, on its own, as is shown below, there is no guarantee that companies will move from a relatively incompetent level of practice to a more professional one. For this to occur (and for it also to occur in the public sector even without privatisation) it would appear that there must be at least two factors in place for the opportunity to be fully grasped, and for a high level of static and dynamic efficiency to be achieved through phase-1 and phase-2 learning.

The first necessary condition is that there must be personnel within a company (or in a public agency), at both the main board and purchasing levels, who understand the opportunity which purchasing and supply functional professionalism provides for rapid improvements in static and dynamic efficiency, and who know what must be done to bring it about. If this occurs then there is already a high probability that the scope for, and scale of, purchasing and supply improvement will (when compared with companies or public agencies that do not understand the opportunity) be very high indeed. The quantum here will be the comparison one might make between privatised and public bodies that are only operating at the phase-1 learning level of cost reduction, and those that are developing phase-2 learning around functional professionalism.

From our research, however, the scale of, and scope for, static and dynamic efficiency gains may also have a high correlation with a company's capacity to develop an understanding of how transformational efficiency gains are achieved. As one of the current authors has argued elsewhere (and as alluded to in Chapter 2, pp. 31–34, with the discussion of the difference between single-loop and double-loop learning) the second factor that appears to have a significant potential impact on a company's ability to maximise its capacity to achieve high levels of static and dynamic efficiency gains may, ironically, also be linked to its ability to achieve an understanding of supply alignment and procurement competence (Cox, 1997a, 1997b, 1998).

Once a company understands strategically what this competence means (phase-3 learning in the model outlined above), and what quantum of cost improvement is available through transformational efficiency gains, it also becomes more obvious what the proper role for purchasing and supply as an operational function should be. It also becomes more obvious what the quantum of static efficiency gains are that are achievable. This is because individuals in the company come to understand the difference between *short-term* operational cost reduction and the capacity for *long-term* cost improvement, through proactive management of the boundary of the firm and the effective leverage of supply chain resources and assets.

Since none of the case study privatised companies and public bodies in this project appear to understand fully this need for a synchronised approach to effective business management, this leads to the conclusion that privatisation, on its own, cannot be the basis for the development of this level of business understanding and competence. Since companies in the private sector only rarely appear to be able to develop this level of strategic and operational competence, it is clear that this must be an ideal to which only some companies will aspire. Given this, it is possible to develop a template in order to understand the degree to which the short case study companies and public bodies in this project have been able to approach this ideal through their ability to link their needs for static and dynamic efficiency (through an operational focus on different levels of purchasing and supply competence), with an awareness of the potential for transformational efficiency, through a focus on supply alignment and procurement competence in supply chain resource and asset management.

As can be seen from Figure 13.1, based on the initial ten case studies in Chapters 5–7, few of the privatised companies or public bodies analysed here have, as yet, fully understood the need for a synergistic approach to strategy and operational practice. The research also demonstrates that companies do learn, and that they can move from one category to another, once the initial strategic and operational mistakes made after privatisation have been digested. Despite this, the case study organisations appear to fall into two broad types. There are those which have decided on a particular approach and which are stuck in this strategic and operational mindset. These can be referred to as *static organisations*. The second group are those which, for whatever reason, have a capacity to recognise their initial mistakes strategically and operationally, and which have fundamentally changed their way of doing business. These can be referred to as *learning organisations*. Clearly within these broad types there are a number of subcategories as explained below.

It is important to make the point at the outset that being a static or a learning organisation does not, in itself, convey anything about the appropriateness of either type of categorisation for business success. A company that is

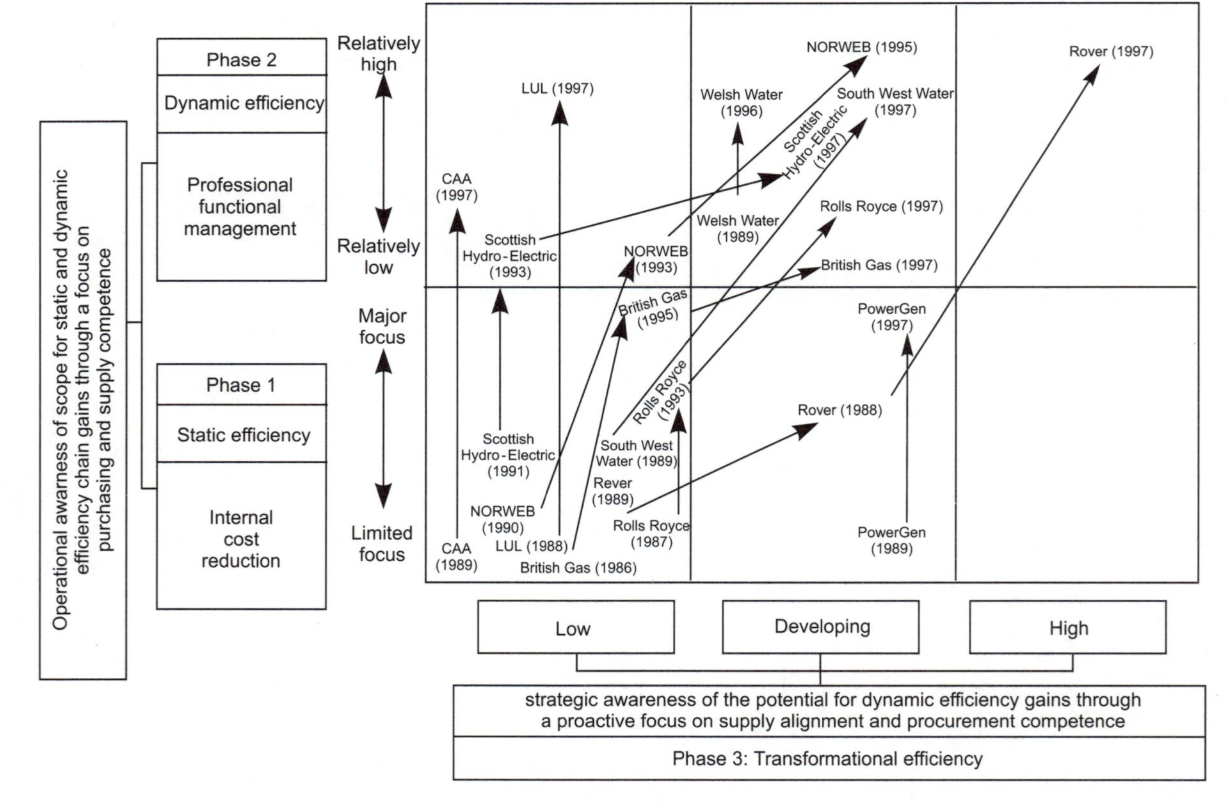

Figure 13.1 Procurement and purchasing competence analysis in eight privatised and two public sector bodies.
Source: Cox, 1998 'The Four Faces of Procurement Competence'.

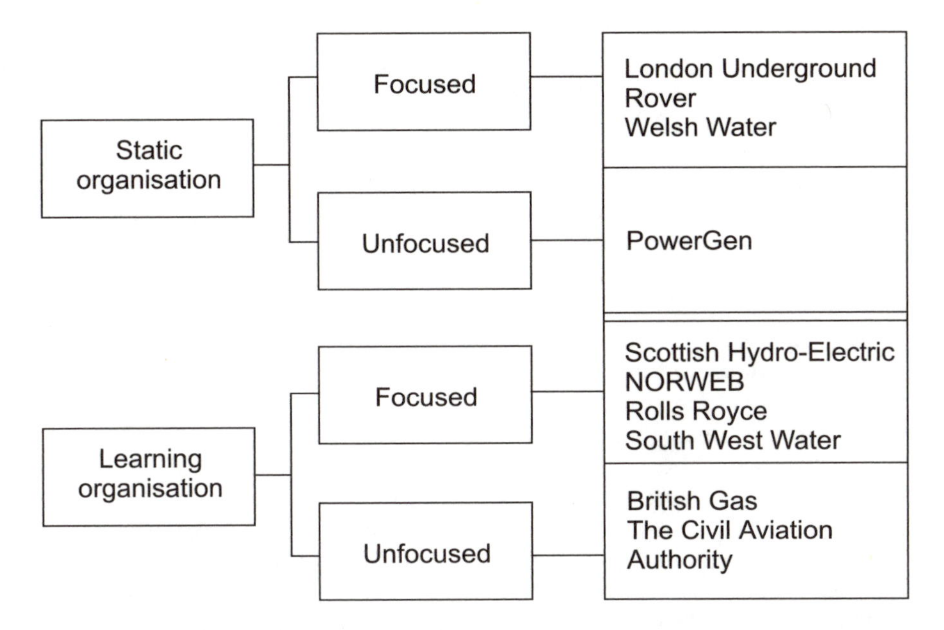

Figure 13.2 The appropriateness of static and learning approaches for the ten initial cases.

static may be very successful if it knows what it is doing strategically and operationally. On the other hand, a company that constantly has to learn may very well be one that does not know what it is doing. It may simply be jumping from one misaligned strategic and operational focus to another, perhaps on the basis of the latest business management fad. Such a company could, therefore, be seen as highly incompetent; whereas a static company may well have developed a high degree of focus in its internal and external relationships and competencies. This being the case, as well as categorising case study organisations in terms of static and learning categories, it was felt appropriate to differentiate them further into those which appeared to be focused or unfocused. Figure 13.2 demonstrates how the ten organisations in the study have been classified using this methodology. Each of these classifications is discussed briefly below.

Focused static organisations

In this category one can locate Welsh Water, between 1989 and 1996. During this period, the essential feature of corporate strategy and operational practice was a focus on static and dynamic efficiency gains. This was achieved through some headcount cost reduction but, primarily, by the continuation of a well-established policy of improving the functional professionalism of purchasing and supply management. This approach did not involve any substantial change in the role and responsibility of the function in the business after privatisation. On the contrary, it resulted in an increase in the importance of what was already in place, as the senior purchasing and supply staff focused on the more strategic aspects of their responsibilities and devolved lesser important practices to other parts of the business.

This is a sign of a relatively mature and professional purchasing function. The adoption of advanced purchasing and supply tools and techniques, and the recognition of the operational benefits of the outsourcing of many non-strategic support functions, is further evidence of a high level of operational competence. Despite this, there is little evidence of a focus on transformational efficiency gains. This is hardly surprising, given that the water companies do not face effective competition and, therefore, have no immediate driver for strategic innovation. In the future, it will be interesting to see how the company – now called Hyder plc since the merger with South Wales Electricity – deals with the need to mange efficiency gains in two very different supply chains, with dissimilar competitive environments. The need for a focus on supply alignment and procurement competence will be of paramount importance in the future, even though it has not been so in the past.

Although it is too early to know the long-term impact of the takeover of Rover by BMW, the Rover case is one of a focused company that, up until the takeover, was relatively static in its perception of the need for operational and strategic change. In the Rover case this should not be seen as a criticism of the competence of the company. On the contrary, it is clear that since the 1970s the company has been a learning organisation, which, by the time of privatisation, had already undergone considerable reappraisal of its internal and external competence needs. There is no doubt that privatisation and the increased competition from Japanese car manufacturers, as well as the assistance of Honda internally, had a profound impact on the company's activities. Despite this, by the 1980s the company had already accepted the need for that form of supply alignment and procurement competence which has been presented here as the ideal to which all companies ought to aspire.

It is not surprising, therefore, that of all of the cases in this book, Rover stands out as the clearest example of strategic and operational alignment. Privatisation had some impact on this, but it is the common-sense approach taught by Honda and started initially by significant individuals, like Sir Michael Edwardes in the 1970s, that are probably of most significance in the transformation of the company. Given the collective learning in the company, and its gradual evolution under private ownership through phase-1 and phase-2 learning, it is not surprising that it is Rover which is the closest of our case studies to the ideal of strategic and operational alignment.

London Underground Ltd (LUL) provides a particularly instructive case study of a public sector body that has a static focus on short-term efficiency improvement, which is particularly focused on the delivery of this goal. LUL has developed a high level of purchasing functional professionalism in the way in which it has tackled the need to achieve static and dynamic efficiency gains, given the operating constraints within which it exists.

This case, therefore, belies the normal stereotype of public sector bodies as being incapable of developing a high level of practitioner competence. Despite this, the case shows that because of the political and financial pressures LUL operates under – national and EU rules and short-term cost reduction targets – it has proved impossible for the company to develop a synergistic focus on transformational and static and dynamic efficiency. The difficulty this creates is that the company is not able to learn *how* to achieve transformational efficiency and may, under some circumstances, be failing to control critical supply chain assets (Cox, 1997a), through a need to outsource to achieve short-term cost reduction. This problem at the strategic level may well hinder necessary 'learning', and may also militate against the effective operationalisation of purchasing professional competence.

Unfocused static organisations

PowerGen can be located in this category. This is not to argue that the company is incompetent, as such. Rather it is to argue that this is a case of company which seems to have become locked into a fixed view of strategy, and that this has had a profound impact on the capacity of the purchasing professionals in the business to contribute to operational improvement. The major reasons for this corporate myopia arise because immediately after privatisation the company decided to create SBUs to challenge the overly centralised structure of the former CEGB. While this may have been appropriate at the time, as an initial starting point, since that time the fixation with this approach has had serious consequences for functional professionalism in the company. The corporate strategy was immediately focused on aggressive cost reduction through headcount reductions and the outsourcing of what were regarded as non-core activities. There was also an attachment to aggressive arm's-length contractual negotiations with all suppliers.

While there is evidence that this approach achieved considerable initial benefits, in terms of cost reduction, and has improved the share price of the company, a more long-term view of business success might suggest that this devolved and cost management approach has limitations. The primary reason for this is that there is evidence that outsourcing may well have reduced costs, but only at the price of passing potentially critical assets to powerful suppliers. Relatedly, the downsizing of the purchasing and supply role in the company may well have contributed to a growing level of functional incompetence rather than professionalism. This is because the SBU structure militates against a consolidation of spend and ensures that purchasing remains an engineering- and production-dominated function. For these reasons, while there has been a considerable short-term improvement in costs, it is likely that this will have been obtained at the cost of an understanding of the scope for continuous improvement, through supply innovation in the purchasing and supply function.

Focused learning organisations

In this category can be located South West Water. Although this regional water company is one of the smaller of those privatised in 1989, it provides a case study of developing operational alignment and functional professionalism. The company had little competence in purchasing and supply management at privatisation, but the new senior management was able to recognise the relative importance of this function to a regional monopolist of water supply. Given this fact, and the company's ability to recruit a competent purchasing professional, who demanded and was able to achieve a more functionally important role in the business than had been the case in the past, the case demonstrates the ability of a company to learn in a focused way. This focus has centred on the development of operational effectiveness and competence through the development of new processes, better purchasing tools and techniques and improved purchasing practitioner skills and capabilities. This way of thinking has also been heavily weighted against fad management, in favour of an understanding of the appropriateness of particular operational practice under specific circumstances (on the significance of this way of thinking see Cox, 1997a). As a result of this focused learning about functional professionalism, there has been considerable evidence of significant improvement in static and dynamic efficiency. The need for transformational efficiency gains is not, however, at a premium, given the company's lack of effective competitive pressures.

Interestingly, the Scottish Hydro-Electric case shows some clear similarities with the South West Water case. The major similarity is the fact that the company has recognised that, in order to achieve significant long-term cost improvement, it must employ people of high calibre and with the requisite intellectual qualifications. The other major similarity has been the desire to understand what is appropriate for the company to do, given the circumstances that it faces. Due to this way of thinking, the company has adopted a two-stage approach to its development of purchasing professionalism. In the first stage, it developed aggressive cost reduction. The major reasons for this aggressive and arm's-length approach to suppliers arose from an historic lack of any purchasing professionals in the business before privatisation, and the fact that many suppliers had taken advantage of this fact in the past.

The company has not, however, become locked into this way of thinking about static and dynamic efficiency gains. After 1993, Scottish Hydro-Electric recognised that it needed a different internal structure, and that the resulting devolution of operations provided the opportunity to develop a more sophisticated approach to long-term cost improvement. Since then, the company has become more professional in its development of advanced purchasing and supply tools and techniques. Importantly, however, some of the senior practitioners in the purchasing function have recently begun to develop an understanding of transformational ways of thinking. This may be of emerging significance in the future as the electricity industry is opened to increasing levels of competition and supply innovation is at a premium.

NORWEB (as it was called before the 1995 merger with North West Water and the company's renaming as United Utilities) is also a case that demonstrates the benefits that can flow to a company once it has recognised the static and dynamic efficiency gains that an appropriate focus on purchasing functional professionalism can achieve. Like the South West Water and Hydro-Electric cases outlined above, there are clear similarities with the way in which NORWEB was able to develop its purchasing professionalism. Like Scottish Hydro-Electric, the company only gradually came to understand the benefits of a more appropriate focus on purchasing functional improvement after an initial focus on cost reduction. NORWEB also had a history of having virtually no real purchasing competence in the business before privatisation. After 1993, however, the company was able to understand the need for a supply chain integration approach, and there is little doubt that the ability to think in this way materially benefited the company's development of purchasing professionalism.

Like both of the two cases already outlined in this section, NORWEB also recognised the importance of adopting and developing advanced purchasing tools and techniques, as well as the need to recruit and train its purchasing practitioners to a high level of competence. Like the other examples of developing a high level of professional competence, it is clear that the focus in NORWEB has been primarily on static and dynamic rather than transformational efficiency gains. Given that the company was (like the other examples discussed here) a relative monopolist before 1995, this is not surprising. The fact that the company faces growing competition in electricity supply in the future, and has merged with a company that (while likely to remain a regional monopolist in water supply) is operating within a very different primary supply chain, may cause the new company to reassess its approach to efficiency gains in the future.

Rolls Royce falls on the cusp between the focused and unfocused learning organisation categories. The reason for this lies in the fact that it continues to operate within a relatively oligopolistic market for aero-engines, but has in recent years begun to recognise the need for significant improvements in static and dynamic efficiency. After 1992, the company also recognised that it must re-engineer its businesses after its takeover of NEI. Given this strategic refocus, it has been inevitable that a re-engineering of the internal operational structure would be required. This has been hastened by privatisation rather than occasioned by it. It is still true to say, however, that the company has some way to go in understanding what the proper focus for purchasing professional competence should be. It is still learning about strategic supply alignment and procurement competence.

Unfocused learning organisations

In this category we place British Gas. Despite the fact that the company decided to split into two separate businesses from February 1997, there is little doubt that the company has been through a period of constant change and learning since its privatisation in 1986. Arguably, this has been partially due to an inability by senior management to understand how to achieve transformational efficiency gains through supply alignment and procurement competence. The fiasco of the 'take or pay' gas supply contracts are but the most visible manifestation of this failing. Over the years since privatisation it seems, however, that, when allowed to (see the movements in Figure 13.1, page 218) purchasing and supply professionals have used whatever opportunities have been available to them to achieve static and dynamic efficiency gains through the further development of their functional professionalism. Despite this, there is still substantial evidence that both the old integrated company (and, presumably, the two companies that have been recently created – British Gas plc and Centrica) do not wholly understand what a fully professional approach to purchasing and supply management looks like. This is due to the unfocused learning that has been in train since privatisation, and the lack of understanding within the business about supply alignment and procurement competence. It remains to be seen whether either of the two newly created companies can develop a more strategically and operationally aligned focus in the future.

The Civil Aviation Authority provides an excellent example of the problems of operating within the public sector, when the organisation is a relative monopoly provider of goods or services. The lack of competitive pressures, and the absence of a commercial focus on purchasing functional competence by those individuals historically responsible for the function, has ensured that the CAA lags considerably behind the privatised companies in this study. Although there has been some improvement in purchasing function professionalism in the last few years, until the recent past, the organisation had all the hallmarks of an unfocused and static organisation. It has now begun to learn but there is still considerable evidence that its lacks focus. This is partly created by the constraints imposed on practitioners by national and EU purchasing legislation, as well as due to a lack of awareness about how static, dynamic and transformational efficiency is achieved within the public sector as a whole (a discussion about how this might be achieved in the public sector is outlined in *Managing Healthcare Strategically*, Nottingham Health Authority, 1997).

Supply alignment and procurement competence: the evidence of transformational efficiency gains in five cases

It is apparent from the above discussion that the development of an appropriate operational focus on static and dynamic efficiency gains through the enhancement of purchasing professional functionalism is not confined to privatised companies. The evidence from our research demonstrates that when there is a conducive environment in the public sector, and the appointment of suitably competent individuals, then similar levels of purchasing functional professionalism to that which is apparent in better managed private sector companies can be developed in the public sector too.

It is also the case, however, that privatisation does appear to have a significant impact in stimulating the timing and pace of change. In the absence of the appropriate political and financial stimulus in the public sector, it is likely – as the CAA case demonstrates – that only halting steps will be taken in the direction of purchasing and supply functional professionalism. There is, therefore, a correlation between privatisation and an operational improvement in purchasing and supply competence. Within this broad generalisation it is clear, however, that while most privatised companies do, eventually, arrive at a higher level of purchasing functional professionalism, there is no certainty that this will occur – as the Powergen and British Gas cases demonstrate.

More importantly than this, is, it seems from the cases studied, that only Rover so far has fundamentally understood the link between strategy and operational practice. Rover has operated under tremendous cost pressures and has been given considerable assistance in refocusing the corporate effort by its joint venture with Honda. It is the only company in this study that seems to have begun to understand the synergies that flow from the development of a supply alignment and procurement competence approach to business management. It would appear, therefore, that, notwithstanding the desire of governments when they privatise, the capacity for such companies to develop a high level of business competence, rather than achieve operational functional improvement, may be limited. Of course, this failing may have more to do with a poor general level of business competence among British managers than it has to do with the act of privatising itself.

In order to understand why there is a high probability of companies that have been privatised only achieving significant improvements in their operational functions, rather than in their understanding of supply alignment and procurement competence, a further five case studies were undertaken. These, more detailed, cases studies (Chapters 8 to 12) sought to understand why there has been only a halting development of an understanding of transformational efficiency through supply alignment and procurement competence. The main findings from the four privatisation and one public sector case studies are summarised below, using the same methodology as in the previous section.

Figure 13.3 on page 226 and Figure 13.4 on page 227 indicate that, of the five more detailed cases studied, there are significant differences between those that can be categorised as either static or learning organisations, and whether or not they are focused or unfocused in this respect. Similarly, there is a wide discrepancy between them in terms of the degree to which they have developed either a high level of purchasing and supply functional professionalism to

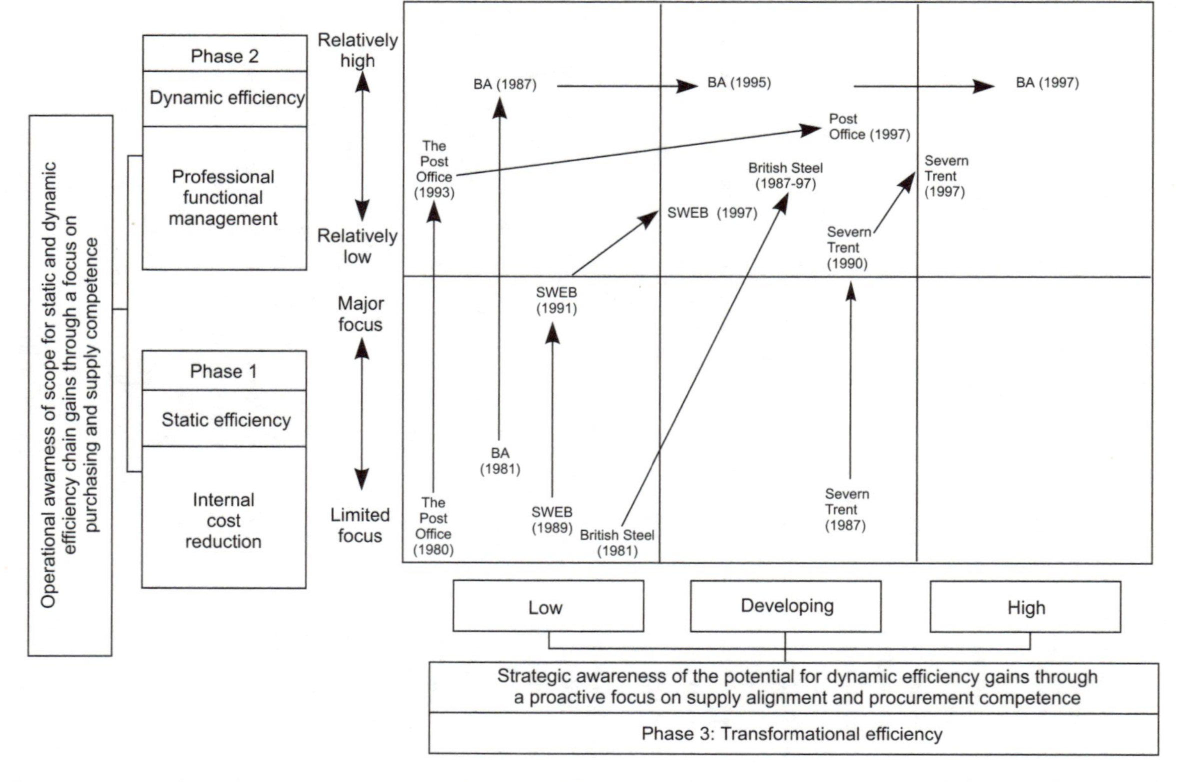

Figure 13.3 Procurement and purchasing competence analysis in the four privatised companies and one public sector body which were studied in detail.
Source: Cox (1998) 'The Four Faces of Procurement Competence'.

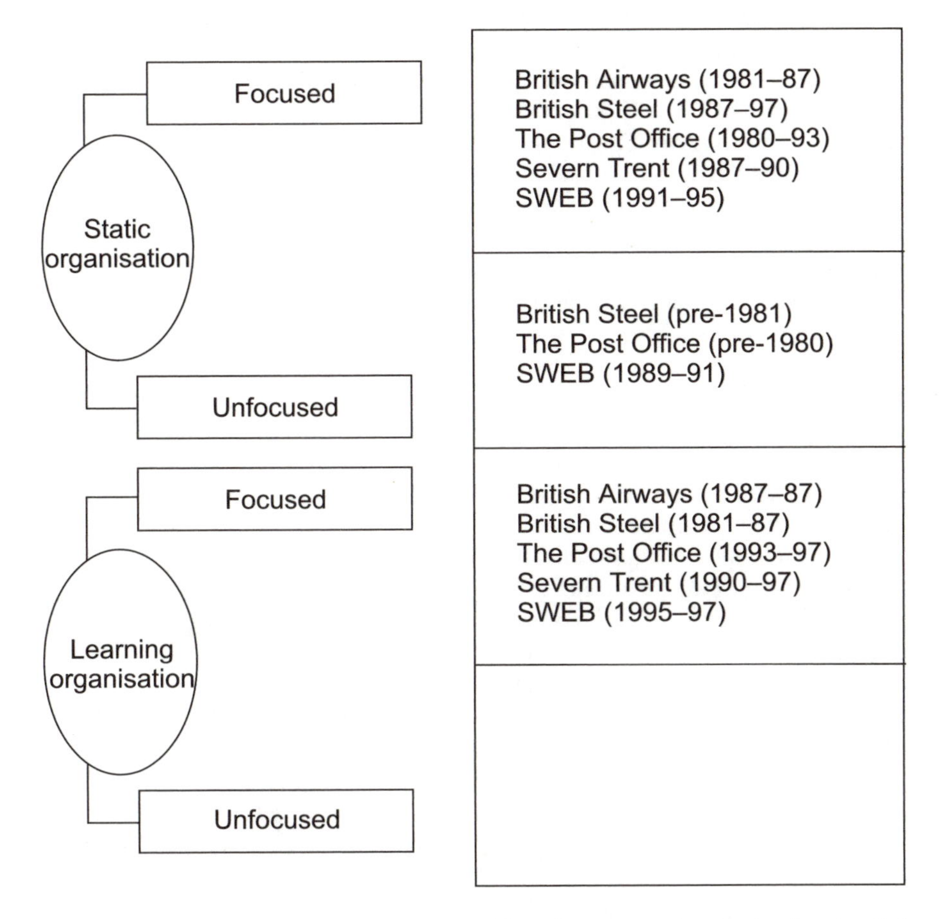

Figure 13.4 The appropriateness of static and learning approaches for the five detailed cases.

achieve static and dynamic efficiency gains, and/or a high level of awareness of how transformational efficiency can be achieved through supply alignment and procurement competence. The results of this analysis are described below.

The Severn Trent case

The Severn Trent case demonstrates conclusively why even privatised companies may find it difficult to change their way of thinking so that they rapidly develop an understanding of procurement competence and supply alignment. The primary reason why the company has only recently been prepared to think about procurement competence, rather than its post-privatisation focus on functional professionalism in purchasing and supply, is probably due to the structure of the industry in which it operates.

Severn Trent is privatised, but it does not face proximate competitive pressures. The company is a relatively permanent monopolist in its geographic position in the water industry with a dependent customer base. Such competitive pressures that it does experience are primarily surrogate constraints, which are imposed by Ofwat, the regulator to the industry. Obviously, the pressure from shareholders for value accumulation and the potential threat of takeover provide additional surrogate pressures, but the company does not experience the same need to innovate as experienced by companies in competitive industries, with survival and profitability at fundamental risk.

Despite these potential forces for inertia, it appears that the regulatory and shareholding pressures have had some impact on the company since privatisation. This is evidenced by the fact that the company has recognised the need for purchasing and supply functional improvement, by the development of an initial focus on internal reorganisation and cost reduction and, later, through the development of a more sophisticated approach to purchasing training and development. This has seen the development of an embryonic understanding of procurement competence in the business.

This development of an understanding of the potential for a more effective approach to leverage in supply offerings has not, as yet, however, resulted in any clear evidence of an understanding of the need for supply alignment, as the company's reactive approach to business development and outsourcing demonstrates. The company remains, then, a fairly static organisation that has arguably become highly focused on static and dynamic efficiency, rather than transformational efficiency improvement since privatisation in 1990. More recently, the desire by the company to acquire companies and to diversify into other analogous businesses demonstrated the emergence of this transformational way of thinking. It remains to be seen, however, whether the company will be able to develop the appropriate focus on supply alignment within the very different supply chains that these businesses represent.

The South West Electricity case

The SWEB case demonstrates that it is not just public sector bodies that can be complacent and ignore the opportunities for static efficiency gains that confront them. After privatisation in 1989, from the evidence presented in this case study, SWEB was an unfocused and static organisation seemingly with little interest in operational performance improvement. But by 1991 all of this began to change and, due to a combination of regulatory pressures, and growing competition in electricity supply, a more aggressive approach to static and dynamic efficiency improvement developed. This was focused primarily on functional performance improvement.

After 1995, and the takeover of the company by US owners, there was a move to integrate the purchasing and supply function more strategically into the business, and to align the still essentially reactive management of supply markets to the aggressive cost reduction focus of the new management. In the process, there is evidence, through the focus on outsourcing in the company, that there was a better understanding of how dynamic, if not, transformational, efficiency might be achieved.

It is still too early to say whether or not this focus on dynamic efficiency gains will be fully effective because the operating focus of the company is still largely on static efficiency improvement in the short term. The short history of the company demonstrates, however, that companies can move through a variety of phases, as Figure 13.4 indicates. SWEB has been, in our analytical framework, both a focused and unfocused static organisation, and it may now be developing, like Severn Trent, a more focused, learning orientation.

The British Airways case

BA is a company that, initially before, and immediately after, privatisation, developed an approach to organisational change and operational performance improvement that focused on short-term cost reduction. As a result, the company can be categorised as a focused learning organisation. The reason for this is that the initial learning in the company was directed towards immediate improvements in static and dynamic efficiency, through radical reorganisation of the way in which (and by whom) internal and external resources were managed.

After this initial stage, and upon privatisation in 1987, the company maintained its aggressive approach to functional professionalism in supply management. It also demonstrated its ability to extend its search for functional excellence through a strategy of reviewing all major areas of activity using an outsourcing methodology. This demonstrates a continuous improvement emphasis in the company but within existing operational and functional constraints.

After 1995, with the completion of the initial operational outsourcing review and the appointment of a new CEO, a more radical business efficiency plan was introduced. This was occasioned by the recognition of the fact that radical changes in the relatively benign regulatory structure would occur by the turn of the century, for example as the EU looked for a more open and competitive marketplace among national carriers in Europe. In this environment it is clear that the scope for competitive advantage through static and dynamic efficiency gains was likely to be limited. As a result there is evidence that the new leadership at the company decided to seek out transformational efficiency gains. This led them to revisit the initial outsourcing review undertaken operationally in the purchasing and supply function but now at a strategic level.

The dominant view currently in place in the company is based on core competence thinking and outsourcing practice. The company is considering radical outsourcing of key areas of what were, in the past, regarded as core operational activities. There seems little doubt that this thinking may well have contributed to the recent industrial relations conflict that lost the company several million pounds worth of operating revenue, in the early summer of 1997. Also, the reliance on this strategically static way of thinking indicates that while the company has recognised the need to achieve transformational efficiency, it is still at the development stage of a proper understanding of how this can be achieved. (For a more inclusive analysis of this problem, through which companies focus on core competence thinking as the basis for outsourcing decision making, interested readers are directed to the recent work in this area by one of the authors; Cox, 1997a; Lonsdale and Cox 1998; Cox and Lonsdale, 1998).

Despite this, the company continues to out-perform many of the other companies and public organisations in this study, in terms of procurement competence, because it clearly has the capacity to act in advance of the strategic threats which the company faces in the future. It is, therefore, proactive but it still has a great deal to learn.

The British Steel case

While British Airways is an interesting case because it has begun to anticipate the consequences of an increase in competition on its operational activities and strategic focus, British Steel is an example of a former, relatively dominant national player responding aggressively to the consequences of competitive failure. British Steel's improvement approach to outsourcing and purchasing and supply functional professionalism was not generated by privatisation, but rather by the need to survive and downsize before privatisation occurred. This happened while the company was still publicly owned, and this case amply demonstrates the fact that organisational and performance improvement in purchasing and supply can occur in the public, as well as in the private sector, if the appropriate financial drivers and competent individuals are in place.

Despite the rapid improvement in functional performance before 1988, our research indicates that British Steel is probably best categorised as a static, but highly focused organisation. The reason for this conclusion lies in the strategy adopted by the company after 1981 and due to the relative maturity and national concentration of the industry worldwide. Since British Steel had to adopt an aggressive outsourcing strategy to downsize the company at a time of major financial and economic pressures, it seems that it adopted a core competence view of the world, and focused mainly on a highly competitive processing role in the steel supply chain. This has, in a sense, tied the company's hands because it must develop an aggressive short-term cost reduction focus in its operational activities, due to increasing global competition for what is a relatively simple and technologically imitable product. This is the case notwithstanding British Steel's attempts since the early 1980s to move away from a dependence on bulk steelmaking towards specialist steel products.

Given this competitive environment, plus the sheer size of the company in the UK marketplace, the operational focus of the company has tended to be on static and dynamic efficiency gains at the expense of a more supply aligned and procurement competence approach. The search for transformational efficiency has been limited by the structural features of the supply chain position that the company is locked into. Moreover, there is evidence that, even in the search for static and dynamic efficiency, there is little evidence of an understanding at the operational or strategic levels in the company of the forces that shape innovation in supply. The thinking appears to be heavily focused on a highly professional, but still essentially reactive, approach to supply market offerings outside of the boundary of the firm.

The Post Office case

There is evidence that, while The Post Office has little historic awareness of how to achieve static, dynamic or transformational efficiency, in recent years it has begun to understand what each of these competencies requires. As a result, after 1993 there has been a rapid change in the organisation's awareness of what is required to move from a relatively focused static organisation, pursuing short-term cost reduction targets, to a more focused, learning organisation.

Interestingly, most of the *efficiency* improvements that have been generated in The Post Office appear to have arisen directly as the result of three forces. The first of these is the threat of privatisation (which has recently receded). The second is the tightening of the financial targets under which the government forces the organisation to operate. The third, and perhaps the most important in the context of the recent improvement in the level of awareness of purchasing and supply functional professionalism, has been the recruitment of leading practitioners with private sector experience.

Since 1993 there has been, therefore, a major development in the competence of the purchasing and supply function in the business. This has coincided with further developments in the search for transformational efficiency gains in the business as a whole. This search for these major efficiencies has been hindered, however, by political factors. In the mid-1990s, the lack of willingness by the government to privatise The Post Office, and its recognition that any increase in competition from the private sector might have a debilitating impact on the rural electorate, significantly reduced the competitive pressures on the business. As a result, it is not surprising that the focus has been primarily on static and dynamic efficiency gains with limited recourse to outsourcing.

Perhaps the most important finding from a detailed study of The Post Office is the confirmation provided for the general conclusion in our other case studies of public sector organisations. In our three shorter case studies it was argued that functional professionalism is not solely dependent on private ownership, it can also be created by proactive and competent individuals in key positions in the public sector. The Post Office case further demonstrates that transformational efficiency can be achieved even when an organisation remains in the public sector. While The Post Office has been constrained in its search for supply alignment and procurement competence, there is little doubt that the surrogate competitive pressures imposed upon it, and the recruitment of commercially minded practitioners from the private sector, have stimulated transformational thinking about strategy and operational practice. This means that privatisation on its own is not necessarily the only way in which transformational efficiency is achieved. It can be achieved in the public sector if the right incentives and penalties are put in place.

As the discussion above indicates, there is evidence in our five detailed case studies that the one control, public sector body and the four privatised companies have all demonstrated the same level of ability to achieve static and dynamic efficiency gains by shifting through phase-1 to phase-2 learning. The Post Office was able to achieve a significant improvement in purchasing professionalism as a result of the aggressive short-term financial pressures induced by government, through having a competent individual in place in the business, and by the threat of privatisation and the loss of existing monopoly services to private sector providers. This environment operated as a stimulus for static and dynamic efficiency gains to be achieved because it was a surrogate for competitive market forces.

The four detailed privatisation cases also demonstrate the impact that a shift from public to private ownership can achieve in stimulating a significant transformation in purchasing and supply functional professionalism. All four companies moved through phase-1 to phase-2 learning over a relatively short period of time, and achieved significant static and dynamic efficiency gains in the process. Of these four case study companies, however, only British Airways has really begun to address the need for transformational efficiency through the development of a supply alignment and procurement competence approach to purchasing. Even for BA, it is still the case that the company has some way to go in achieving a proper understanding of how this is achieved through an appropriate focus on supply alignment and procurement competence. Why this should be so for a focused learning organisation like BA, as well as for those less-focused and more static companies in this study, is now discussed.

On the problems of achieving static, dynamic and transformational efficiency gains

There is a correlation in the findings from this study between the degree of competitive pressure and the development of an understanding of the need for supply alignment and procurement competence. The fact that only Rover and British Airways have begun to approach an appreciation of what this might entail, and even they, in our view, are some considerable way from fully achieving it, emphasises the need for companies and public organisations to develop an understanding of how transformational efficiency can be achieved.

In so far as the privatised companies and indeed most of the public bodies in this study are concerned, it seems that the exposure to competitive and market disciplines does have a profound impact on the search for static and dynamic efficiency gains. Virtually all of the organisations in our study have demonstrated a capacity to move through an initial focus on internal cost reduction, to an understanding of the need to develop a more sophisticated approach to purchasing functional improvement. This has normally involved the development of a range of tools and techniques associated with the more professional segmentation and management of different types of supply relationships.

The major reason for the relatively poor showing of the public sector organisations in our study is probably due to the lack of the capital and product market disciplines impacting on the business that are found in the privatised companies (while recognising that competitive product market pressures are very limited in the water sector). Despite this, where senior managers understand the potential for the static, dynamic and transformational efficiency gains that can flow from a more professional approach to purchasing and supply then, once professionally competent individuals have been recruited (as in The Post Office and London Underground cases) the public sector can develop similar levels of purchasing functional professionalism as those found in the private sector.

It is in the area of transformational efficiency that the public sector organisations in our study tend to fall down the most in comparison to the private sector companies. It is in those private sector companies most under product market competitive pressure that the beginnings of an understanding of supply alignment and procurement competence can be discerned. Elsewhere, in those companies that have been privatised but which have operated, at least until relatively recently, with monopoly or oligopoly control over supply chain resources (like the water, electricity and gas industries), there has been the least evidence of an awareness of the need for transformational efficiency.

This is an interesting conclusion because it implies that there may still be considerable efficiency gains available in many of the industries that have been privatised. The fact that most of the privatised companies are still only operating with a focus on static and dynamic efficiency, and do not fully understand how to innovate to achieve transformational efficiency needs explanation. While it is not the purpose of this study to undertake this task, it is the case that many private sector companies, and not just the recently privatised ones, are guilty of a failure to understand how to develop an appropriate approach to achieving transformational efficiency.

There are many reasons why practitioners in companies do not fully understand what is meant by supply alignment and procurement competence. Explaining in detail why this is so in particular supply chains, industries and markets remains a challenging agenda for future research. It is clear, on the basis of this study, however, that there are likely to be two primary causal factors. These are, first, the relative degree of competitive pressure in the product markets that any company faces and, second, the competence of individuals within companies. That competitive pressure on its own is not a sufficient stimulus for the development of a proper understanding of the causes of business success, through successful strategic and operational innovation, is an interesting conclusion from our study and deserves further testing.

The research reported in this book demonstrates that those individuals managing the formerly privatised companies, and those operating in the public organisations studied, can have a considerable impact on the development of an understanding of operational effectiveness. So much so that, the role of individuals in this study shows that human knowledge and understanding may act as a surrogate for competitive pressures in public bodies and in those companies not exposed to significant competition after privatisation. As encouraging as this may be, it is still true, as this study has shown, that human competence is likely to be most developed, in relation to static and dynamic efficiency gains, through reactive marginal improvements to operational performance. It is, therefore, still the case that, on the basis of the evidence presented here, most practitioners have some considerable way to go before they develop a sophisticated understanding of the key forces that shape transformational innovation in business.

Appendix: The Postal Questionnaire

SECTION 1 HOW HAS THE PURCHASING FUNCTION CHANGED?

For all sections, read 'around the time of privatisation' where 'privatisation' is mentioned, as it is clear that many of the changes discussed took place over an extended period. Please tick appropriate boxes unless otherwise instructed.

1.1 Please describe the structure of the purchasing department before and after privatisation, and where purchasing would like to position itself in the future.

Structure of purchasing	*Before privatisation*	*Since privatisation*	*Aim for the future*
Centralised (all organisation's purchasing carried out centrally)			
Devolved–controlled (controlled & co-ordinated from centre)			
Devolved–enabled (autonomous purchasing units with a strategic centre)			
Decentralised (little or no authority at centre)			
Other (please specify below)			
Don't know (see below)			

Other ....

....

Don't know: *If you do not know how the purchasing department was structured before privatisation, can you think of anyone who does?*

....

....

1.2 When did the above changes take place?

> 3 yrs before	*0–3 yrs before*	*During year of privatisation*	*0–3 yrs after*	*> 3 yrs after*	*No change*

1.3 Does the purchasing department have a 'mission statement'? If so, please describe it, and explain if it has changed since privatisation.

....

....

1.4 Please describe the strategy of the purchasing department, and how this fits in with overall company strategy.

....

....

If there have been any major changes in strategy since privatisation, please explain these.

....

....

1.5 What is the title of the most senior purchasing manager? Please describe his or her position in the company, and give any major changes since privatisation.

....

....

1.6 Again regarding the position of the most senior purchasing manager, please tick the appropriate boxes.

Position	*Before privatisation*	*Since privatisation*
Main board director		
Reporting directly to main board director, either:		
Managing director		
Finance director		
Mktg/sales director		
Ops/production director		
HR/personnel director		
Other director (specify)		
Other (specify below)		

Other ....

....

1.7 When did the above changes take place?

> 3 yrs before	0–3 yrs before	During year of privatisation	0–3 yrs after	> 3yrs after	No change

1.8 How many employees are there in the purchasing department (excluding clerical and support staff), and how has this changed since privatisation?

Before privatisation	*Since privatisation*

If there has been a change, why do you think this is so?

....

....

SECTION 2 INVOLVEMENT OF PURCHASING IN COMPANY SPEND

Please read the following definitions before completing this section.

Total spend refers to the total value of all bought-in goods and services. This can be divided into:

Traditional spend: goods and services related directly to production such as components, spare parts, machinery and maintenance, and

Non-traditional spend: ancillary expenditure such as advertising, consultancy fees, hotels and travel expenses.

2.1 What is your company's Total annual spend, and how does this divide into Traditional and Non-traditional expenditure? Please give an estimate if this information is not available.

Total annual spend (£)	*Traditional (%)*	*Non-traditional (%)*

2.2 What percentage of the Total annual spend is the purchasing department responsible for, and how has this changed since privatisation?

	Before privatisation (%)	*Since privatisation (%)*
Percentage of total annual spend attributable to purchasing department		

2.3 Similarly, what percentage of your company's traditional and non-traditional spend is the purchasing department responsible for?

	Before privatisation (%)	*Since privatisation (%)*
Percentage of traditional spend attributable to purchasing dept. Percentage of non-traditional spend attributable to purchasing dept.		

2.4 Who else in the company carries major responsibility for purchasing these types of goods, and how has this changed since privatisation?

Traditional: ....

....

Non-traditional: ....

....

2.5 If there have been notable changes in your responsibility regarding any of the above, please give details.

....

....

2.6 What proportion of your company's total spend is sourced from foreign suppliers?

	Before privatisation (%)	*Since privatisation (%)*
Percentage of total spend sourced from foreign suppliers		

SECTION 3 WHY HAS THE ROLE OF PURCHASING CHANGED?

3.1 If you feel that the role of purchasing *has* changed since privatisation, please describe how it has changed.

....

....

3.2 Which factors have driven this change?

Factor driving change?	*Yes*	*No*
A fundamental review of organisational structure included changes in purchasing		
Consultants recommended changes in purchasing		
A new MD introduced changes in purchasing		
A new head of purchasing was brought in		
Existing head of purchasing was given more power		
The need to reduce overhead costs		
Other (specify below)		

Other factors/further explanation:

....

....

3.3 If you feel that the role of purchasing *has not* changed since privatisation, why is this so?

Factor inhibiting change?	*Yes*	*No*
Senior management do not understand the needs of purchasing		
Reflects lack of change throughout the organisation		
Lack of professional training & qualifications for purchasers		
No need for change		
Other (specify below)		

Other ....

....

SECTION 4 OUTSOURCING OR VERTICAL INTEGRATION?

4.1 Has your company moved towards more in-house production or more outsourcing since privatisation?

More in-house production	*More outsourcing*	*No change*

4.2 On what criteria were the above decisions made?

Criteria	*Yes*	*No*
The decision that you/other companies can produce certain goods or services more efficiently		
Need for liquidity leading to the sale of manufacturing facilities		
Release from government intervention allowing management to make the decision		
The need to reduce employment costs in your company		
Other (specify below)		

Other/further explanation ....

....

4.3 Was purchasing involved proactively, reactively, or not at all in the above make–buy decisions? Please give examples of decisions made and state your level of involvement.

Specify decision	*Proactive involvement*	*Reactive involvement*	*No involvement*

Explanation ....

....

SECTION 5 PROCUREMENT TECHNIQUES AND SUPPLIER PERFORMANCE

5.1 Which of these tools and techniques are most commonly used by purchasing? A description of some of these is given in Appendix 1.*

Tools & techniques	*Before privatisation*	*Since privatisation*
Writing tender specifications		
Organising bids		
Negotiating		
Awarding contracts		
Expediting		
Inspection of goods on arrival		
Vendor accreditation		
Formal vendor selection		
Benchmarking/best practice		
Purchasing portfolio analysis		
Strategic source planning		
Purchase price cost analysis		
Strategic supplier alliances		
Partnership sourcing		
Network sourcing		
Relational competence analysis		
Other (specify below)		

*Not reproduced in this book, but see this book's Glossary on pp. 242–4 for explanation of certain terms.

Other ....

....

5.2 Since privatisation, what initiatives have there been to develop the use of these tools and techniques?

....

....

5.3 Since privatisation, how has supplier performance changed in the following areas?

Performance indicator	*Major improvement*	*Slight improvement*	*No change*	*Slight deterioration*	*Major deterioration*
Cost competitiveness					
Product/service quality					
Cycle times					
New-product development time					
Flexibility					
On-time delivery					
Access to new technology & innovation					
Other (specify below)					

Other – please note any other measures that you use, and whether supplier performance has improved or deteriorated since privatisation.

....

....

5.4 What criteria are used to measure the performance of the procurement department, and how have these changed since privatisation?

....

....

SECTION 6 'ANY OTHER BUSINESS'

6.1 If you have any other thoughts that might add insight into our study, and you feel have not been covered by the questionnaire, please write them here.

....

....

~~~~~~~~~~~~~~~~ Many thanks for your time ~~~~~~~~~~~~~~~~

Note

This questionnaire was sent to senior executives in the purchasing departments of 48 privatised companies in the UK. It was completed by executives in 28 companies, a response rate of 58 per cent.
~~~~~~~~~~~~~~~~

Glossary of terms

Benchmarking/best practice A methodology that seeks to achieve performance improvement by comparing the performance of suppliers for a given product/service against the leading suppliers in the industry. It can also be used to compare and adapt the practices of other companies to improve existing operational practices.

Business process re-engineering (BPR) A concept associated with consulting companies attempting to sell fundamental change in companies. Based on the simple idea that business is a process not a series of functions, so that the business should be re-engineered to align with processes. Most major companies have tried it with limited evidence of significant long-term success. Works best when companies understand the processes they are in (thus, works best when they understand supply alignment and procurement competence).

CIPS Chartered Institute of Purchasing and Supply.

Core competence thinking The idea that companies should not concentrate on everything but should focus their resources on the development of those things that they are best at, and which will provide a way of delighting future customers. The idea was developed by Hamel and Prahalad, but has been usurped by those interested in downsizing and head-count cost reductions in companies.

Customer–supplier development programme A process by which customers and suppliers work together to develop an understanding of each other's businesses in order to develop efficiency in their relationships, or in the products and services they jointly provide.

Devolved controlled structures A process by which operational responsibility for purchasing and supply chain alignment is given to lower, relatively autonomous levels of the business.

Devolved enabled structures As with **devolved controlled structures**, but the degree of autonomy and access to independent resources is greater, allowing the business unit to operate with tremendous freedom.

Dynamic efficiency An improvement in a company's performance by a major change in the current operational process and procedures within the existing production system. For example, by changing the way in which supply expenditure is consolidated internally, or by realigning the existing specification and expediting processes into multi-functional team-working with internal customers and suppliers.

Functional (purchasing) professionalism See purchasing functional professionalism below.

Lean manufacture The application of Japanese thinking about waste reduction in manufacturing processes and integrated supply relationships.

Leveraged spend or buying A process by which expenditure in a company is consolidated internally so that it can be used in volume to negotiate better deals from suppliers. Many major companies have used this thinking to create global commodity councils to focus their spend in particular areas in order to improve their buying performance.

Make–buy The decision whether to produce something in-house ('make') or to purchase from a separate supplier ('buy'). This is one of the most fundamental decisions taken by any company strategically and operationally.

Network sourcing Building an extended network of suppliers, with much mutual dependence between customer and supplier. Similar to the so-called Japanese 'pyramid system'. Involves open information flows, a tiered supply structure, and much customer effort in developing suppliers. May also involve risk-sharing and joint design between customer and supplier, some shared ownership and profit-sharing.

Outsourcing A decision to purchase from an external supplier. This may involve a process of buying externally or of sourcing a complete process or service – that was formally undertaken internally – from external suppliers.

Partnership sourcing A joint commitment between customer and supplier to invest in a long-term relationship. Involves trust, much openness and access to each other's internal structures and information, and possibly joint risk-sharing agreements, co-ordinated project teams, sharing design capabilities, and quality and delivery performance standards.

Preferred customer status A process by which a supplier seeks to win a preferred status from a buying company by promising performance improvement in return for a long-term contractual relationship.

Preferred supplier status A selection by the buyer of one or two suppliers who will be provided with regular, long-term and high-volume business if they sustain the required performance targets.

Purchasing functional professionalism (functional professionalism) A way of organising essentially selective and reactive ways of managing supply in a systematic, coherent and rigorously professional way.

Purchasing cards The replacement of paper purchase order and invoice systems with buying through the use of corporate credit cards. Most companies have begun to use this system, although VAT reconciliation in the UK has hindered its widespread development.

Purchase price cost analysis Rather than just negotiating on the price of the product or service, the buyer analyses all of the costs and margins in the supply of a product or service.

Purchasing portfolio analysis matrix A purchasing tool or technique which allows the practitioner to analyse bought-in products according to the importance of the products to the company, and the 'risk' in the supply market (i.e. the number of suppliers, possibility of substitution, etc.). Based on this analysis a supply strategy can then be framed for each product purchased.

Relational competence analysis The process by which a company understands the competencies it needs to buy from the external suppliers and its defining a strategy to link different types of competence need with appropriate types of supply relationships.

Relationship management programmes A process by which the buying company trains its own personnel in the ability to manage supply relationships. It can also be extended into joint relationship assessment by and with suppliers.

Risk and revenue-sharing partnerships The most extensive form of **partnership sourcing** in which both parties to the relationship share risks and rewards.

Single sourcing Purchase from one supplier or a preferred supplier.

Static efficiency An improvement in a company's performance by the achievement of contractual efficiency without a major change in existing operational processes or procedures. For example, by awarding a contract for the same product or service to a more efficient and effective supplier.

Strategic source planning A process by which a buying company understands the specific supply chain for a given product and works within it to improve cost reduction or the quality of product or service delivery.

Strategic supplier alliances Collaboration, mergers or joint ventures with suppliers (or other forms of cross-share ownership) that are likely to lead to joint investment strategies, or joint design and production over the long term.

Supply alignment A process by which a company understands how to align its strategic and operational practices and processes with the structure of the supply chain(s) within which it operates.

Supply alignment and procurement competence An entrepreneurial focus on the structure of power and leverage within supply and value chains that allows the company to develop a flexible response to supply and value-chain positioning. A strategic and operational methodology that emphasises the iterative importance of the make–buy decision marking out the effective boundary of the firm. Explained in more detail in Andrew Cox, *Business Success*, Earlsgate Press, 1997.

Transformational efficiency An improvement in the company's performance by a focus on, and understanding of, the importance of supply alignment and procurement competence.

Vendor accreditation A quantitative method of assessing supplier performance, measuring elements such as price, quality (rejection percentage etc.), and delivery reliability (e.g. number of late or early deliveries), and rating suppliers according to their score on these criteria.

Whole-life costing Rather than concentrating only on the initial bought-in cost of a product or service the buyer analyses the whole-life costs of acquiring the item.

Notes

2 Privatisation, business restructuring and purchasing and supply management

1. All nationalised industries are public corporations but not all public corporations are nationalised industries. Nationalised enterprises are state-controlled bodies with most or all of their revenues derived from trading activities. This is not necessarily true of public corporations.
2. While the main financing of state industries was through loans, from the mid-1960s 'public dividend capital' (PDC) was introduced, first at British Airways and a little later at British Steel. These enterprises were particularly subject to business cycle effects and found the payment of interest on loan capital difficult in the years of trade recession. In return for PDC, 'dividend' payments were made out of profits in place of interest charges. The 'dividend' was agreed with the Treasury and the sponsoring department and therefore was only notionally similar to a dividend payment in the private sector.
3. *The Financial and Economic Obligations of the Nationalised Industries*, Cmnd. 1337: HMSO.
4. *Nationalised Industries: a review of economic and financial objectives*, Cmnd. 3437: HMSO.
5. NEDO (1976) *A Study of UK Nationalised Industries: their role in the economy and control in the future*, HMSO.
6. *The Nationalised Industries*, Cmnd. 7131.
7. The term privatisation was not widely used until the early 1980s.
8. Of course, ensuring competition when a state industry exists, backed by taxpayer funding, may be difficult. From 1982/83 it was possible for private firms to supply gas and electricity, but the dominance of British Gas and the state electricity businesses in the energy markets meant that competition did not develop. The size and special status of the incumbent producer proved to be an effective barrier to market entry.
9. In terms of raising the percentage of the population holding shares the policy was effective. The numbers rose from 6 per cent to a peak of 20 per cent in 1990. Before the flotation of building societies in 1997 the figure was around 17 per cent. However, most of the new shareholders own shares in only one or two companies and the percentage of total shares quoted in the stock market held by the large institutional investors (e.g. pension funds and banks) has continued to rise, to almost 80 per cent.
10. The literature does assume that incumbent managers fear takeovers. The existence of 'golden parachutes' and similar executive compensation packages may remove this fear. Also, 'poison pills' and other barriers to takeovers exist in some capital markets to reduce the threat from unwelcome bids.

11 There are also problems associated with small shareholders censuring management. The costs of mounting opposition to management, canvassing support from among other shareholders and attending AGMs are likely to dwarf the gain to any individual small investor from improving managerial performance. Censuring is usually not an economically rational activity for individual small investors.
12 A similar argument appears in Austrian economics. The 1970s and 1980s saw a revival in interest in Austrian economists such as Hayek and Schumpeter in right-wing circles in Britain. For a review of Austrian economics, see Parker and Stead, 1991, ch. 5.
13 The extent to which the Conservative Party in the 1970s and 1980s was influenced by these theories is unclear. However, they appear to have had some influence. They were popularised by free-market think-tanks such as the Institute of Economic Affairs and the Adam Smith Institute, both in London, with which a number of leading Conservatives such as Keith Joseph had links.
14 Competition could take the form of potential competition. Where the market is 'contestable' a monopoly supplier can be expected to price and minimise production costs so as to forestall market entry by a new competitor (Baumol *et al.*, 1982).
15 In Oliver Williamson's terminology, an M-form (multi-form) rather than a U-form (uni-form) structure (Williamson, 1971) would be one possible response.
16 Strategy can be analysed at the corporate, strategic business unit or functional levels. Here the emphasis is on corporate level strategy, but this in turn has similar implications for business and functional strategy.
17 Some early findings were reported in Cox *et al.* (1998) and Harris *et al.* (1998).

3 The research project and methodology

1 Resource constraints prevented a full-scale study of either the public sector or of companies residing permanently in the private sector.
2 For the public sector organisations the time period for 'change' was the outcome of discussion between researcher and interviewee; this is explained further in the individual case studies.

4 The impact of privatisation on the purchasing and supply function

1 Three respondents gave a figure for the minimum number of procurement staff before privatisation.
2 On 19 November 1987 a major fire at King's Cross Underground station led to thirty fatalities and a major review within London Underground of safety procedures.

5 The impact of privatisation on utilities' purchasing and supply management

1 Restructuring prevents meaningful comparisons with pre-1993 figures, according to the company's 1996 *Annual Report and Accounts*.
2 This figure represents loss on ordinary activities before taxation and after exceptional charges.
3 Another factor influencing the restructure was the 1993 MMC Report on British Gas. Following the report and negotiations with Ofgas and the government, the company agreed to separate gas supply from transportation (pipelines and storage) to facilitate market entry by new gas suppliers. Initially, this was to be achieved by having two separate businesses – supply and pipeline – within British Gas. Later, the restructuring was replanned by management and British Gas was broken up into two separate companies.

4 The 1997 demerger will obviously have caused a further transformation in purchasing strategy and structure. This occurred, however, after our fieldwork was completed.
5 As explained, this report refers mainly to changes before the effects of the merger were strongly felt.
6 Purchasing managers were presented with a taxonomy of purchasing structures in tabular form and asked to mark any changes since privatisation.
7 Membership of the Chartered Institute of Purchasing and Supply.
8 Before an exceptional restructuring charge of £35.5m. (SWW plc, 1995).
9 This period coincides with the period until the price cap is next changed by Ofwat, in the year 2000. Ian Byatt, director general of Ofwat, has already confirmed that he intends to tighten the price cap on water companies at his next review and this is leading to a further search for cost savings within the water and sewerage companies.
10 This figure includes £121m. in exceptional credits.
11 In May 1998, PowerGen announced that it had begun detailed merger talks with Houston Industries of the US to further its transatlantic ambitions (*The Financial Times*, 4 May 1998, p. 1).
12 PowerGen had less than fifteen power stations at the time of the interview; some had been leased or sold to smaller, newer competitors.
13 Chartered Institute of Purchasing and Supply.
14 It is interesting to note that the 1995 merger has resulted in further radical changes in purchasing structure and strategy. The supply chain business was merged with the purchasing function of North West Water and moved into a new facilities management division called Vertex Data Science Ltd. Within this division, which operates as a separate company, purchasing sells its services both within United Utilities and to external customers.
15 Words used by a management interviewee within purchasing.

6 The impact of privatisation on non-utilities' purchasing and supply management

1 This refers to Rolls Royce aerospace company. Rolls Royce motor vehicles, owned by Vickers plc and sold to the German vehicle company Volkswagen in June 1998, has never been in public ownership.
2 The company did make losses in 1992, due mainly to the severe recession in the civil aircraft industry.
3 Something economists call the 'hold up' problem in contracting (Hart and Moore, 1988).

7 Developments in public sector procurement

1 The CAA has an interface with the Ministry of Defence because the Royal Air Force also uses the air space.
2 Eurocontrol calculate the full charge to the airline for flying over European airspace, then divides this proportionately between the countries involved and allocates it to their air traffic control services.
3 London Buses retains responsibility for providing a transport service even though the routes have been franchised. This involves monitoring service levels, among other duties.
4 The same government reversed its decision after this research had been undertaken, announcing its intention in February 1997 to privatise London Underground (*The Times*, 26 February 1997). Following the election of a new Labour government in May of that year, policy switched to one of introducing private capital by fran-

chising the rail infrastructure while leaving train services within public ownership.

8 Severn Trent Water

1 Chartered Institute of Purchasing and Supply.
2 In water, the price cap is RPI +K, where $K = -X+Q$ (X is an efficiency improvement factor and Q reflects the need for investment in improved water quality).

10 British Airways

1 The words of a purchasing manager interviewed at BA.
2 There was only one BA kitchen remaining at Heathrow by late 1996.
3 To counter the potential threat from discount, no-frills airlines, in 1998 BA introduced its own such operator, called 'Go'.

References

Argawal, A. and Mandelker, G. N. (1987) 'Managerial Incentives and Corporate Investment and Financing Decisions', *Journal of Finance*, 43, pp. 823–37.

Argyris, C. and Schon, D. (1978) *Organisational Learning: a theory of action perspective*, Reading, Mass., Addison-Wesley.

Arrow, K. J. (1963) *Social Choice and Individual Values*, New Haven, Yale University Press.

Arthur, W. B. (1988) 'Positive Feedbacks in the Economy', in Anderson, P., Arrow, K. and Pines, D. (ed.), *The Economy as an Evolving Complex System*, Reading, Mass., Addison-Wesley.

Aylen, J. (1994) 'The Privatisation of British Steel', in Bishop, M., Kay, J. and Mayer, C. (eds), *Privatisation and Economic Performance*, Oxford, Oxford University Press.

Ayub, M. A. and Hegsted, S. O. (1986) *Public Industrial Enterprises: determinants of firm performance*, Washington, DC, World Bank.

Bailey, E. E. (1973) *Economic Theory of Regulatory Constraint*, Lexington, DC, Heath.

Bain, J. S. (1959) *Industrial Organisation*, New York, Wiley.

Baker, S. and Weiner, E. (1992) 'Latin America: the big move to free markets', *Business Week*, 15 June, pp. 50–55.

Barry E. E. (1965) *Nationalisation in British Politics: the historical background*, London, Jonathan Cape.

Baumol, W. J., Panzar, J. C. and Willig, R. D. (1982) *Contestable Markets and the Theory of Industry Structure*, New York, Harcourt Brace Jovanovich.

Bishop, M. and Kay, J. (1993) 'Introduction', in Bishop, M. and Kay, J. (eds), *European Mergers and Merger Policy*, Oxford, Oxford University Press.

Bishop, P. (1997) 'Fighting for Freedom', *New Civil Engineer*, 27 February.

BMW (1994) (1995) *Annual Report and Accounts.*

Bos, D. (1991) *Privatization: a theoretical treatment*, Oxford, Clarendon Press.

Bouverie-Brine, C. and Macbeth, D. K. (1995) 'Managing Supply Chains: a collaborative project between London Underground Ltd and the Supply Chain Management Group', in Lamming, R. and Cox, A. (eds), *Strategic Procurement Management in the 1990s: concepts and cases*, Boston, UK, Earlsgate Press.

British Airways plc (1994–95) and (1995–96) *Annual Report and Accounts.*

British Gas (1997) *Annual Report and Accounts.*

British Steel (1995) *A Brief History*, published by British Steel.

British Steel (1995–96) *Annual Report and Accounts.*

Buchanan, J. M. (1968) *The Demand and Supply of Public Goods*, Chicago, Rand McNally.

Buchanan, J. M. (1978) 'From Private Preferences to Public Philosophy: the development of public choice', in Buchanan, J. M. *et al.*, *The Economics of Politics*, Institute of Economic Affairs Readings 18, London, Institute of Economic Affairs.

Burns, T. and Stalker, G. M. (1961) *The Management of Innovation*, London, Tavistock Press.

Caddick, J. R. and Dale, B. G. (1987) 'The Determination of Purchasing Objectives and Strategies: some key influences', *International Journal of Physical Distribution and Materials Management*, 17 (3), pp. 5–16.

Chief Executive (1990) 'Air Wars', pp. 43–45.

Civil Aviation Authority (1995) *Annual Report and Accounts*.

Cowen, T. and Parker, D. (1997) *Markets in the Firm: a market process approach to management*, Hobart Paper Number 134, Institute of Economic Affairs.

Cox, A. (1996a) 'Relational Competence and Strategic Procurement Management: towards a contractual and entrepreneurial theory of the firm', *European Journal of Purchasing and Supply Management*, 2 (1), pp. 57–70.

Cox, A. (ed.) (1996b) *Innovations in Strategic Procurement Management*, Boston, UK, Earlsgate Press.

Cox, A. (1997a) *Business Success: a way of thinking about strategy, critical supply chain assets and operational best practice*, Boston, UK, Earlsgate Press.

Cox, A. (1997b) 'On Power, Appropriateness and Procurement Competence', *Supply Management*, 2 October, pp. 24–27.

Cox, A. (1998) 'The Four Faces of Procurement Competence: managing dynamic and static efficiency in public and private sector supply', Proceedings of the 2nd Worldwide Symposium on Purchasing and Supply Chain Management, Forum Hotel, London, 1–3 April, Easton-on-the-Hill, Stamford: Chartered Institute of Purchasing and Supply.

Cox. A. and Hines, P. (1997) *Advanced Supply Management: the best practice debate,* Boston, UK, Earlsgate Press.

Cox, A., Lonsdale, C. and Watson , G. (1999) *Managing Transformational Efficiency: lessons from experience in the management of makebuy and outsourcing risk*, Boston, UK, Earlsgate Press.

Cox, A. and Thomson, I. (1998) 'On the Appropriateness of Benchmarking', *Journal of General Management*, 23 (3), spring, pp. 1–20.

Cox, A. and Thompson, I. (1999) *The Contract Selection Toolkit*, Boston, UK, Earlsgate Press.

Cox, A., Harris, L. and Parker, D. (1996) 'Confusion and Uncertainty in Procurement Management: the impact of privatisation on buyer and supplier relationships', *Occasional Paper in Industrial Strategy,* Birmingham Business School, No. 38, June, ISBN 0–7044–1718–9, ISSN 0961–7698.

Cox, A., Harris, L. and Parker, D. (1998) 'The Impact of Privatisation on Procurement Management: evidence from seven privatised companies in the UK', *European Journal of Purchasing and Supply Management*, 4 (2–3), pp. 87–96.

CRI (1995) *The UK Regulated Industries: financial facts 1993/94*, London, Centre for the Study of Regulated Industries.

CRI (1995–96) *On the UK Electricity Industry: financial and operating review*, London, CIPFA.

CRI (1997) The UK Water Industry: financial and operating review 1995/96, London, Centre for the Study of Regulated Industries.

Downs, A. (1957) *An Economic Theory of Democracy*, New York, Harper Row.

Dunsire, A., Hartley, K. and Parker, D. (1991) 'Organisational Status and Performance: a summary of the findings', *Public Administration*, 69, pp. 21–40.

Dunsire, A., Hartley, K., Parker, D. and Dimitriou, B. (1988) 'Organisational Status and Performance: a conceptual framework for testing public choice theories', *Public Administration*, 66, pp. 363–88.

Economist, The (1996) 'British Gas – hot air?', 10 February, p. 85.

Economist, The (1996) 'London Underground Limited – new destination?', p. 34.

Economist, The (1997) 'Rolls Royce flies high', 28 June, p. 97.

Economist, The (1997) 'Business-class socialist', 19 July, p. 74.

Edwardes, M. (1983) *Back from the Brink*, London, Collins.

Eisenhardt, K. M. (1989) 'Agency Theory: an assessment and review', *Academy of Management Review*, 14, pp. 363–425.

Fama, E. (1980) 'Agency Problems and the Theory of the Firm', *Journal of Political Economy*, 88 (2), pp. 288–307.

Financial Times, The (1996) 'United Utilities sees £474m cost savings', 29 March, p. 22.

Financial Times, The (1996) 'Severn Trent outlines growth plans', 12 June.

Financial Times, The (1996) 'Branson upsets BA wedding', 11 July, p. 9.

Financial Times, The (1996) 'BA to outline £1bn savings', 18 September, p. 22.

Franks, J. R. and Harris, R. S. (1989) 'Shareholder Wealth Effects of Corporate Takeovers: the UK experience, 1955–1985', *Journal of Financial Economics*, 16, pp. 225–49.

Garret, P. (1997) 'Culture is the Key to Privatisation', *Utility Europe*, January, pp. 13–14.

Ghamawat, P. and Costa, J. E. R. (1993) 'The Organisational Tension between Static and Dynamic Efficiency', *Strategic Management Journal*, 14, pp. 59–73.

Green, R. and Vogelsang, I. (1994) 'BA: a turnaround anticipating privatisation', in Bishop, M., Kay, J. and Mayer, C. (eds), *Privatisation and Economic Performance*, Oxford, Oxford University Press.

Grossman, S. J. and Hart, O. D. (1980) 'Takeover Bids, the Free Rider Problem and the Theory of the Corporation', *Bell Journal of Economics*, 11, pp. 42–64.

Gurassa, C. (1995) 'BA stood for bloody awful' – 1994 speech reported in *Across the Board*, January.

Hamel, G. (1991) 'Competition for Competence and Inter-partner Learning with International Strategic Alliances', *Strategic Management Journal*, (special issue), 12, pp. 83–103.

Harper, J. (1997) *Monopoly and Competition in British Telecommunications*, London, Cassell.

Harris, L., Parker, D. and Cox, A. (1998) 'UK Privatisation: its impact on procurement', *British Journal of Management*, 9 (special issue), pp. S-13–S-26.

Hart, O. and Moore, J. (1988) 'Incomplete Contracts and Renegotiation', *Econometrica*, 56, pp. 755–85.

HMSO (1956) *Report of the Committee on Electricity Supply* (Herbert Committee), Cmnd. 9672, London, HMSO.

HMSO (1961) *The Financial and Economic Obligations of the Nationalised Industries*, Cmnd. 1337, London, HMSO.

HMSO (1967) *Nationalised Industries: a review of economic and financial objectives*, Cmnd. 3437, London, HMSO.

HMSO (1978) *The Nationalised Industries*, Cmnd. 7131, London, HMSO.

Hughes, A. (1993) 'Mergers and Economic Performance in the UK: a survey of the empirical evidence 1950–1990', in Bishop, M. and Kay, J. (eds), *European Mergers and Merger Policy*, Oxford, Oxford University Press.

Hyder plc (1996) *Annual Report and Accounts.*
Jenkins, S. (1997) 'Burying the Family Silver', *The Times*, 26 February.
Jensen, M. C. and Meckling, W. H. (1976) 'Theory of the Firm: managerial behaviour, agency costs and ownership structure', *Journal of Financial Economics*, 3, pp. 305–60.
Johnson, G. and Scholes, K. (1997) *Exploring Corporate Strategy: text and cases*, London, Prentice Hall.
Kennedy, D. (1997) 'The Evolution of Electricity Generation Prices', Occasional paper 6, Centre for the study of Regulated Industries, London.
Kindel, S. (1988) 'Knights with Bare Knuckles', *Financial World*, 1 November, pp. 38–40.
Kochan, T. A., McKersie, R. and Capelli, P. (1984) 'Strategic Choice and Industrial Relations Theory', *Industrial Relations*, 23 (1), pp. 16–39.
Laffont, J. J. and Tirole, J. (1993) *A Theory of Incentives in Procurement and Regulation*, Cambridge, Mass., MIT Press.
Lamming, R. (1993) *Beyond Partnership: strategies for innovation and lean supply*, London, Prentice Hall.
Lamming, R. and Cox, A. (1995) *Strategic Procurement Management in the 1990s: concepts and cases*, Boston, UK, Earlsgate Press.
London Transport (1994–95) *Annual Report and Accounts.*
London Underground (1991) *A New Dawn for London*, London Underground Limited Company Plan, November.
Lonsdale, C. and Cox, A. (1998) *Outsourcing: a business guide to risk management tools and techniques*, Boston, UK, Earlsgate Press.
McMaster, R. and Sawkins, J. W. (1996) 'The Contract State, Trust Distortion and Efficiency', *Review of Social Economy*, 54 (2), pp. 145–67.
Magrath, A. J. (1991) 'Born-again Marketing', *Across the Board*, June.
Martin, S. and Parker, D. (1997) *The Impact of Privatisation: ownership and corporate performance in the UK*, London, Routledge.
Mayer, C. (1997) 'The City and Corporate Performance: condemned or exonerated?', *Cambridge Journal of Economics*, 21 (2), pp. 291–302.
Meeks, G. (1977) *Disappointing Marriage: a study of the gains from merger*, Cambridge, Cambridge University Press.
Mintzberg, H. (1987) 'Crafting Strategy', *Harvard Business Review*, 65 (4), pp. 65–75.
Mitchell, W. C. (1988) *Government As It Is.* Hobart paper No. 109, Institute of Economic Affairs, London.
MMC, Monopolies and Mergers Commission (1980) *The Inner London Letter Post*, London, HMSO.
MMC, Monopolies and Mergers Commission (1984) *The Post Office Letter Post Service*, Cmnd. 9332, London, HMSO.
MMC, Monopolies and Mergers Commission (1988) *Gas*, Cmnd. 500, London, HMSO.
MMC, Monopolies and Mergers Commission (1993) *Gas and British Gas plc*, 3 volumes, London, HMSO.
MMC, Monopolies and Mergers Commission (1995) *South West Water Services Ltd: a report on the determination of adjustment factors and infrastructure charges for South West Water Services Ltd.*, London, HMSO.
MMC, Monopolies and Mergers Commission (1997) *British Gas plc: a report under the Gas Act 1986 on the restriction of prices for gas transportation and storage services*, London, HMSO.

Morrison, H. S. (1933) *Socialisation and Transport*, London, Constable.

Nanda, A. and Williamson, P. J. (1995) 'Using Joint Ventures to Ease the Pain of Restructuring', *Harvard Business Review*, 73 (6), November–December, pp. 119–28.

NEDO (1976) *A Study of UK Nationalised Industries: their role in the economy and control in the future*, London, HMSO/National Economic Development Office.

Nelson, R. R. and Winter, S. G. (1982) *An Evolutionary Theory of Economic Change*, Cambridge, Mass., Harvard University Press.

NORWEB (1995) *Annual Report and Accounts.*

Nottingham Health Authority (1997) *Managing Healthcare Strategically*, Nottingham, NHA, Standard Court.

O'Connell Davidson, J. (1994) *Privatisation and Employment Relations: the case of the water industry*, London, Cassell.

Ott, A. and Hartley, K. (eds) (1991) *Privatisation and Economic Efficiency: a comparative analysis of developed and developing countries*, Aldershot, Edward Elgar.

Parker, D. (1985) 'Is the Private Sector More Efficient: a study in the public v. private debate', *Public Administration Bulletin*, 48, pp. 2–23.

Parker, D. (1987) 'The New Right, State Ownership and Privatisation: a critique', *Economic and Industrial Democracy: an International Journal*, 8, pp. 349–78.

Parker, D. (1994) 'Privatisation and Business Restructuring: change and continuity in the privatised industries', *The Review of Policy Issues*, 1 (2), pp. 3–27.

Parker, D. (1995a) 'Privatisation and Agency Status: identifying the critical factors for performance improvement', *British Journal of Management*, 6, pp. 29–43.

Parker, D. (1995b) 'Chaos Theory and the Management of Change', *Proceedings of the Lunar Society*, 8, September, pp. 1–19.

Parker, D. (1997) 'Privatisation and Regulation: reflections on the UK experience', *The Review of Policy Issues*, 3 (3), pp. 3–38.

Parker, D. (1998) 'Price Cap Regulation, Profitability and Returns to Investors in the UK Regulated Industries', *Utilities Policy*, 6 (4), pp. 303–15.

Parker, D. and Hartley, K. (1997) 'The Economics of Partnership Sourcing Versus Adversarial Competition: a critique', *European Journal of Purchasing and Supply Management*, 3 (2), pp. 115–25.

Parker, D. and Martin, S. (1996) 'The Impact of UK Privatisation on Employment, Profits, and the Distribution of Business Income', *Public Money and Management*, 16 (1), January–March, pp. 31–38.

Parker, D. and Stead, R. (1991) *Profit and Enterprise: the political economy of profit*, London, Harvester Wheatsheaf.

Parker, D. and Wu, H. L. (1998) 'Privatisation and Performance: a study of the British steel industry under public and private ownership', *Economic Issues*, 3 (2), pp. 31–50.

Pearson, J. N. and Gritzmacher, K. J. (1990) 'Integrating Purchasing into Strategic Management', *Long Range Planning*, 23 (3), pp. 91–99.

Pendleton, A. and Winterton, J. (eds) (1993) *Public Enterprise in Transition: industrial relations in state and privatised companies*, London, Routledge.

Porter, M. E. (1985) *Competitive Advantage: creating and sustaining superior performance*, New York, Free Press.

Post Office, The (1996) *Annual Report and Accounts.*

PowerGen (1996) *Annual Report and Accounts.*

Price, C. (1994) 'Gas Regulation and Competition: substitutes or complements?', in Bishop, M., Kay, J. and Mayer, C. (eds), *Privatisation and Economic Performance*, Oxford, Oxford University Press.

Prokesch, S. (1995) 'Competing on Customer Service: an interview with British Airways' Sir Colin Marshall', *Harvard Business Review*, 73 (6), November–December, pp. 101–16.

Pryke, R. (1981) *The Nationalised Industries: policies and performance since 1968*, Oxford, Martin Robertson.

Robertson, I. (1995) 'Developing Lean Supply in the Rover Group', in Lamming, R. and Cox, A. (eds), *Strategic Procurement Management in the 1990s: concepts and cases*, Boston, UK, Earlsgate Press.

Rolls Royce (1994) (1995) *Annual Report and Accounts.*

Ross, S. A. (1973) 'The Economic Theory of Agency: the principal's problem', *American Economic Review*, 62, pp. 134–39.

Scherer, F. M. (1970) *Industrial Market Structure and Economic Performance*, Boston, Houghton Mifflin.

Scottish Hydro-Electric (1996) *Annual Report and Accounts.*

Senior, I. (1989) 'Liberating the Letter', in Veljanovski, C. (ed.) *Privatisation and Competition: a market prospectus*, London, Institute of Economic Affairs.

Severn Trent (1996) *Annual Report and Accounts.*

Singh, A. (1975) 'Take-overs, Economic "Natural Selection", and the Theory of the Firm: evidence from postwar UK experience', *Economic Journal*, 85, pp. 497–515.

South West Water (1995) *Annual Report and Accounts.*

Spicer, B. W. and Ballew, V. (1983) 'Management Accounting Systems and the Economics of Internal Organisation', *Accounting, Organisations and Society*, 8 (1), pp. 73–96.

Swann, D. (1988) *The Retreat of the State: deregulation and privatisation in the UK and US*, London, Harvester Wheatsheaf.

SWEB (1996) *Annual Report and Accounts.*

Syedain, H. (1991) 'Rolls Model', *Management Today*, April, pp. 45–48.

Tullock, G. (1976) *The Vote Motive*, London, Institute of Economic Affairs.

Vickers, J. and Yarrow, G. (1988) *Privatisation: an economic analysis*, Cambridge, Mass., MIT Press.

Walking, R. A. and Long, M. S. (1984) 'Agency Theory, Managerial Welfare and Takeover Bid Resistance', *Journal of Economics*, spring, pp. 54–68.

Wallis, E. (1995) 'Managing Privatisation at PowerGen', *Long Range Planning*, 28 (6), pp. 10–18.

Waterson, M. (1997) 'Implementation Practices in Regulation: an analysis of UK experience', in Lehro, E. (ed.), *Natural Monopolies and Competition*, Helsinki, SITRA.

Welsh Water (1995) *Annual Report and Accounts.*

Williamson, O. E. (1971) 'Managerial Discretion, Organisation Form and the Multi-division Hypothesis', in Marris, R. and Wood, A. (eds), *The Corporate Economy: growth, competition and innovative potential*, London, Macmillan.

Index

Note: Page numbers in italics refer to figures or tables where these are separated from their textual reference